Illawarra escarpment scenery looking from Summit Tank north towards Mt. Kembla.

Wollongong's NATIVE TREES

Leon Fuller

Photography by Russell Badans

KINGSCLEAR
BOOKS

Kingsclear Books
36 Kingsclear Road, Alexandria 2015
Phone (02) 5574367
(02) 439 5093

First published 1980 Weston and Co., Kiama
Second Edition 1982
Reprinted 1995 Kingsclear Books

Copyright © Leon Fuller
Copyright © photographs Russell Badans
Cover photographs Barry Smith
Cover design Michelle Havenstein
Printed in Australia by McPherson's Printing Group
NATIONAL LIBRARY OF AUSTRALIA
ISBN 0 908272 39 1

Foreword

This reprint of *Wollongong's Native Trees* appears almost exactly as it did in the last printing twelve years ago. This is in spite of changes having occurred in nomenclature and new material on the trees having come to light in the intervening period. The reasons for simply reproducing the last edition are largely concerning difficulties in financing the publication of a complete revision coupled with difficulties with copyright of the book.

However considering the demand for the book a reprint was overdue. To make the book available it was necessary to drop the idea of a complete revision.

It is expected that shortly following this printing of *Wollongong's Native Trees* there will be a supplement published with all the information to bring the book up to date. Largely due to the efforts of Anders Bofeldt there are numerous changes in the distribution of species, mainly extending to those shown on the maps of the last edition. Anders has also found about twenty more uncommon and rare species of tree that weren't included in the last edition.

The supplement will also include new scientific names for seven or so species and other minor miscellaneous information.

LEON FULLER
January 1995

Acknowledgements

In preparing this book help was sought and generously given by a large number of people. It would be impossible to list everyone who assisted and it is hoped that those whose names are not included below will not feel forgotten since their help has been greatly appreciated. The fact that no one ever doubted that this project was worthwhile in itself gave me great support.

The names of those who helped in a most conspicuous way appear below and thanks are expressed for their time, patience and expertise.

Many thanks to:

Members of the University of Wollongong, Geography Department — Dr. G. Nanson for carefully checking and commenting on the draft manuscript; the changes as a result making a significant contribution. Mrs. A. Young for providing notes and comments on the physical aspects of the area which make up part of the text and also for allowing reproduction of maps and diagrams. Dr. R. Young for information and comments on the physical aspects of the area. Professor M. G. A. Wilson for checking the final draft and for making available assistance. Mrs. T. Woodward for cartographic work on the base map used for the distribution of species and the wind rose for Wollongong.

Mr. N. Mitchell for comments on the draft manuscript.

Miss D. Black for provoking initial inspiration and for commenting on the descriptions of the trees.

Mr. D. Gibson for writing the section on birds and trees.

Miss A. Speirs for the majority of draft typing and various drawings which are indicated through the book by the symbol ‡.

Mr. D. Walsh for his help in providing photographic material.

Mr. V. Klaphake for sharing his interest in the knowledge of trees.

Betty for typing, patience and endless hours checking manuscripts.

The University of Wollongong for providing support and assistance particularly in the final assembly stage of the book.

The C.S.I.R.O., Division of Forest Research and the Australian Government Publishing service for permission to reproduce drawing from *Eucalyptus Buds and Fruit* edited by G. M. Chippendale. Drawings extracted from this publication are indicated throughout this book by the symbol ★.

Staff of the National Herbarium, Sydney for identifying plant material and providing other information on the trees.

LEON FULLER,
May, 1980

Acknowledgements for Second Edition

The printing of this edition has been sponsored by the University of Wollongong and the University's continuing support is gratefully acknowledged.

I would also like to especially thank the director of the N.S.W. National Herbarium Dr. L. A. S. Johnson for the many constructive comments and suggested additions and alterations. Staff of the Herbarium as well were most helpful in providing information particularly Mr. D. Blaxell and Mrs. G. Harden.

Two of the additional species in this edition were found by Mr. K. Mills and I express thanks to him for informing me of these and a number of other changes and extensions of distribution.

Mr. C. Pavich I thank for help and access in various escarpment areas.

LEON FULLER,
October 1982

Contents

	Page
ACKNOWLEDGEMENTS FOR 2nd EDITION	
ACKNOWLEDGEMENTS	1
INTRODUCTION	5
HISTORY	7
Origin of Illawarra Landforms	7
Just Prior to the Arrival of Europeans	8
Enter Lieutenant James Cook	8
The First Settlers	9
The Cedar Getters	9
Land Settlement	10
Coal Mining	11
Industrial Development	12
Other Historical Factors which have Influenced Present Vegetation	12
Summary	13
LANDFORMS, GEOLOGY AND CLIMATE	15
The Main Physical Features	15
Plateau	15
Escarpment	17
Coastal Plain	18
Climate	19
General Patterns	19
Drying Winds	23
Insolation	23
Temperature	23
Summary	23
PATTERNS OF DISTRIBUTION	25
General	25
Overall Patterns	26
Coastline Zone	26
Coastal Plain	31
Escarpment	34
Escarpment Cliffs	40
Plateau	40
Rainforest	42
Classification and Distribution of Rainforest in the Wollongong Area	44
Conclusion	45
TREES IN OTHER ROLES	46
Trees and Birds	46

	Page
Birds and Blossoms	46
Seed Dispersal	47
Insect Suppression	48
Local Trees in the Garden	49

WOLLONGONG'S NATIVE TREES — DESCRIPTIONS . 53

TREES LISTED IN COMMUNITY GROUPS 317

Coastline Zone	317
Seacliff Communities North of Thirroul	318
Coastal Plain Sclerophyll Forest	318
Rainforest along Coastal Plain Creeks	319
Rainforest on Volcanic Soils on Coastal Plain (Berkeley and Flagstaff Hills)	319
Escarpment Foothills (Sclerophyll Forest)	320
Upper Slopes of Escarpment (Sclerophyll Forest)	321
Escarpment Cliffs	321
Rainforest of the Escarpment and Plateau Gullies	322
Plateau (Sclerophyll Forest on Hawkesbury Sandstone)	323
Sclerophyll Forest of Plateau (On Soils Below Hawkesbury Sandstone)	324
Rainforest Trees found in Sclerophyll Forest and More Exposed Situations	324

MISCELLANY 326

Shrubs which Occasionally Reach Tree Proportions in the Wollongong Area	326
Additional Trees found just Outside the Area Covered in this Book	326

GLOSSARY 327
REFERENCES AND FURTHER READING 333
INDEX 335

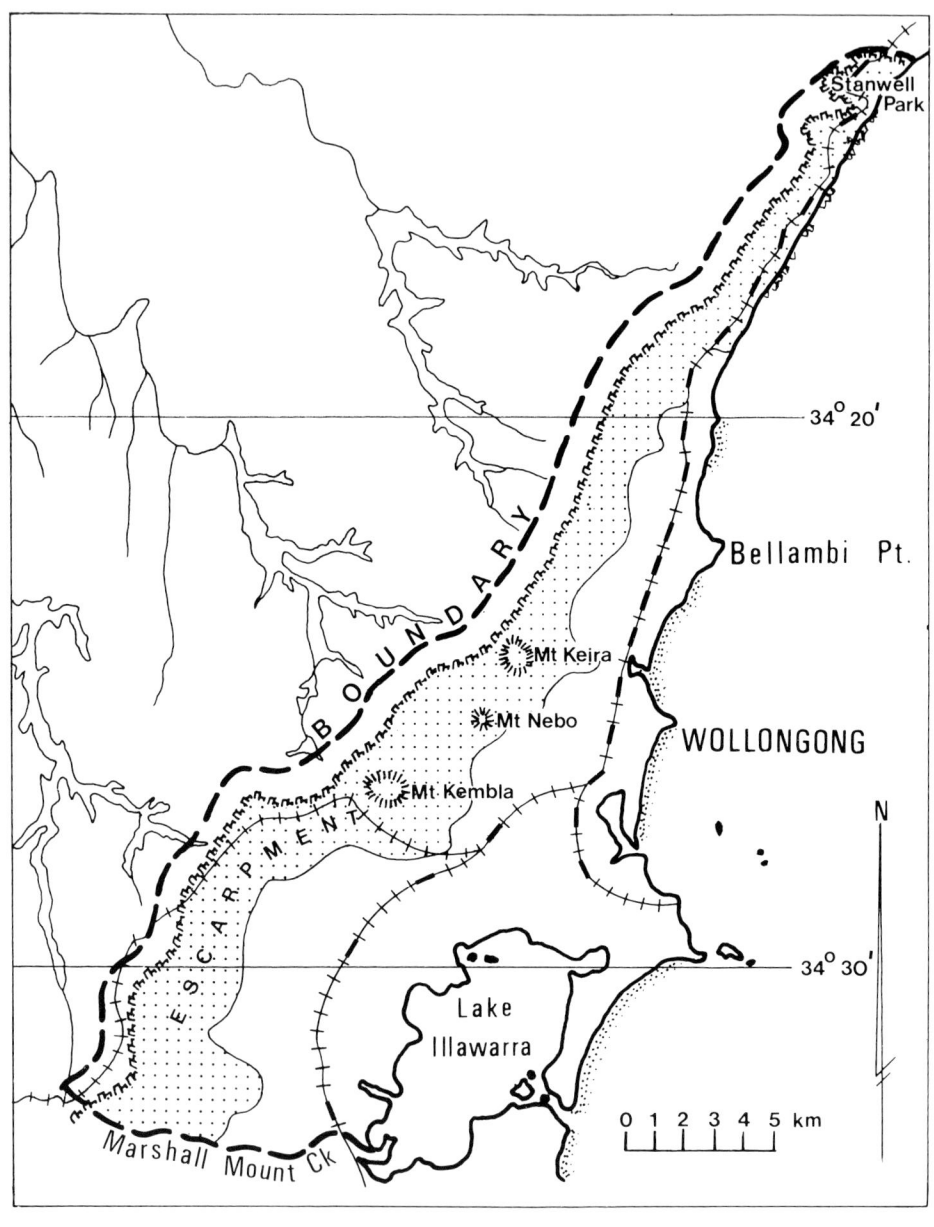

Fig. 0.1 Surrounds of Wollongong showing area covered by this book.

Introduction

Despite the highly urbanised and industrialised nature of the Wollongong area, the remnants of the natural landscape still show great diversity and inherent beauty. The main aim of this book is to try to bring an understanding of this landscape closer to those who would wish to know it better. The information presented here has a wider application than just the Wollongong area, since most of the species occur commonly elsewhere along the New South Wales coast.

Wollongong is approximately eight kilometres south of Sydney (34°27'S). The area which is described in this book is shown on Fig. 0.1 and stretches from Stanwell Park in the north to the southern end of Lake Illawarra. The coastline forms the eastern boundary, and the western boundary is an imaginary line following the escarpment crest, but one kilometre to the west of it. This western boundary extends from Stanwell Park to Marshall Mount Creek in the south. Illawarra Lake, Macquarie Rivulet and Marshall Mount Creek form the southern boundary. This section of the Illawarra is at the south-eastern edge of the Sydney Basin, with rainfall dropping off to the west and a corresponding tendency towards drier plant communities. To the north, Royal National Park and coastal Sydney are largely underlain by Hawkesbury Sandstone and carry characteristic plant communities, although there are some gullies which contain rainforest. To the south the moister communities of rainforest and wet sclerophyll forest extend along the coast to the Shoalhaven River, from where the annual rainfall decreases in a southerly direction.

The latitude, physical features, climate and rich soils have bestowed upon the area a setting for quite diverse and luxuriant vegetation, ranging from rainforest to dry sclerophyll forest. This is evidenced by the large number of tree species (140 odd including 90 rainforest trees) the region supports. While stories of rainforest once covering the area are probably exaggerated, no doubt the complexity and luxuriance of the area in its natural state must have made it truly a wonderland. It is of little surprise that this should be so, with the Illawarra escarpment rising to over 400 metres only a few kilometres from the sea. These abrupt mountain slopes intercept moisture laden winds blowing onshore and cause rainfall in excess of 1500mm per year near the crest.

This high rainfall, rich soils and infrequent fires contribute to the growth of extensive rainforest on the escarpment slopes.

At the other end of the scale, on the sandstone soils of the plateau, dry sclerophyll forest dominates. The main reason for having chosen the western boundary of the area under study as being west of the escarpment is to give a glimpse of the contrast in vegetation above and below the escarpment cliffs.

Of the area examined in this book east of the escarpment crest there is only 16% of the total land area left as natural forest. The remainder is either urban, pasture or depauperate forest bearing little similarity to the original forest. even so one could be excused for thinking that there is still considerable bushland left in this area. The high, forest covered escarpment dominates the landscape, yet despite this, it is staggering to look on a map and see the diminutive area that actually is covered by forest. the wooded escarpment slopes, along with the beaches, are the most valuable natural assets this region possesses. Assets such as these need to be guarded jealously by local citizens.

This book is designed mainly for the person wishing to learn about trees native to the Wollongong area and if nothing else, is an inventory of the tree species that occur here. An inventory for a given area can be very useful as an aid for identification by limiting the number of species to check through. then as species are identified the check list becomes smaller and the mystery of all those unknown plants progressively dissolves.

Features of this book aimed at making identification easier are the photographs of each species and also the fact that emphasis is placed on leaves. All too often one meets the frustrating situation of having a plant to identify and only leaves to do it with. On going to an appropriate key it is found that flowers and fruit are the all-important features for identification. Leaves are the most readily available parts of plants, and because of this, identification is simplified in this book.

Because biological organisms are ignorant of classification efforts and tend to produce frequent exceptions to rules, questions of definition of a tree arise. For the purposes of this book, the definition of a tree is taken as "a woody plant which grows or has the potential to grown taller than four metres, and has more or less a single trunk and a distinct crown". To a small degree, however, some licence has been used to include or exclude some species such as the inclusion of tree ferns and mallee eucalypts. Where doubt arises it may be resolved by referring to the small list of tree-like shrubs which occur in the area.

Finally, this book is only a written description based largely on the author's personal observations. Because of this it can at best be an outline of what is there. The simplest way to overcome this limitation is to go out and see the trees for yourself.

History

European occupation has most certainly had a massive effect on the landscape of Illawarra. The last 150 years has resulted in changes possibly more severe than for any similar period in geological history. However, it is on this last 150 years that this description of history must concentrate because of these dramatic changes and because it is only for this period that reliable information is available. While on the subject of reliable information, a note of caution must be sounded, for the aspect of the history we are interested in here, namely the vegetation, has sometimes been misinterpreted throughout the records. There are many colourful descriptions from pioneers of "thick brush" and "jungle" which no doubt convey the feelings of these people to the difficulty in travelling through the bush in the early days, but these words do not convey any real meaning when it comes to differentiating one type of forest from another. It is obvious there are misconceptions regarding the bush when these descriptions include eucalypts in their stories of "brush" (rainforest).

Despite inaccuracies there is still enough reliable information left to give us an idea of the composition of the original forests. In fact, from the fragmentary pieces of forest which are left standing today, it is possible to build up a reasonably clear picture of the probable forest cover before the appearance of Europeans.

Origin of Illawarra Landforms

The foundations of the landforms, the sediments and volcanic rocks, were laid down during Permian and Triassic times, some 180 to 280 million years ago. The final uplift which brought the landscape to its present level occurred about 30 million years ago. Since uplift, the area has been dissected by streams so that very little flat, high land now survives. Rock falls have caused the cliffs to retreat and landslips were a common occurrence on the escarpment slopes long before they became noticed as a problem in the urban area. Stream cutting and slope erosion probably have been more active at times in the past since we know that climate has fluctuated markedly in geological time, but we do not know exactly how these variations have affected the Illawarra area. During the Ice Ages the streams would have been cutting down to a much lower sea level.

Over the last 20,000 years there has been a general climatic warming which melted glacial ice and brought the sea up approximately 100 metres to its present level. This rise in sea level, finishing some 6,000 years ago, resulted in inundation of previously dry land probably covered with a continuation of the coastal plain forests. The sand dunes which have had such a profound effect on conditions and vegetation along the sea front were probably deposited during the last 6,500 years.

The two most dominant features of the forests of the district are the eucalypts and the rainforests. Development of the eucalypts occurred during the Tertiary period (60 million years ago to two million years ago). The adaptive radiation of this genus is rather complex and is still active today, so it is impossible to locate a time slot for any of the species of Eucalyptus invading Illawarra.

Some years ago the origin of the sub-tropical rainforest element was thought to be Indo-Malaysian and the entry of these species was believed to have occurred while Australia and New Guinea were closely associated with Asia ten to fourteen million years ago. However, there is some evidence now to show that a large part of the sub-tropical rainforest component may have actually had its origin in Australia.

Just prior to the arrival of Europeans
Observations of alluvial deposits have indicated climatic changes in the geological history of the area. There is also evidence to show that rainfall has increased over the last fifty years. The vegetation exhibits quite a diversity and in some cases, such as rainforest on the escarpment and moorlands on the plateau, a change in rainfall would possibly have the effect of varying the extent of these communities.

The effects of aboriginal occupation on the coastal area can only be speculated. They apparently fired forests and also used the environment to obtain food and produce tools, weapons, canoes, shelter, etc., but what impact this had is largely unknown. Records from early settlers of large trees and much rainforest indicate the aborigines lived in sympathy with their environment.

The dry eucalypt forest of the plateau is believed to have been burned regularly by the Aborigines. Burning promotes new grass growth and this in turn encourages animals. The moorland areas particularly would probably have been a target for burning. The major impact of regular burning would probably only have been the perpetuation of the forest as we see it today, i.e. a few species of eucalypts being the dominant trees and rainforest confined to the moist gullies, which do not readily burn.

Enter Lieutenant James Cook
Captain Cook was off Wollongong on 25th to 28th April 1770, and apart from naming Red Point, Hat Hill and attempting a landing, gave the area little note. The major impact of Captain Cook's voyage, of course, was that it was the single stone that started the avalanche of migration which populated this country.

The next visitors to the area were Bass and flinders in 1796, and some shipwrecked sailors who walked overland from Cape Howe to Wattamolla. As a result of a report from these shipwrecked sailors of coal in the cliffs along the coast, Bass revisited the area in 1797 to report on the coal to the Governor. During this visit Bass made note of the vegetation and how different it was to that about Sydney. He commented on the cabbage palms, tree ferns and stinging tree, and was obviously impressed by the general effect the rainforest gave.

G. W. Evans, on journeying from the Shoalhaven to Appin via Five Islands in 1812, also made notes of the forests through which he travelled. He commented on the "thick brush"; rainforest where sunlight didn't reach the ground, where tall cedar and sassafras grew, and the bare forest floor. His most notable observation when he ascended the mountain "6 miles north of Five Islands Point" was the contrast in vegetation between the mountain slopes and the plateau.

"I proceeded up a ridge of very good land better than a Mile when it became stoney and higher Ground. Ascended it was thick with Underwood and very large trees, continued so far a great distance over the Mountain until I met a steep Rock which we got over, afterwards the land was rather high but extremely wet*, low, miserable trees, and Prickly Bush; …"

* The wet lands were most probably the moorland swamps on the plateau.

The First Settlers

Following a few years of drought during 1814 and 1815, stories of ample pastures at "Five Islands" led Charles Throsby Smith to make a journey to the area in 1815. Finding pastures he soon afterwards drove the first mob of cattle into Illawarra.

It is interesting to note that these extensive pastures existed since it is most probable that the land east of the escarpment, except for swamps and beaches, carried tall forest. The pastures then would have been a ground cover of such species as kangaroo grass *(Themeda australis),* wallaby grass *(Danthonia sp.)* and various legumes and herbs growing under a tree canopy of the coastal plain. This type of community can still be found today scattered in fragments over the plain.

The Cedar Getters

The cedar getting era was one of the more colourful periods in the history of Illawarra. It was the lure of earning big money, fast, which attracted men to this way of life. No doubt many absconding convicts found their way to the district as did other "undesirables", for descriptions of the life of cedar getters suggest a carefree pirate-like existence.

By 1819 so much cedar was being removed that the Governor issued an order:

"It is hereby notified, that any person or persons who shall after Monday, the 23rd Instant, be found in possession of, cutting, sawing, or removing Cedar or other timber either in Logs, Planks, or Boards, from the said Districts of Appin or Illawarra, will be prosecuted accordingly for Felony."

Later in 1821 cedar cutting was permitted for a set quantity after receiving permission from the Crown.

It seems that the major area for cedar was along the escarpment west of Kiama. However, since red cedar occurs and is rapidly regenerating in the rainforest of the escarpment from Stanwell Park to the Shoalhaven, it could be expected that cedar was obtained to a greater or lesser degree throughout the length of Illawarra.

It is difficult to gauge the impact of cedar getting on the rainforests of the area. On the one hand it represents selective removal of a species which must have an effect on the ecology of a forest. On the other hand, the large number of tree species and the complexity of the rainforest would probably minimise an ecological upset.

The actual removal of the trees is only one part of the impact of cedar getting. Access roads for transport of cut timber became deep mud slurries during wet weather. Constant deviations would have been made and associated clearing for roads would have carved up the forests to a fair degree, even though road construction during the last century was not the massive earth moving operation it is today. When felling large cedar trees, it was, as it is today, the practice to clear a path for the falling tree. This is especially necessary in the rainforest because of the tangle of strong vines among the trees which may misdirect its fall.

Reporting in 1872, a press correspondent had this to say about the sawyers of the North Coast, and there is no reason to believe those in Illawarra were any different.

"The sawyers are a wasteful set of men. They destroy more timber than they use. They cut and square only the best parts of a tree, leaving great masses of cedar, which would fetch a great price in the market, to rot unheeded in the brushes. They destroy young trees too, with most culpable carelessness, and wishing only to seize the present advantages, care not a button how many trees they destroy in cutting down an old one." (*Sydney Morning Herald*, November 11, 1872.)

In opening up the forest for timber, great harm may be, and probably was done to the remaining trees, but because of the absence of introduced weeds in the early 19th century, the rainforest probably regrew in a couple of decades, not to its original height, but to something lower such as we see today.

There must have been some magnificent red cedars felled for timber. Many stories exist of trees 10 feet in diameter and judging from specimens still standing today of this order of size, the tree canopies are well over one hundred feet high and the tallest ones were possibly over one hundred and fifty feet high. Governor Macquarie on visiting Illawarra in 1822, had one noble tree measured. It was 120 feet high and 21 feet in circumference ten feet from the ground.

Red cedar, contrary to common belief, is by no means rare in Illawarra at the present time. In fact, it is quite common, with trees present in almost all the pockets of rainforest along the escarpment, and some rainforest gullies carrying almost pure stands of red cedar. Because of past exploitation of this tree, there are few large old specimens to be found and most trees are young, up to 200mm trunk diameter and under fifty feet tall. Red cedar occurs on the mountain slopes from just under the cliff faces of the escarpment to the gullies on the coastal plain. If anything, there is a concentration of this species in the region of the benches on the escarpment. It grows in wet sclerophyll forest but reaches its best development in climax rainforest.

Consett Davis, 1941, made special note of red cedar **not** occurring in his study area at Bulli. However, it is quite common there. Just below the top of Bulli Pass there is an extensive stand of the trees. This of course, means that either this species has become common since 1941, or that Davis made an oversight.

It is also interesting to note that even as early as 1822, while on a tour of Illawarra, Governor Macquarie wrote that red cedar was scarce because of exploitation.

Land Settlement

At the same time as cedar was being cut out of the forests, settlers were arriving in Illawarra. Throsby was reputed to be the first, although other reports indicate that Joseph Wilde, one of Throsby's stockmen, drove cattle into the area as early as 1803. This occupation under free grazing permit continued right up to 1817 when the first land grants were issued. It appears that this was a move only to formalise what had existed for some time.

During the 1820's land settlement seems to be a little obscure. Land grants were taken up and by 1831 the majority of choice lands on the coastal plain were occupied. Some grants were large, but many were quite small — a hundred acres or less. The only land left, even as far north as Bulli, was the relatively inferior land of the escarpment slopes. Right up to the mid thirties the scene was still one of grazing on largely uncleared country. Some attempts were made at cultivating the land, but transport problems and Aborigines making off with crop yields made it a very risky business.

One of the major limitations to development was the lack of a proper road to Sydney, and following a visit to the area in 1834 by Governor Bourke, the Surveyor General, Sir Thomas Mitchell, was sent to Illawarra to survey a road.

Between the years 1830 and 1860 the real land development in Illawarra district took place. There was a large influx of assisted immigrants into the district. Holders of land grants took advantage of this, and grants were divided and sold as smaller farms or the land-holders leased the land under "Clearing Leases". About 50 acres or less were allotted to a man for usually five years. The "rent" on the land was that it be cleared by the end of the five years. These were the real pioneers of the district. Sometimes they were provided with initial rations, but if they weren't, it is a wonder how they survived. Their contribution to the district was development at a cost of what must have been extremely hard work, since all clearing was then by axe. An area would be felled and then burnt. The rainforest with its expectations of rich soil was the first to be cleared, and then the eucalypt forest later. The trees of some forests were ringbarked and left. As soon as an area was felled and burned, it was planted with wheat, maize, potatoes or turnips. Nearly all the major estates in the area were cleared in this way. And although it is a tribute to the hardiness of these early pioneers, it is a sorry state to contemplate now when the world's forests are diminishing rapidly.

After clearing, many of the estates were divided into smaller farms of 100 acres or less. These were the beginnings of many dairy farms and through the decades following the forties, almost the whole district became a centre for dairying. As dairy farms were developed, the need for imported grasses arose, and clover, rye and prairie grass were sown with paspalum and others coming in the twentieth century

Coal Mining

Whereas agriculture was responsible for the development of the area south of Wollongong, it was coal mining which brought the majority of settlers to the northern part of the area. Because of the narrower coastal plain in the north, there was actually less land for agriculture, and this same fact meant coal mines on the escarpment were closer to the sea and hence sea transport. The first coal was mined on a small scale at Mount Keira in 1849. A second mine was opened 30 metres above this seam when coal was a more sought after commodity in 1857.

It wasn't till 1862 when four more mines were opened that coal mining and their associated villages began to have an impact on the landscape of the district. These other mines were at Mount Pleasant, Bellambi, Woonona and Bulli. While the mines in the Mount Keira area had villages near the workings, the Woonona and Bulli mines housed their workers in villages on the coastal plain.

The story of coal mining in the area is one of a continual rise in coal production, with various mines closing down and others opening. The net result of increased output meant an increase in the number of workers, and an increase in the size of the villages. Once again the area prospered, with a corresponding degradation of the natural surroundings. For every mine on the escarpment meant a hole punched in the forest, as well as clearing for tramways, villages and roads. Some of this development, of course, was done on land already cleared for agriculture. However, as coal mining extended north, particularly as far as Coalcliff, the development was more and more in virgin forest. Present day residential development has almost completely obscured the effects of coal mining on the coastal plain, but as evidence of the damage of the past, one has only to look at the effects of one hundred years of coal mining on the escarpment.

Industrial Development

The industrial development of Illawarra began with the Dapto Smelting Works, at Kanahooka Point in 1898. From here development moved to Port Kembla with Electrolytic Refining and Smelting Company (1907), Metal Manufactures (1918) and Australian Fertilizers (1921) becoming established. The Hoskins steel works began production in 1928. Other industry of the area rose through the years, such as Newbold Refractories at Thirroul, and metal, machinery and clothing factories.

Despite the industrialisation of the area, and the visual impact on the landscape, most of the effects of industry have been localised. Factories have been confined to the coastal plain area where the land was initially cleared for agriculture. It could not be said that industrial development has done more to degenerate, directly, the natural surroundings than other influences such as agriculture and coal mining. One exception to this is the tragedy of Tom Thumb Lagoon. A water body which was beautiful beyond belief, teeming with aquatic and bird life, is now reduced to a deep harbour and polluted drainage channels.

Of course, what industry has done to the area in an indirect manner has created the enormous residential area which now covers the coastal plain. The very presence of this large population puts a heavy strain on those elements of the natural world still remaining. The slopes of the Illawarra escarpment, Lake Illawarra, and the beaches, are all under pressure. We see today an almost continuous mass of housing from the hind dune area, where many past lagoons have suffered extensive filling operations, to the lower slopes of the escarpment where development has only been limited by landslip. As if the agriculturalists of the last century did not do enough, housing developers of this century have finished the job by clearing any worthwhile patches of bushland left on the coastal plain. It will never be known what unique prizes of beauty went down under these destructive forces. There is reason to believe that some species disappeared from the area. Now is the last chance for any information to be gathered. Urban development, while still expanding is also growing more intensive and it can be expected that in possibly two more decades, the City of Wollongong on the coastal plain, will be the complete suburban desert.

Other Historical Factors which have Influenced Present Vegetation

Since the arrival of Europeans, Illawarra, indeed the whole of Australia, has absorbed hundreds of introduced plants and animals. Many introductions have been for economic or ornamental reasons, and with subsequent escape from cultivation they have become established as weeds in the Australian bushland. Others have been introduced unintentionally.

Illawarra over the years has seen a great change in the composition of its natural forests as a result of these weeds. Lantana, crofton weed, inkweed, blackberry, and in recent times, privet have all invaded the rich soils of the area over the last 150 years. Bushfires, and the penetration of roads, railways and power lines into the forest have accelerated the spread of weeds dramatically. In fact, weed invasion will probably be the final death knell for the remainder of the typical Australian forest ecology in Illawarra.

Bushfires have probably played the major role in changes brought about in post European settlement times. This is only after the stage was set by preceding events. Fires have a direct and long term destructive effect; however, given time the forests will regenerate. This, of course, only applies when "natural" conditions prevail, and only the seeds of those plants killed in fire are present. Today we have lurking in the background a tremendous pool of seed from introduced weeds mentioned above. When a fire ravages the forest these weeds quickly take advantage of the weakened forest and easily overrun the native plants. This happens particularly in wet sclerophyll forests and rainforests which clothe the escarpment. As well as this direct invasion, there is secondary degeneration from the fringe of weeds accompanying fire trails cut through the bush. Control burning in wet sclerophyll forest probably has detrimental effects on the vegetation, since there is evidence of degeneration from this activity.

With the high human population in the area, great pressure has also been put on the ecology of the bush in the form of vandalism and theft. Staghorn ferns, tree ferns and orchids are attractive and easy prey to the first greedy vandal that happens along. Not only are these species selectively removed from the rainforests, but many magnificent old trees are needlessly cut down to make the acquisition of these epiphytes easier. Also, it is not uncommon to see trees cut down to satisfy desire for pure destruction. Those people surely cheat themselves.

Summary

Compared to occupation by the Aborigines the forests of Illawarra district have suffered from the time white man first set foot in the area.

The landscape has seen dramatic changes from grazing, cedar getting, industry and urban development. On top of this, there have been the insidious degenerative effects from introduced weeds, bushfires and vandalism.

Despite this, there is still very worthwhile beauty and grandeur left in the scenery and the bush itself. It is to be hoped that moves such as the Illawarra Escarpment management plans will provide the necessary impetus for the future to preserve what is left.

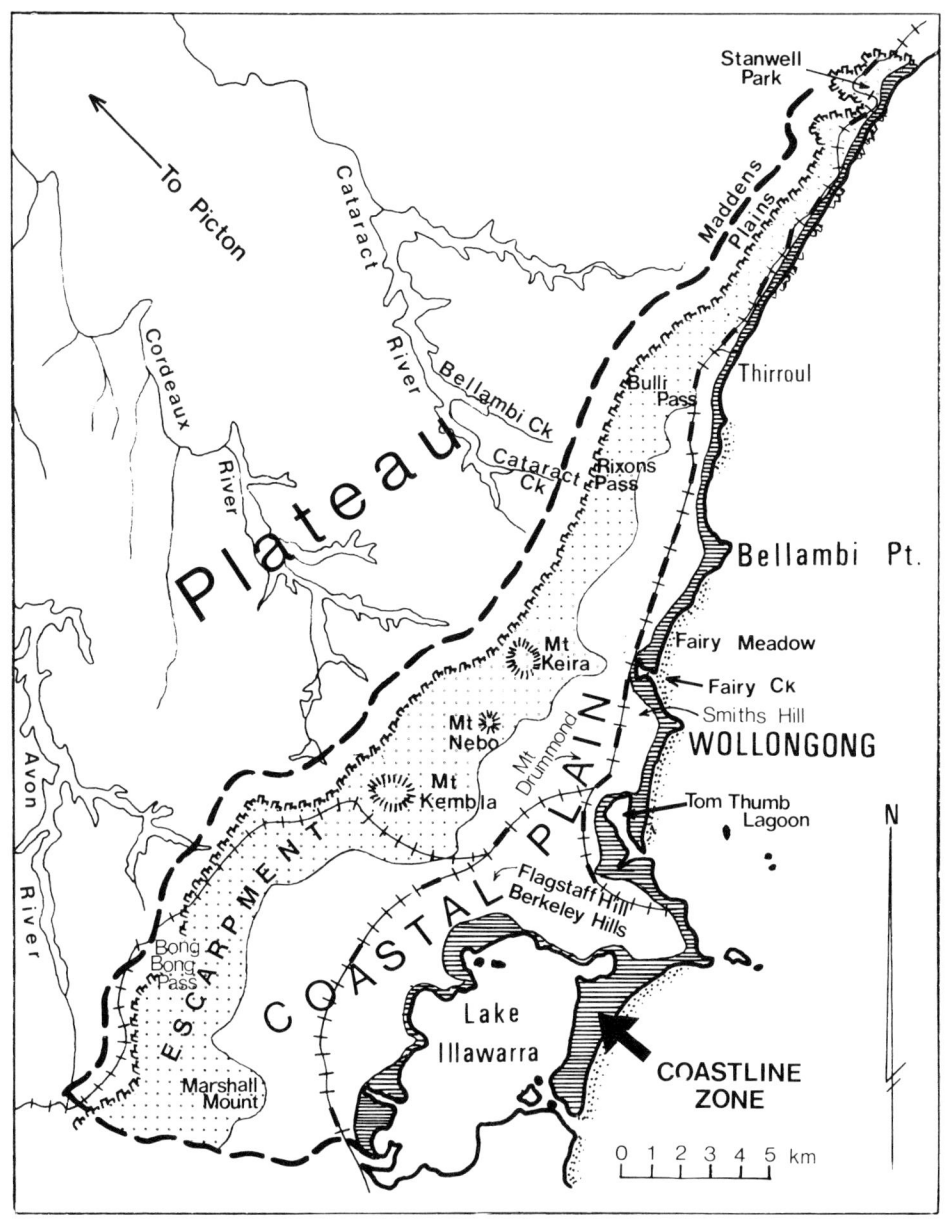

Fig. 2.1 Main physiographic subdivisions and other features and places of the area.

Landforms, Geology & Climate

Topography, geology, latitude, climate and proximity to the sea are probably the major influences which determine the character of the vegetation in the Illawarra area. This section is aimed at outlining these elements. The next section "Patterns of Distribution", will show some of the relationships between the physical features and the distribution of tree species. In doing this it must not be forgotten that the vegetation itself has an influence on the physical world and that Illawarra is not an island but a part of a vast continent so that cause and effect relationships may exist on a widespread scale.

The Main Physical Features

The area as shown on Fig. 2.1 can be divided into: a plateau; an escarpment; a coastal plain; and a coastline composed of sandy beaches alternating with rocky headlands. (See also Fig. 2.2.)

The major geological groups are, the Hawkesbury Sandstone, the Narrabeen Group, the Coal Measures and the Shoalhaven Group. Fig. 2.3 shows the distribution of these various groups.

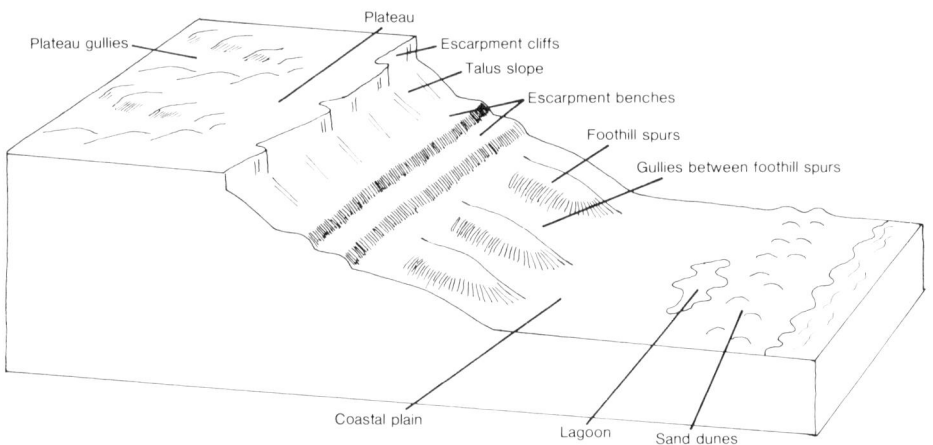

Fig. 2.2 Relief drawing of main physical features of the area. ‡

Plateau

Although it is often called a plateau, the area west of the escarpment is more like a ramp that slopes down gently from behind Wollongong towards Picton. Rivers such as the Cordeaux and Cataract have cut so deeply into the ramp that their gorges were dammed for water supply early this century. It may seem odd that rivers which rise so close to the sea flow away from the coast and into the long Hawkesbury-Nepean system, but they flow down the fall of the ramp. This fall roughly follows the 2-3° north-westerly dip of the Hawkesbury Sandstone, so the sandstone forms the surface of most of the ramp.

On the Hawkesbury Sandstone the soils are thin, acidic and sandy and carry dry sclerophyll eucalypt forest. Quite often though, the shallow upland valleys are swampy open moorland with groves of small eucalypts, for example at Maddens Plains. Here the soils are still sandy but deeper and black with organic material.

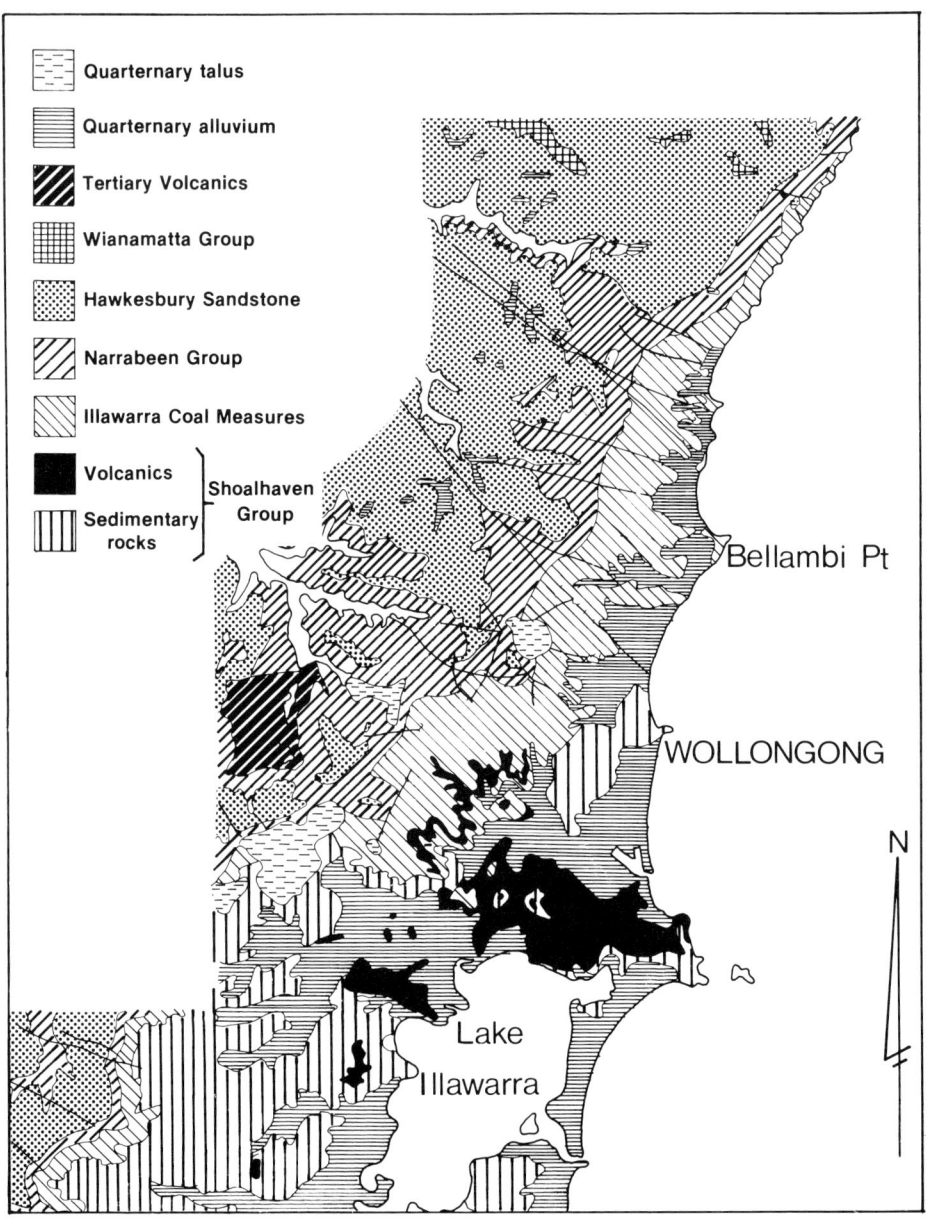

Fig. 2.3   Geology of the area (after Bowman, 1974).

Some streams, even those quite close to the escarpment like Cataract and Bellambi Creeks, have cut right through the Hawkesbury Sandstone into the Narrabeen Group below. These valleys and the main river gorges offer some shelter and usually deeper, more clayey soils so that wet sclerophyll forest and rainforest are common.

Escarpment (See Fig. 2.4)

The escarpment forms a remarkably even line running generally NNE-SSW with only two major outlying mountains in Mount Keira and Mount Kembla; Mount Nebo, between these two represents a similar vagrant projection in an advanced state of erosion.

For much of its length, the escarpment crest is an impressive line of cliffs formed by the Hawkesbury Sandstone. Sometimes the cliffs are obscured by trees and where the Hawkesbury Sandstone cuts out (for example Bulli and Rixons Passes) the Narrabeen Group rocks form the escarpment edge. The sandstone cliffs stand in high nearly-vertical faces but large blocks often fall away as the softer stratum beneath them (the Bald Hill Claystone) is eroded. These rockfalls tear the forest cover but do not usually travel very far. Erosion of the cliff line is not fast but evidence of it can be seen in numerous places along the escarpment.

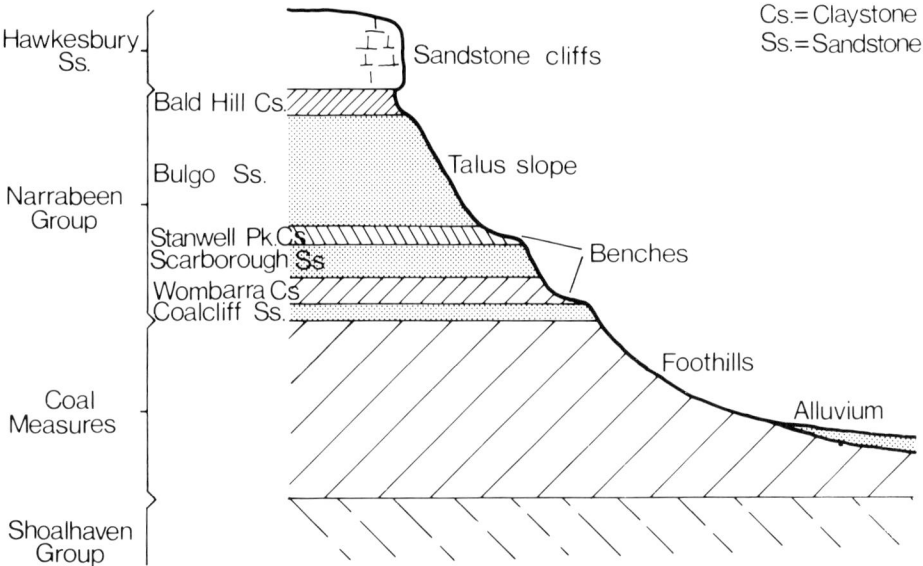

Fig. 2.4 Section of escarpment showing how stratigraphy relates to topography.

Below the cliff line of the escarpment, a long steep (30°-40° from the horizontal) slope extends for up to 100 metres over the Bulgo (in the north) or Colo Vale (south of Bong Bong Pass) sandstones. The soil is usually thin but fallen blocks and patches of finer debris cling to this slope. Most of the coachwood *(Ceratopetalum apetalum)* is found here.

Below this steep slope, north of Mt. Kembla, two prominent benches can be easily seen from the coastal plain, partly because of their characteristic vegetation patterns (see Fig. 3.13). The lower bench has formed on the Wombarra Claystone and the higher one on the Stanwell Park Claystone, and both benches have quite deep clayey soils. In some places debris from the steep slope and cliffs has been washed or has gradually tumbled down onto the benches. South of Mt. Kembla the Narrabeen Group becomes higher on the escarpment and much thinner consequently the benches grade down in prominence and are not discernible at about Bong Bong Pass. Instead, however, resistant strata of the Coal Measures and Shoalhaven Group form rather wide benches in lieu of the two previously mentioned. All of the benches have suffered some clearing for agriculture and this, as well as fire trails, serve as a means to locate them from maps and from the air.

Finally there are the escarpment foothills, long broad spurs that sometimes run out onto the coastal plain. The lower sections of Bulli Pass and Mt. Ousley Road follow two of these spurs which are cut in the Illawarra Coal Measures. North of Mt. Keira the foothills carry magnificent blackbutt *(Eucalyptus pilularis)* forests. South of Mt. Keira the forest is dominated by a mixture of forest red gum *(Eucalyptus tereticornis)* and, coast white box *(Eucalyptus quadrangulata)*. In the area west of Lake Illawarra, the foothills are mainly Shoalhaven Group rocks.

The benches and escarpment foothills have clayey acidic soils which are usually thin in steep areas but may be a few metres thick on gentle slopes. Often the slopes are covered with material called taluvium, which is a mass of boulders set in sandy clay and has accumulated over a very long time from debris off the slopes above. This material is redder and more bouldery than the soils which have weathered on the underlying rocks but it has a similar texture. Because the clayey soils hold moisture, they support tall wet sclerophyll forests.

It is interesting to look at the drainage pattern of the escarpment and plain. The escarpment forms a sharp divide between the large rivers flowing to the north-west and the smaller streams flowing eastwards to the sea. Where the east-flowing steams are large — i.e. in the south of Macquarie Rivulet especially, but also Mullet Creek — the crest has been pushed away from the coast as the streams have cut back and formed sizeable channels throughout the height of the escarpment. In the north, by contrast, the creeks are small and many of them only form channels up as far as the lower (Wombarra Claystone) bench. Only a few, such as Fairy Creek, cut right up to near the cliffline. While small creeks certainly flow on the upper parts of the escarpment and across the benches, they do not drain water very efficiently down to the plain. So, water can seep very deeply into the soils of the benches. It is the availability of water at the back of the benches which supports rainforest.

Coastal Plain

The coastal plain is roughly triangular. North of Thirroul there is no real plain and the suburbs cling to the escarpment foothills. Although the coastal plain extends northward to Thirroul the vegetation typical of the greater part of the plain stops a few kilometres to the south. Southward from Thirroul the plain widens gradually until, 25km to the south around Marshall Mount, it is 14km wide. It is crossed by easterly flowing streams at intervals which become more frequent towards the north.

West of Illawarra Lake the coastal plain has a flat to undulating surface which is underlain by rocks of the Shoalhaven Series except where watercourse floodplains occur which are composed of alluvial soil. Immediately north of

Illawarra Lake lie the Berkeley and Flagstaff Hills on which volcanic rocks outcrop and therefore produce quite fertile soils which readily support rainforest in the sheltered gullies and recesses. However, a great percentage of these hills have been cleared. The hills of Mount Drummond and Smiths Hill are also part of the Shoalhaven Series and geologically they are volcanic sandstones. One clue to the different character of these hills is the occurrence of spotted gum *(Eucalyptus maculata)* on Mount Drummond. The Berkeley/Flagstaff Hills and Mount Drummond/Smiths Hill rise out of surrounding Coal Measures and represent the northernmost outcrops of the Shoalhaven Series. Apart from these hills the surrounding coastal plain is flat to undulating and is "typical" coastal plain.

North from Fairy Meadow escarpment foothill spurs extend out further onto the plain; in fact occasionally at the northern end the spurs reach the sea. Between the spurs are flat areas associated with creeks.

The coastline itself is a series of alternating sandy beaches and rocky headlands. The southern beaches are long but the northern ones are shorter and tucked in between prominent headlands. Sand dunes have accumulated behind the longer beaches and these sandy barriers have ponded the streams to form lagoons. Illawarra Lake is the largest lagoon; but others include the once-beautiful Tom Thumb Lagoon and smaller examples such as Fairy Creek and Stanwell Park lagoon.

Soils on windblown sands, like those on the Hawkesbury Sandstone, have very sharp drainage and poor water-holding capacity so the vegetation partly reflects that on the plateau. Species common to both areas include *Banksia serrata, Acacia terminalis* and *Allocasuarina littoralis*. But closeness to the sea and other factors modify the community; *Eucalyptus botryoides, Banksia integrifolia* and *Leptospermum laevigatum* occur only near the sea except in the north where the former two species extend to the plateau.

CLIMATE

General Patterns

Figure 2.5 shows the average monthly rainfall for Wollongong on the coastal plain and from it can be seen clearly the high summer-autumn rainfall and low spring rainfall. During the months August to November dry westerly winds blowing from inland are responsible for the lower average monthly rainfall. It is quite fortuitous however that this dry period occurs in cooler months of the year when water requirements of plants are lowest.

While annual rainfall does not peak in the hottest months (Figs. 2.5 and 2.6) there is usually adequate rainfall during January-February-March to ensure that good growth is made and that rainforest has enough water to survive.

Figure 2.7 further clarifies the rainfall pattern with respect to winds which bring precipitation. Although seasons are not taken into account, it can be seen that the westerly winds are for a great percentage, dry — whereas southerly winds bring rain on a fair number of days, as do easterly winds. As well as the easterly and southerly winds bringing good rain, the north easterly seabreezes, while not actually associated with much rain, certainly maintain atmospheric humidity which is conducive to growth of the moister plant communities.

The implication on comparing Figs. 2.5 and 2.7 is that summer has a greater number of days of rain bearing winds which generally originate from SSW round

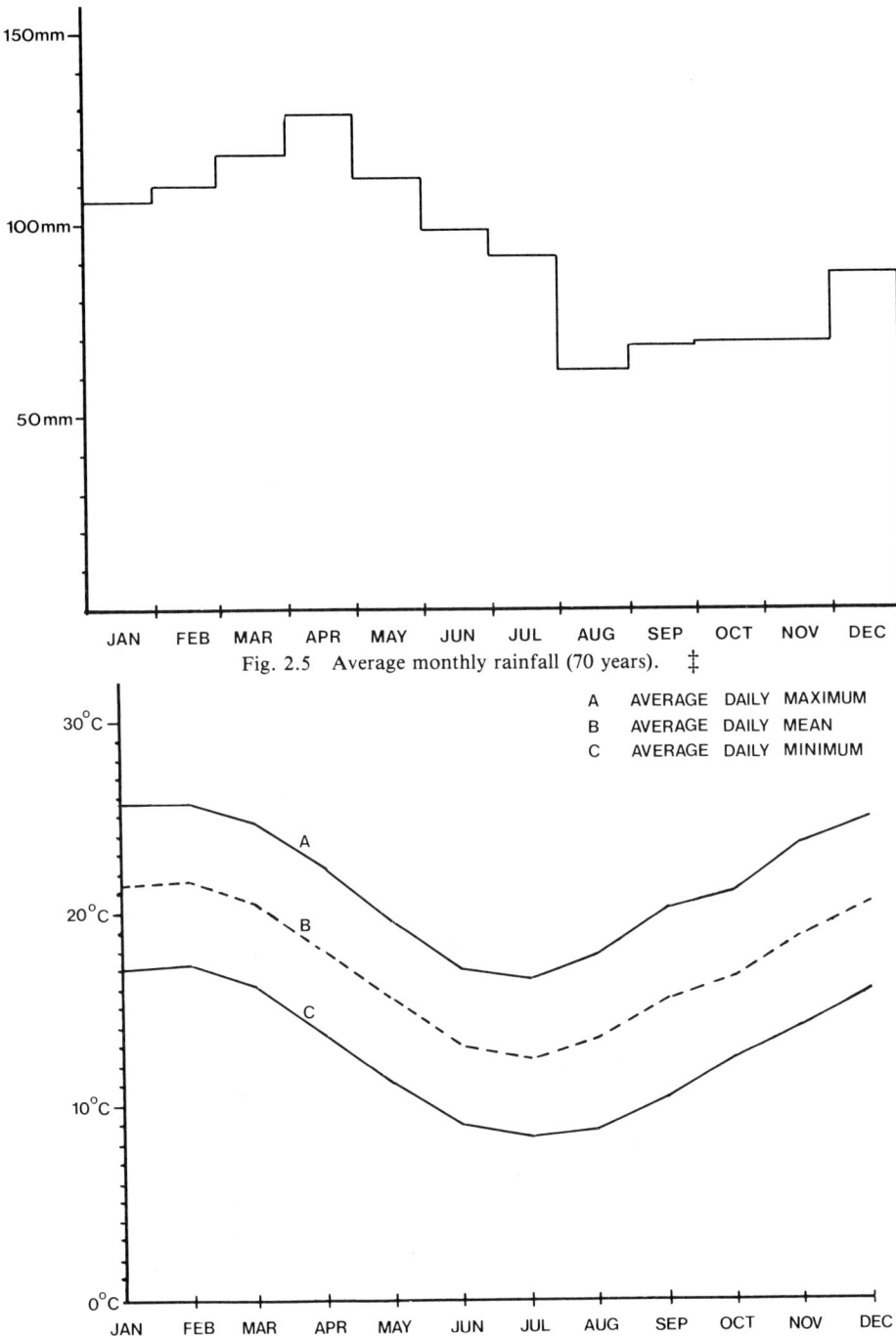

Fig. 2.5 Average monthly rainfall (70 years). ‡

Fig 2.6 Average monthly temperature (30 years) [data for Figs. 2.5 and 2.6 extracted from *University of Wollongong Climatological Station, Annual Report, 1978*. M. J. Boyd, Department of Civil Engineering].

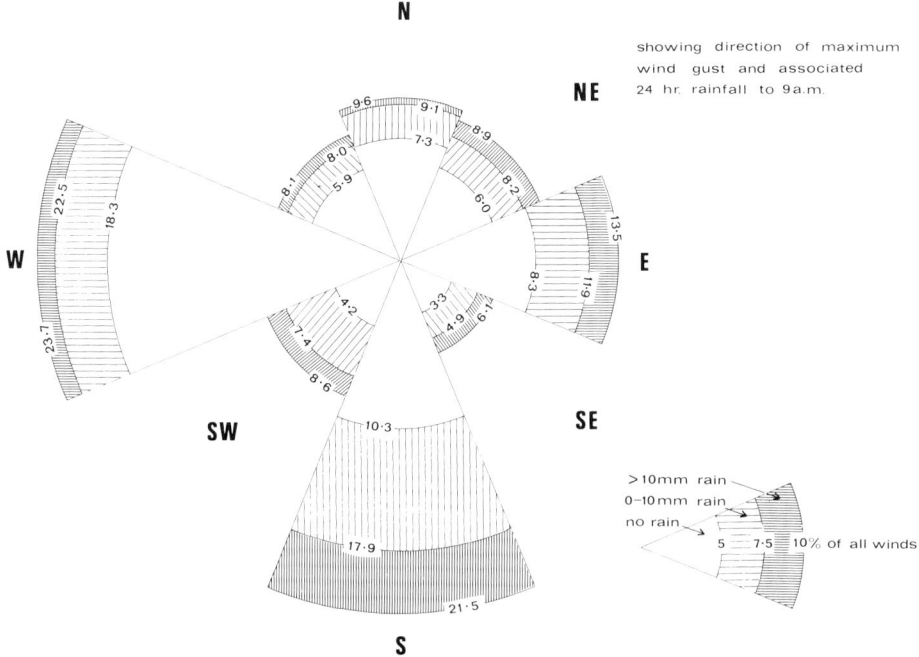

Fig. 2.7 Wind rose for the University of Wollongong weather station [reproduced by courtesy of Mrs. A. Young].

to the NE. Blowing in this sector these winds are strongly influenced by the escarpment and the corresponding uplift gives rise to the distribution of annual rainfall shown on Fig. 2.8. As winds sweep up the slopes, more and more rain falls to a maximum of a yearly average of 1600mm on the edge of the plateau. This is in contrast to 1000-1200mm on the coastal plain. Also of note is the localised effect gorges and ravines have on rainfall. Funnelling associated with these features can cause higher rainfall still on the upper slopes of the escarpment. A prime example of this is Mt. Keira Scout Camp where the gorge between Mt. Keira and the main range causes a greater precipitation from humid south to south-easterly winds. As a direct reflection of the greater supply of water, extensive rainforest is found at the Scout Camp.

Also associated with moisture laden winds and the uplift due to mountains are mists and it is not unusual during wet or very humid weather to see mists obscuring the mountains down to 200 metres and sometimes lower. Often mists are present where there is no actual precipitation in large droplets. However, as far as the trees are concerned, and particularly the rainforest species these mists add a significant amount of moisture to the water supply of the trees. Rainforest or mesophytic plants have a higher degree of spongy tissue and it is believed that they behave virtually like a sponge to the water of the mist.

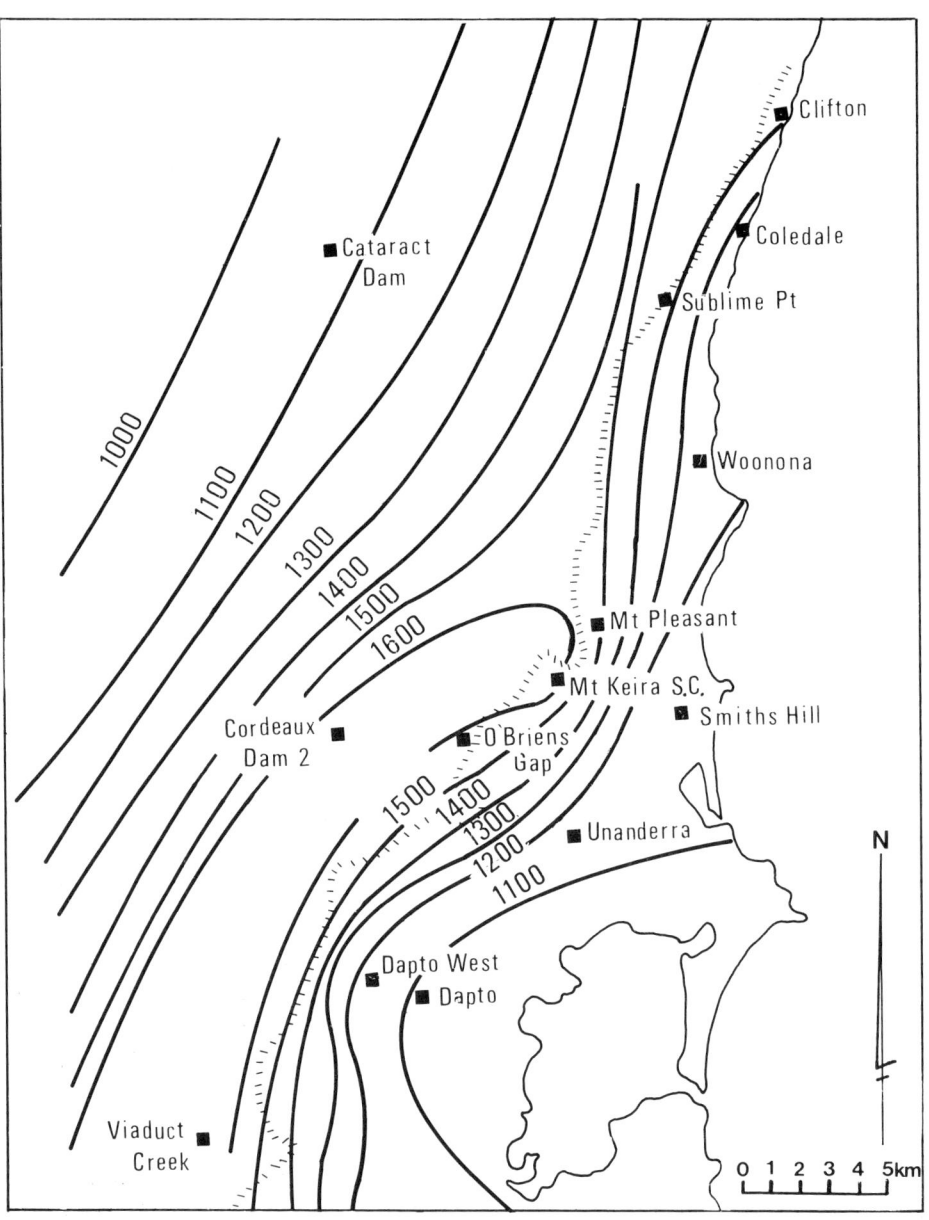

Fig. 2.8 Distribution of average annual rainfall (in mm) [reproduced by courtesy of Mrs. A. Young from her M.Sc. Thesis *The Distribution, Characteristics and Stability of Debris-mantled Slopes in Northern Wollongong*, University of Wollongong, 1976].

Drying Winds

The rainforests of the Wollongong area have taken advantage of the combination of mountains and winds. While the mountain stimulates precipitation from on-shore winds it also gives protection from drying offshore winds.

Of greatest importance though is the protection the escarpment offers against the sizzling hot north-westerly winds associated with low pressure troughs inland in the summer. These winds can dessicate soft plants in a matter of hours, if they are exposed. Any exposed position on the coast carries sclerophyll forest and at a glance it can be seen that rainforest grows only in areas protected from these particular winds. Hot summer north-westerly winds are not frequent or prolonged but generally blow only for one or two days with a week or so between. Summers with virtually no north-westerly wind are not unknown. Another important aspect of north-westerly summer winds is their association with hot dry bushfire conditions. The worst bushfires in this area have been as a result of drought and these winds.

Insolation

The directional aspects of the ground and the latitude of the Wollongong area have a significant influence on the vegetation because of the angle of the sun's rays. These two factors combine to give a length of time of direct sunlight each day and the angle at which the sun strikes the ground.

With the high escarpment this is yet another factor producing conditions for rainforest on the south and east facing slopes and sclerophyll forest in the less shaded areas. Immediately east of the escarpment there can be two to three hours difference in sunlight per day between the plateau and the beach. In some cases such as the southern sides of Brokers Nose, Mt. Keira and Mt. Kembla there are areas which are in continual shade through the winter months.

During summer a limiting factor to vegetation types is later afternoon sun. Early morning sun strikes most of the area and since this is the cooler part of the day, especially after a hot day before, most plants can make use of this sunlight, because of recuperation of their water balance during the night before. On the other hand, by late afternoon the air has warmed up, the plants are possibly coming under some water stress and the sun continues to beat down. Therefore it is reasonable to expect only plants more resistant to hot and dry conditions can be found in this situation.

The plateau, the coastal plain and the sea shore are generally exposed to sun for the whole day and also they carry sclerophyll forest. The escarpment cliffs and slopes which are in shade from mid afternoon on, carry moister communities including rainforest.

Temperature

Wollongong does not experience extremely low temperatures at any time of the year. Frosts are not common or severe and they do not appear to cause limitations on the growth of native trees. The higher temperatures that are associated usually with north-westerly winds in summer, are occasionally in the high 30°'s, and exposed to these winds without adequate moisture and protection from the sun, rainforest plants wilt severely and possibly die. The high temperatures would not normally or adversely affect sclerophyll plants.

Summary

The major elements of the weather affecting plant growth in the Wollongong region are; the moderately high rainfall with a maximum in summer, the warm humid summers, dry winters, and orographic effects that induce a higher rainfall at the escarpment crest than on the coastal plain.

Of particular note with respect to the distribution of forest types is aspect. The east to south facing sector favours the development of wetter types of forests including rainforest, because of protection from dry north-westerly winds and exposure to moist SSW to NE winds in summer. The north and west facing aspects favour the development of sclerophyll forest, because of exposure to the sun and drying north-westerly winds in summer. Temperature extremes are not usually severe, however some days with temperatures in the high 30°'s can be expected each year.

The humid, mild climate is generally ideal for plant growth; evidence of this is the large variety of introduced species which thrive here.

Patterns of Distribution

General

An analysis of patterns of vegetation must in effect be an analysis of the relationship between the plants and their environment. This of course is a two-way arrangement in that plants modify the environment in which they live, often to their own advantage. An example of this can be found on the Wollongong coast where estuarine mangrove communities occur. Mud is trapped and stabilised by the dense array of mangrove roots and by this means the mangroves further extend their own community.

On the Illawarra escarpment rainforest has a modifying effect, creating an environment more suited to its own perpetuation. The dense canopy of leaves casts full shade over the ground and this inhibits other than rainforest plants growing, all to the advantage of the rainforest community. In contrast, the eucalypt forest produces a combustible type of community adapted to survive fire. When a bushfire does occur the eucalypts regenerate rapidly, but when fire attacks the edges of rainforest it dies back, allowing the eucalypts more room to expand.

As well as the physical-biological relationships, the relationships between the physical factors themselves can be very complex and sometimes very circuitous. The fundamental factors influencing the vegetation in this area under study are:

1. Latitude and altitude.
2. Proximity to sea.
3. Climate.
4. Topography and aspect.
5. Geology and soils.
6. Historical influences (European).
7. Introduced weeds.
8. Present man-induced influences such as pollution, disturbance etc.
9. Bushfires.

Latitude and proximity to the sea are largely responsible for the climate of the area. Topography is responsible for both the altitudinal gradation of vegetation and the thickness and composition of the soils. Conversely the vegetation has a marked effect on erosion and stability of slopes. Once again the vegetation tends to stabilise its own environment.

However, one of the major contributions of topography in determining vegetation patterns in this area results from shelter and exposure to insolation and dry westerly winds. Although there is an array of different aspects covering 360° the escarpment running NNE-SSW is responsible for slopes which are both high and continuous, and facing generally east or south-east. Orientated in this direction they are protected from dessicating westerlies, particularly the hot north-westerly winds in summer, but they also accept the moist on-shore winds from the sea. These two factors, in addition to the presence of relatively fertile soils, are responsible for the formation of sub-tropical rainforest in the area.

Where fire and aspect prevent the establishment of rainforest, wet sclerophyll forest is maintained harbouring an understorey of certain rainforest species.

In addition to the "natural" physical and biological influences on the vegetation there are influences arising from human habitation. Weeds and bushfires have been mentioned in "History". Other continual disturbances are air and water pollution, dumping of rubbish, vehicular and foot traffic through the bush, mining, residential and other development.

What is to be seen today is therefore a product of the above forces. It is far removed from what must have existed prior to European settlement. However speculation as to the extent of past forests must be put aside and only what is here today will be considered. If this were to be looked at in detail the information would fill many volumes, and if some of the original magnificence and grandeur is missing it must be accepted, with every endeavour made to protect what is still here.

Overall Patterns

The most striking contrast in the vegetation of the Wollongong area is between rainforest and sclerophyll forest, the latter dominated in most cases by eucalypts but sometimes by other tree species, e.g. *Banksia integrifolia*. There are however many other more subtle variations particularly in sclerophyll forests. These variations are largely a reflection of the physical features of the area (see Fig. 3.1) and the most useful way to look at the distribution of trees is on this basis. As with the major physiographic features the vegetation can be more or less divided into a coastline zone, a coastal plain, the escarpment, and the plateau with dissecting river valleys.

Only dominant or common tree species in any community are given in this section. For the full inventory of trees see "Trees Listed in Community Groups" at the back of this book.

Coastline Zone

The coastline of the area on Fig. 3.1 can be divided into two sections; firstly the northern third, where seacliff plant communities dominate and grade westward into communities typical of the escarpment (even at the rear of the short beaches the land is steep), and secondly the southern two-thirds, which has long sandy beaches, often with lagoon communities behind them, separated by headlands which carry seacliff plants. The southern two-thirds adjoins a coastal plain which together with beach areas have unfortunately been largely developed for residential use. Consequently little remains of the communities associated with the seafront.

Even those vestiges remaining are so altered by activities such as land filling, draining of wetlands, and the creation of residential estates and caravan sites that an understanding of these past communities will never be had. Therefore no attempt will be made to describe the communities as a whole. It is only possible to indicate those tree species which can be found in the patches of bush remaining.

Figs. 3.2 and 3.3 show two sections of typical gradations in vegetation from the sand dunes, west. It is possible to still see this type of gradation at Puckeys Estate (Fig. 3.2) and Primbee Beach (Fig. 3.3). The main elements of the gradation start with *Banksia integrifolia* and *Leptospermum laevigatum*, both appearing as a front row defence of trees against the salt laden winds from the sea. Because of the sandy soil and the exposed nature of the sand dunes the character of the vegetation cover is low and shrubby consisting of drought resistant plants. On the seaward side the canopy is very low and dense and gains height in a westward direction. As well as tree species the community abounds with shrubs and ground cover plants such as *Spinifex hirsutus* and *Lomandra longifolia*.

The hind dune region supports the above two tree species as well as trees such as *Eucalyptus botryoides, Casuarina glauca* and a number of mesophytic species often found in rainforest. The hind dune area enjoys some protection from the

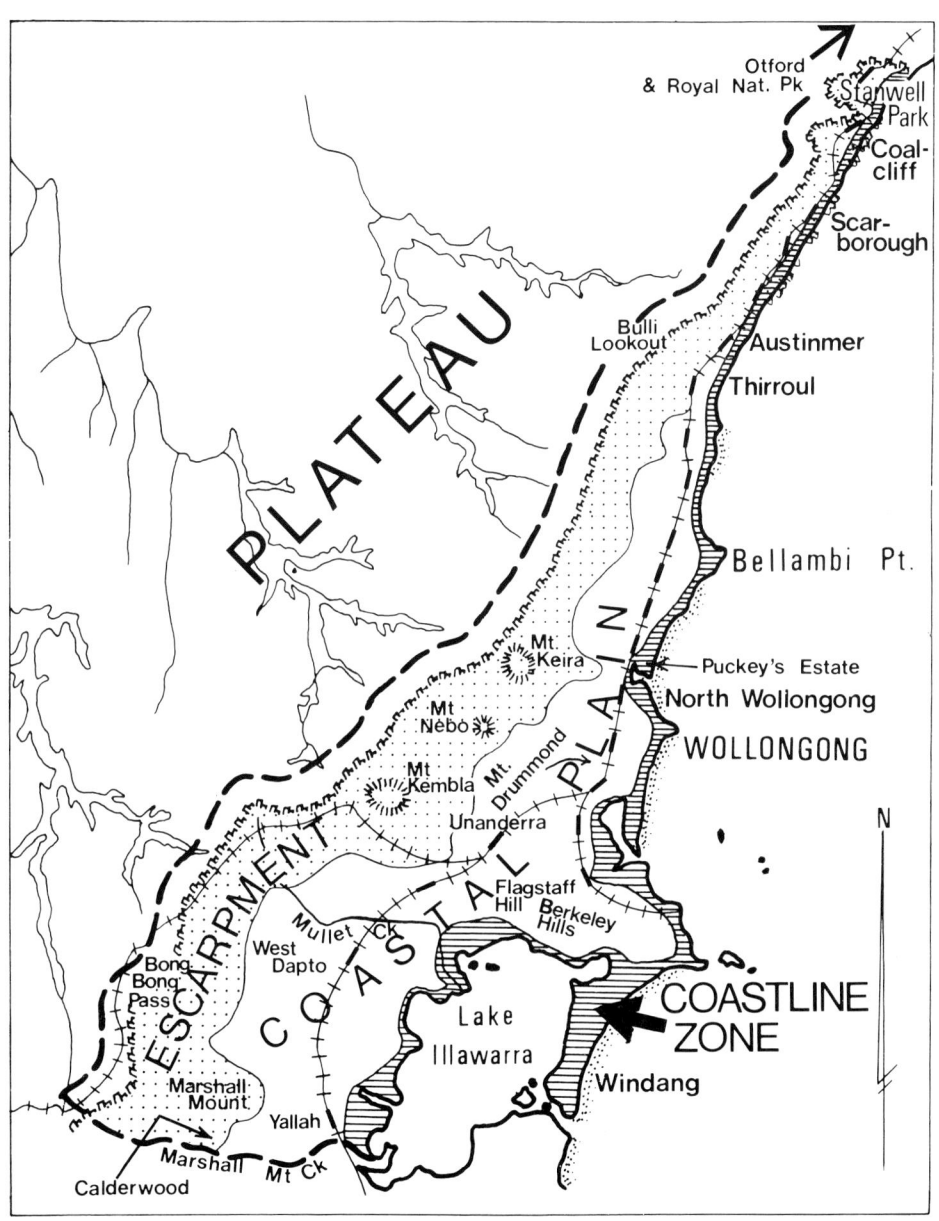

Fig. 3.1 Main subdivisions of vegetation in the area.

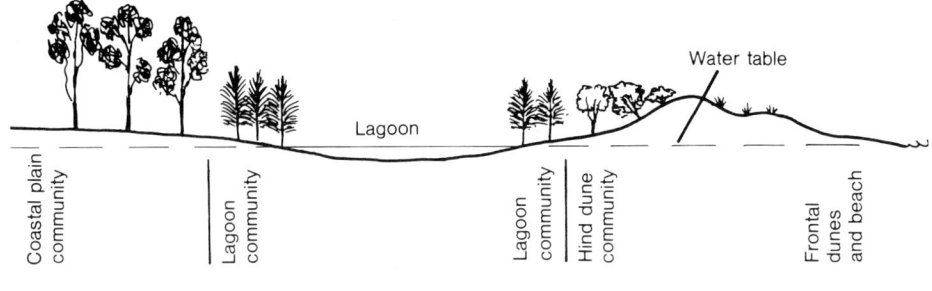

Fig. 3.3 Section of coastline zone — no lagoon but high water table. ‡

blasting salt winds, and the soil is slightly better because it is more stable, moister and usually has a higher organic content. Because of the dune slope, the water table is still relatively low. While there are more and larger trees in the hind dune than the frontal dune community, shrubs still form a substantial part.

Immediately to the west of the dune community is a low lying area containing a lagoon (Fig. 3.4) or a dry soil surface with a high water table (Fig. 3.5). Under these conditions *Casuarina glauca* is by far the most common tree. However *Eucalyptus robusta* and *Eucalyptus botryoides* are also common elements of this area.

The headlands between the long beaches of the southern part of the area are essentially denuded of vegetation. A few miserable plants may still be found and these are mainly *Leptospermum laevigatum* although shrubs such as *Westringia fruticosa* may still be seen tenaciously hanging on against the sea and human interference.

It is from Thirroul northwards that seacliff vegetation is alive and doing well (Fig. 3.6). In this northern third of the coastline, cliffs become more continuous with small sandy beaches in coves. Where the cliffs are steep and close down to the sea *Banksia integrifolia* is common. *Eucalyptus botryoides* is the most common tree higher up the steep slopes and on the gentler inclines. It is on these northern seacliffs that *Allocasuarina verticillata* grows. It is limited to the cliffs and has a distinctive weeping habit.

There appears to be a gradient of vegetation from Austinmer northwards. At Austinmer, sclerophyll plants such as *Eucalyptus botryoides* and *Banksia integrifolia* tend to be dominant. On proceeding north mesophytic (rainforest)

Fig. 3.4 Lagoon community at Puckey's Estate, North Wollongong.

Fig. 3.5 Area behind sand dunes where high water table exists. In the foreground are sedges with swamp mahogany *(Ecualyptus robusta)* behind.

Fig. 3.6 Seacliff vegetation at Clifton.

species form a more and more conspicuous part of the cliff community, especially where the cliffs are the steepest. This gradient is possibly due to the escarpment coming closer to the sea northwards and affording more protection from westerly winds. Mesophytic trees grow on seacliffs as shrubs because of the windy difficult conditions, although where a small degree of protection is afforded by localised gullies the plants are larger. The mesophytic species which do occur here are those found in other coastal regions and include species such as *Guioa semiglauca, Synoum glandulosum, Livistona australis, Acmena smithii* and *Glochidion ferdinandi*. On the seacliffs there is often an odd mixture of sclerophyllous and meosphytic plants with species such as those above growing alongside *Hakea salicifolia, Allocasuarina verticillata* and *Monotoca elliptica*.

Coastal Plain

The major part of urban development has been on the coastal plain. Places free from this type of development are the West Dapto-Yallah area and various small pieces of land. Therefore the generalisations of vegetation for the coastal plain are based on discontinuous occurrences of forests and particular tree species. Due regard must be given this fact although numerous pieces of bushland (small and large) were sampled to build up the following picture.

The coastal plain of the Wollongong area (Fig. 3.1) exhibits some differences between the northern part (north from North Wollongong) and the southern part (south of Berkeley and Flagstaff Hills), with an intermediate zone between. Differences between the northern part and southern part are largely due to the Coal Measures outcropping in the north whereas in the south the underlying Shoalhaven Series outcrop (see Fig. 2.3). Between North Wollongong and Lake Illawarra there is a mixture of these two. North of North Wollongong the coastal plain consists of relatively flat areas with escarpment spurs occasionally intruding. The spurs most often support *Eucalyptus pilularis* with other trees such as *Syncarpia glomulifera* and *Eucalyptus botryoides/saligna*. They are virtually an extension of the escarpment foothills, topographically and botanically. On the flat areas trees more characteristic of the coastal plain occur, such as *Eucalyptus tereticornis, Eucalyptus longifolia, Eucalyptus globoidea* and *Melaleuca styphelioides*. Of course there is some overlap in the composition of forest on the spurs with that on the flats.

The western side of the coastal plain grades into the escarpment foothills forest type, and the eastern side into the lagoon and dune communities. On the coastal plain eucalypts generally dominate although there are some rainforest trees (usually the hardier ones) which grow as an understorey to the eucalypts. Much of the coastal plain forests, particularly the more openly treed types, have a ground cover of grasses such as *Themeda australis, Danthonia sp.* etc., hence the "ample pastures" for the first settlers. The only true rainforest which occurs on the coastal plain (with the exception of Berkeley and Flagstaff Hills) is associated with the watercourses and is confined to the immediate banks of the creeks. This rainforest has a characteristic composition and species such as *Backhousia myrtifolia, Glochidion ferdinandi* and *Acmena smithii* are the most common. It does not contain the lush climax rainforest trees of the escarpment such as *Pennantia cunninghamii, Ceratopetalum apetalum* and *Doryphora sassafras*. Rainforest composition and distribution along creek banks applies to the whole Wollongong coastal plain, not just the northern part.

Between North Wollongong and the Berkeley and Flagstaff Hills the coastal

Fig. 3.7 Spotted gums *(Eucalyptus maculata)* on Mt. Drummond.

plain exhibits a rather mixed character. There are still patches of what could be called typical coastal plain forest dominated by *Eucalyptus tereticornis, Eucalyptus longifolia* and *Eucalyptus globoidea*. Here the spurs of the escarpment foothills do not extend as close to the sea as in the northern part, however in place of the spurs there are outlying hills formed of rocks of the Shoalhaven Series.

These outlying hills have a fair impact on tree distribution. Mt. Drummond in the Coniston area is one such outcrop, and spotted gum *(Eucalyptus maculata)* is locally confined to this outcrop (Fig. 3.7). It is a little surprising why this should be so when in the West Dapto area similar outcrops show no sign of spotted gum.

The other major outlying group of hills in this centre zone is the Berkeley and Flagstaff Hills which is a latite (volcanic rock) outcrop of the Shoalhaven Series. There is not a great deal special about these hills except that rainforest occurs in most of the gullies and recesses (Fig. 3.8). This predisposition to readily form rainforest is due to the fertile nature of the volcanic soil. Other than rainforest species there are a few *Eucalyptus tereticornis* and *Acacia mearnsii* is regenerating in patches.

On the western side of Lake Illawarra the coastal plain between Unanderra and Marshall Mount is generally flat to undulating with the floodplains of Mullet and Marshall Mount Creeks consisting of alluvial soil, while the higher parts are outcrops of rocks of the Shoalhaven Series. While most species of the coastal plain occur on all sites in this area, *Eucalyptus tereticornis* is most common on the higher parts (Fig. 3.9) and also along the escarpment foothills, and *Eucalyptus pilularis* dominates some areas where the soil seems a little richer. On the floodplains

Fig. 3.8   Rainforest on Flagstaff Hill.

Fig. 3.9   Forest red gums *(Eucalyptus tereticornis)* on the coastal plain.

Fig. 3.10 Mixed eucalypt forest on coastal flood plain.

Eucalyptus longifolia, Eucalyptus globoidea, Eucalyptus pilularis, Melaleuca decora and *Melaleuca styphelioides* are the most common (Fig. 3.10).

Eucalyptus bosistoana and *Angophora floribunda* occur on this part of the coastal plain and not in the northern part. Yet *Syncarpia glomulifera* and *Eucalyptus paniculata* have not been observed here.

Escarpment

The vegetation of the escarpment is a mosaic of various forest types. Basically though, the forests fall into two categories; rainforest and sclerophyll forest. A third type, the rainforest ecotone is intermediate between the other two but must strictly be considered sclerophyll forest since it is usually dominated by eucalypts. Often eucalypt forests may have an understorey of rainforest trees and similarly, rainforest may sometimes have eucalypts growing as scattered emergents.

Despite the complexity of forest patterns it is possible to extract some generalisations which hold true under most circumstances. These are based on stratification due to altitude and patterns apparently caused by topography and underlying geology.

Rainforest occurs mainly in three situations on the escarpment (Fig. 3.11); in the deep gullies between foothill spurs (Fig. 3.12), at the rear of the benches (Figs. 3.13 and 3.14) and on the talus slope (Fig. 3.15). Often the rainforest on the talus slope and at the rear of the benches is continuous along the escarpment for up to 1km. In other instances ridges running down the slope and across the benches carry eucalypts because of the better drained nature of soil on the ridges. Yet in other instances eucalypts spread over the entire escarpment from top to bottom.

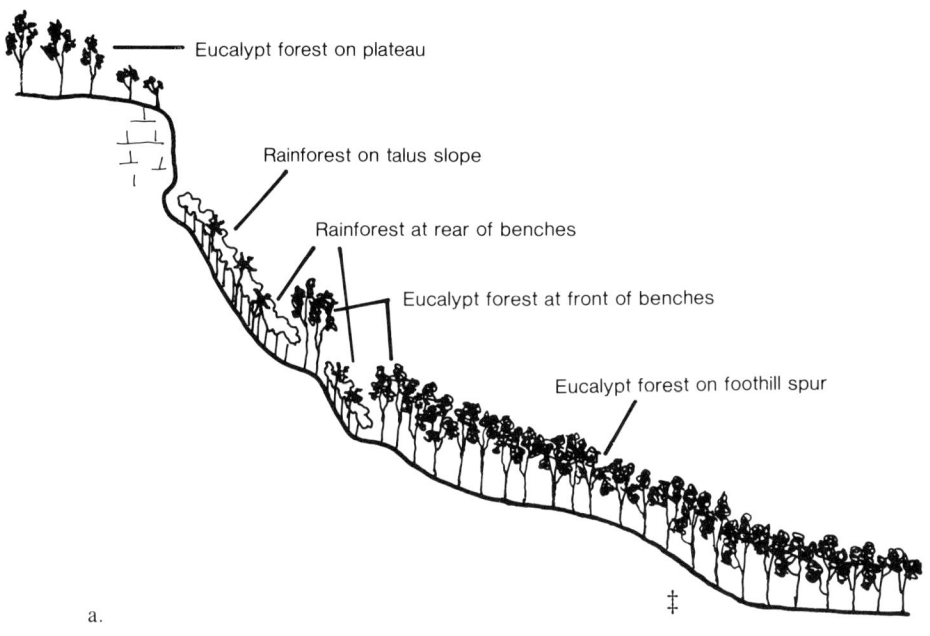

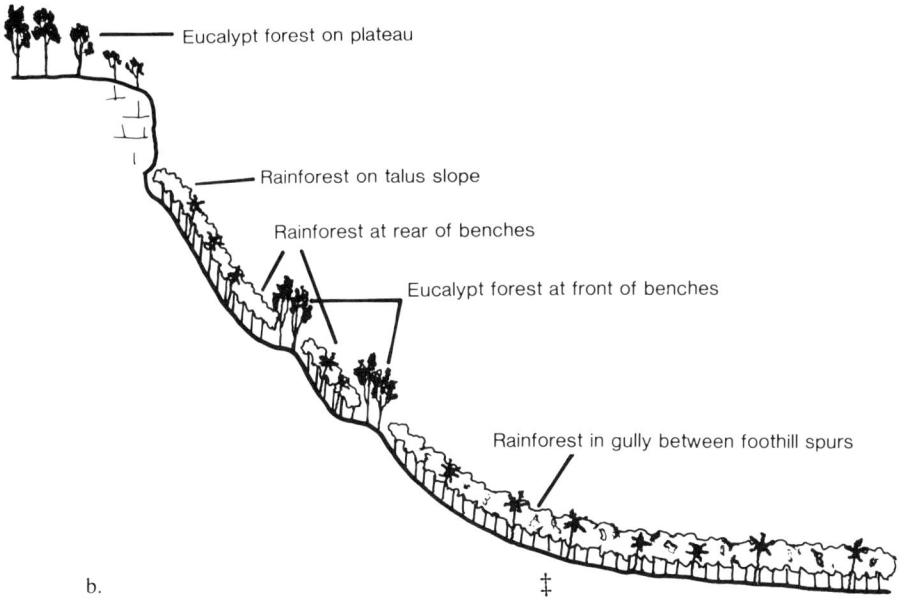

Fig. 3.11 Sections showing vegetation on escarpment, a. Eucalypts on foothill spur; b. Rainforest between foothill spurs.

Fig. 3.12 Rainforest in gully between foothill spurs. The palms indicate the rainforest even though lantana has taken over in the bottom right-hand corner of the photograph.

Fig. 3.13 Benches on the escarpment as seen from below. The rocky cliffs of Hawkesbury Sandstone have been eroded away along this section of escarpment.

Fig. 3.14 Benches on the escarpment as seen from the crest, showing rainforest (Rf) at the rear of the benches and eucalypts (Scf) along the front edges.

Fig. 3.15 The escarpment at Brokers Nose showing rainforest (Rf) on talus slope and eucalypt forest (Scf) on ridges and lower slopes.

Sclerophyll forest on the escarpment is quite different to that on the coastal plain and also stands out distinctly from adjacent rainforest of the escarpment. Eucalypts of this forest on the escarpment are generally tall vigorous trees, with canopies nearly always over 20 metres high and often over 30 metres.

The escarpment foothills support the most extensive sclerophyll forest. Often there is a fringe of eucalypts along the front edge of the benches which actually make the benches clearly visible from the coastal plain (Fig. 3.13). The upper 200 metres of the escarpment has only scattered eucalypts except where a ridge exists or in the section from Austinmer to Stanwell Park where quite dense forest grows composed of *Eucalyptus botryoides* and *Eucalyptus pilularis* as the dominant trees.

The most common species of eucalypt on the escarpment are *Eucalyptus pilularis, Eucalyptus quadrangulata, Eucalyptus saligna* (and its hybrid forms) and *Eucalyptus botryoides*. The distribution of each of these species can be seen on the map accompanying the description of each tree further on in this book. Altitude and proximity to the sea appear to be the major factors controlling these distributions. North of Austinmer the escarpment is closer to the ocean and it is probably this fact which is responsible for *Eucalyptus botryoides* being one of the two commonest trees. The other species here is *Eucalyptus pilularis*.

South of Austinmer and on the escarpment the eucalyptus species have a strong correlation with altitude. Using rainfall (Fig. 3.16), which clearly indicates the effects of altitude, and comparing this with various tree species (Figs. 3.17 to 3.19), a strong correlation can be seen between rainfall and the distribution of those tree species shown. The Figs. are taken generally from the maps accompanying the descriptions later in this book but are modified so that the limits of distribution are for the greatest density of the populations and do not include the scattered outliers. The lower limit of *Eucalyptus smithii* lies more or less between the 1400mm and 1600mm isohyet. With some overlap the upper limit of *Eucalyptus quadrangulata* is along this same line. The lower limit of *Eucalyptus quadrangulata* approximately follows the 1300mm isohyet in the north and the 1200mm isohyet in the south at West Dapto. *Eucalyptus pilularis* only extends into the foothills of the escarpment in the West Dapto area but in the north may be found up to 300 metres. Rainfall is assumed to be a major factor responsible for this gradation since the distributions cross geological changes, although other climatic factors such as temperature may also be important. In some respects the escarpment follows north-south changes similar to the coastal plain. The northern part (north of Mt. Keira) exhibits a relatively simple vegetation structure with the dominant eucalypt species being *Eucalyptus pilularis, Eucalyptus quadrangulata* and *Eucalyptus botryoides*. Between Mt. Keira and Mt. Kembla the patterns of distribution are more complex, with *Eucalyptus quadrangulata, Eucalyptus saligna* and *Eucalyptus saligna/botryoides* hybrids being the most common. The south facing side of Mt. Keira and the north facing side of Mt. Kembla are both largely covered in *Eucalyptus saligna* and hybrids. The southern part, from Mt. Kembla to Marshall Mt. Creek, shows a simple structure again with *Eucalyptus quadrangulata* and *Eucalyptus smithii* being the two most common eucalypts. The occurrence of *Eucalyptus pilularis, Eucalyptus paniculata* and *Syncarpia glomulifera* on the escarpment north of Mt. Keira and their absence south of this point is difficult to explain. It is also interesting to note that at the crest of the escarpment behind Mt. Keira, *Eucalyptus smithii* and *Eucalyptus pilularis* share an overlap zone of only a few hundred metres with *Eucalyptus smithii* occurring south of this point and

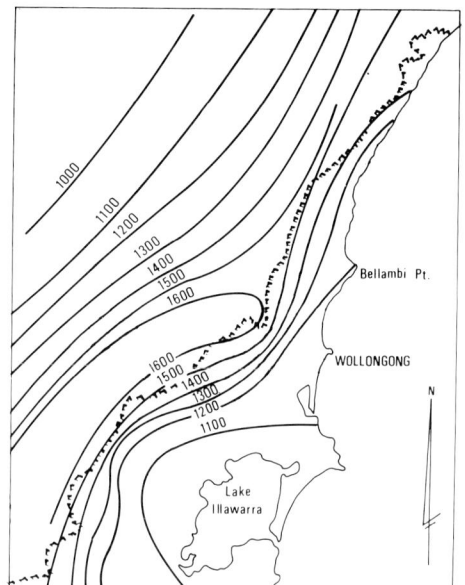

Fig. 3.16 Distribution of average annual rainfall. (Courtesy of Mrs. A. Young).

Fig. 3.17 Distribution of blackbutt *(Eucalyptus pilularis)*.

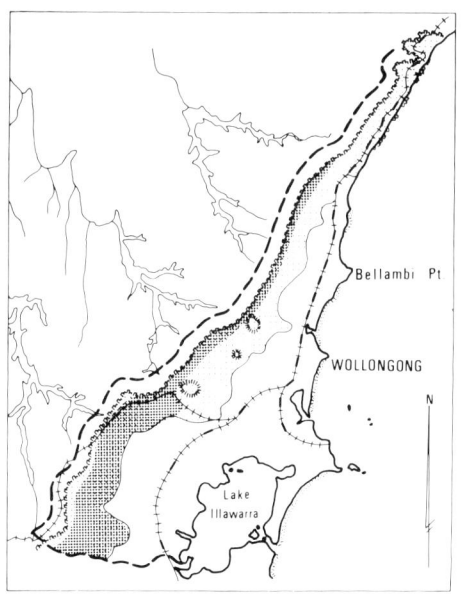

Fig. 3.18 Distribution of coast white box *(Eucalyptus quadrangulata)*.

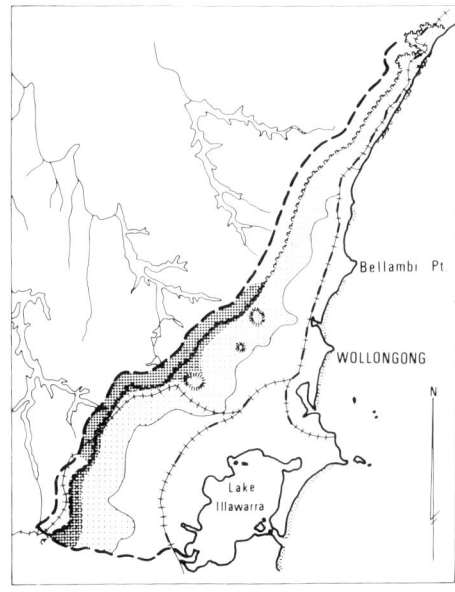

Fig. 3.19 Distribution of gully gum *(Eucalyptus smithii)*.

Eucalyptus pilularis to the north. It appears then that the Mt. Keira area is a changeover point in a north/south direction for conditions which cause these effects.

The northern-most part of the area under study in this book, around Stanwell Park and Coalcliff, is a zone of changeover from vegetation characteristic of Illawarra to that more typical of the Sydney area and differs in some respects to the rest of the Illawarra escarpment. Some of the differences are: the occurrence of *Angophora costata* both on the plateau and lower escarpment, the occurrence of *Tristaniopsis laurina* as a 10 metre tall rainforest tree on the banks of Stanwell Creek where it flows down the escarpment and the occurrence of *Choricarpia leptopetala* at Stanwell Park. The appearance of *Tristaniopsis laurina* as a common tree along the banks of Stanwell Creek is significant since it does not occur elsewhere along the escarpment. *Archontophoenix cunninghamii* occurs at Otford (virtually in this changeover zone). It occurs south of there in Illawarra, and does not grow in the Sydney area but reappears in the Gosford district. *Brachychiton acerifolium* likewise misses the Sydney area.

Escarpment Cliffs

The escarpment cliffs do not have any trees that are unique to them. They have, however, smaller shrubs and herbs which are distinctive of this habitat, but the trees are extensions of communities growing above or below the cliffs.

The soil on ledges on the cliffs is usually sandy and water is commonly found seeping out of joints in the sandstone. These conditions and protection from dry westerly winds along the eastward facing escarpment provide a good habitat for some of the species from the plateau, and since gravity favours dispersal of seed from above, it is not uncommon to find such plateau trees as *Eucalyptus sieberi* and *Allocasuarina littoralis*. It is also worth mentioning that ferns and orchids abound on the escarpment cliffs.

Because of the shallow soil and the exposed nature of the escarpment to strong south to north-easterly winds, tree species growing here often only grow a metre or so high. In some ways the escarpment cliffs are similar to the sea cliffs to the north which are also exposed to high winds. Plants such as *Melaleuca hypericifolia* and *Lomandra longifolia* can be found in both situations.

The vegetation of the escarpment is not uniform along its entire length, for indeed not even the rocky cliffs are continuous. In the north close to the sea, trees such as *Banksia integrifolia* and *Eucalyptus botryoides* grow, whereas in the south quite large trees of *Eucalyptus sieberi* and *Eucalyptus piperita* grow. The height of the cliffs, their aspect and distance from the sea all vary along the length of the escarpment, so it is not completely unexpected that vegetation also varies. A fully detailed ecological study of the escarpment cliffs is beyond the scope of this book, but a list of tree species appears in Trees Listed in Community Groups.

Plateau

The only part of the plateau under scrutiny in this book is the strip contained between the escarpment crest and an imaginary line one kilometre to the west. This is enough to give an impression of the contrast above and below the escarpment crest.

In the very northern part of the area (Fig. 3.1) northwards from a point west of Scarborough, the vegetation on the plateau takes on a character which is similar to the vegetation typical of parts of Royal National Park. It is in this northern corner that *Angophora costata* and *Ceratopetalum gummiferum* are found. Also *Banksia integrifolia* finds its way to the plateau here.

The plateau between the point west of Scarborough and Bulli Lookout has a flat to undulating surface. There are large areas of "hanging swamps" which are covered with low "moorland" plants such as sedges, melaleuca and banksia species (Fig. 3.20). Between swamp areas is forest dominated by *Eucalyptus sieberi, Eucalyptus racemosa/haemastoma* and *Eucalyptus gummifera.* The dry sclerophyll forest over all the Hawkesbury Sandstone of the plateau is dominated by medium sized trees and has a more or less dense undergrowth of sclerophyllous and often prickly shrubs. Investigation into the swamps (Young — personal comment) has indicated that the swamp areas themselves are areas of quite deep sandy soil whereas the forest overlies subterranean rocky outcrops where drainage is better. There is usually a very sharp cut off point between these two plant communities.

Between Bulli Lookout and a point about 1km north of Bong Bong Pass the plateau has quite a variable topography, at least in the one kilometre wide strip being dealt with here. The Hawkesbury Sandstone has been eroded away in many places exposing the underlying Narrabeen Series. This gives rise to more fertile soils and also gullies which provide protection allowing rainforest to form (Fig. 3.21). In many ways this part of the plateau is similar to the escarpment, with rainforest and wet sclerophyll forest forming a complex mosaic of vegetation. Eucalyptus species range from *Eucalyptus sieberi* on the Hawkesbury Sandstone, to massive trees of *Eucalyptus muellerana* and *Eucalyptus smithii* in sheltered areas. Other eucalypts

Fig. 3.20 Plateau-swamp community and adjacent eucalypt forest.

Fig. 3.21 Plateau gully showing rainforest (Rf) on the lower east-facing side of the gully. (East is to the left and the creek is marked (Ck).)

include *Eucalyptus piperita, Eucalyptus gummifera, Eucalyptus cypellocarpa* and *Eucalyptus elata*. Rainforest in this central plateau area is found nearly always on the east and south facing hillsides.

From the southern end of the last described plateau zone to the plateau above Marshall Mt. Creek, the plateau surface is undulating. The surface is all Hawkesbury Sandstone and consequently most of the eastern side ends in abrupt cliffs. As well, the vegetation becomes dry sclerophyll forest. Here again *Eucalyptus sieberi* dominates but other representative species are *Eucalyptus gummifera, Eucalyptus racemosa/haemastoma, Eucalyptus stricta* and *Eucalyptus ligustrina. Eucalyptus piperita* occurs in some sheltered places, particularly where the plateau slopes down to the headwaters of escarpment creeks.

RAINFOREST

Approaching the Illawarra district, particularly from the west, one cannot help but be impressed by an increase in the luxuriance of the natural vegetation, especially that on the escarpment. The eucalypt forest stands tall and thickly crowned but an important contribution to this luxuriance is made by rainforest; even in the eucalypt forest, mesophytic (water loving) species of rainforest can be found in abundance in the understorey.

The definition of rainforest can be rather elusive since the name implies a dependency on high and constant rainfall. This implication is not strictly true because rainforest develops in a wide range of seasonal rainfall patterns under varying temperature and soil fertility. In contrast to the typical Australian eucalypt forest, however, rainforest plants are mesophytic, i.e. they grow under conditions of average water availability and have leaves which are usually "fleshier", larger and with a thinner cuticle than leaves of "sclerophyll" plants. The leaves therefore readily exchange water with the atmosphere.

Rather than defining rainforest in succinct terms, instead let us look at the elements of rainforest and build up a picture of what separates it from other plant communities. The basis for the following description of rainforest features are the characteristics easily observed in local Wollongong forests.

On stepping into rainforest it is immediately apparent that light levels are much lower than in eucalypt forest. The closed canopy is responsible for this with each dense crown of leaves running into the next. However, the canopy may be even or uneven in height or have occasional lateral breaks in it. There may be one, two or three levels of canopy foliage. The net result, however, is usually close to full shade at ground level which inhibits all but the most shade tolerant species, such as ferns, seedlings of rainforest trees and a few other herbaceous plants. Consequently, the ground under rainforest is often bare soil or partially covered with leaf litter or ferns.

Supporting the dense leafy canopy are many straight, closely spaced stems of trees sporting few lateral branches except near the top. The tree trunks are sometimes fluted or buttressed and flare out quickly into a mass of roots near the soil surface. Rainforest trees do not have the deep roots of trees in eucalypt forest. The reason for the shallow rooting of rainforest trees is as follows. With the abundance of organic matter and soil moisture, micro organism activity in the upper soil horizons is very high. This depletes the oxygen supply in the soil and releases abundant nutrients. To take advantage of these nutrients, as well as obtain an adequate supply of oxygen, the tree roots are found very near the soil surface. Tree roots form a dense mat in the top 100mm to 200mm of soil, but below this are largely absent. High rainfall and the efficient release of soil nutrients by organisms means that most of the rainforest fertility is tied up in the plants themselves. There is an almost closed cycle whereby rainforest trees absorb nutrients from the soil and return it temporarily to the soil with leaf fall. Clearing of rainforest breaks this cycle. Exposure of the soil to direct rainfall rapidly leaches out nutrients and within a few years the soil is depleted.

The canopy of the rainforest is an important shield for the soil against the sun and drying winds and the leaves, being mesophytic, have the capacity to transpire freely. Conversely though, the leaves also have the capacity to absorb water, and this is an important mechanism since rainforest often occurs where misty conditions are common. Absorption of mists probably adds a significant amount to the trees' intake of water, but in addition condensation on leaves, forming water droplets that drip to the ground via the drip tips, is a common feature of rainforest species.

Protection which rainforest offers against dessicating outside conditions favours the growth of epiphytes such as lichens, elkhorns, birds nest ferns and orchids, as well as a host of woody climbing plants.

Generally "rainforest" is quite exclusive of eucalypts. In a purist sense, where eucalypts or other sclerophyllous trees such as *Syncarpia glomulifera* occur as scattered specimens in otherwise pure rainforest, this forest cannot bear the name rainforest. However where sclerophyllous elements do exist they are probably relics of a more extensive sclerophyll forest being overtaken by rainforest, and Webb (1968) includes rainforest with sclerophyllous emergents in his classification.

Classification and Distribution of Rainforest in the Wollongong Area

The classification and ecological status of Wollongong's rainforest is presently part of an ongoing study (Bywater 1978 and in prep.). Using Webb's 1968 classification system the rainforest has been separated into two distinct types. Although out of the area included in this book it is worth noting that the rainforest on latite in the Jamberoo area can be placed in the Subtropical Complex Notophyll Vine Forest category. This type is characterised by a minimum of ferns and an abundance of woody vines, vascular epiphytes, three tree layers, emergents, a few deciduous elements and a varied and luxuriant tree element. Rainforest on the escarpment is not as easy to pigeon-hole and represents a mixture of two categories. Bywater has termed it Mixed Notophyll Vine-Fern Forest.

There are, however, subtle variations of rainforest within the escarpment area. Also there are the rainforests of the plateau gullies and those associated with streams across the coastal plain to consider. Because of the almost complete disruption by urban development the coastal plain rainforest must be treated with caution. However there is an outstanding difference between this and rainforest on the escarpment and that is that the coastal plain rainforest contains virtually no *Ceratopetalum apetalum* and virtually no *Doryphora sassafras*, two of the most common species on the upper part of the escarpment. In fact the abundance of these two species seems to be proportional to altitude within the area considered in this book.

Rainforest in the deep gullies between spurs of the foothills (Fig 3.12) is quite luxuriant and contains a large number of species. There are very few examples of this rainforest left, two gullies being at Calderwood and Stanwell Park. Luxuriant rainforest is again to be found at the rear of the benches on the escarpment (Fig. 3.14). It is here some of the largest of the rainforest trees can be seen, such as emergent *Ficus sp., Citronella moorei* and *Toona australis*, all well over 35m tall. There are also many dense stands of *Livistona australis* in the moist conditions of the benches.

Above the benches on the talus slope of the escarpment occurs a simpler type of rainforest (Fig. 3.15). In fact nearly all rainforest above this point (i.e. on the Bulgo Sandstone and above) is similar whether it be on the escarpment or in plateau gullies. This rainforest is dominated by five species; *Ceratopetalum apetalum, Doryphora sassafras, Cryptocarya glaucescens, Acmena smithii* and *Livistona australis*. Of course there are many other species of trees, particularly along watercourses where the diversity may be as great as further down the escarpment, but generally the simpler nature of the rainforest in this upper part can be recognised quite readily.

It is interesting to look at rainforest in the Wollongong area on the basis of plant succession. From recent research Bywater has indicated that bushfire is the major limiting factor on rainforest in this area. Fire attacks the edges, and limits the spread of rainforest, even though the occurrence of fire may have a 200 or 300 year interval. On top of this there is also exposure to drying winds, sun and inhospitable soils which further limit the spread of rainforest. Despite these limitations there is reason to believe rainforest has a successional development in this area.

Evidence for succession lies in the composition of rainforest in various situations. On the coastal plain the "rainforest" consists of species which usually grow on the edge of rainforest on the escarpment and on the escarpment the diversity of rainforest appears to be proportional to the width of the rainforest. That is, as the rainforest spreads the pioneer species at its edge are engulfed by those following and die out or grow to a size comparable to those following. As the rainforest spreads further, species are added to the forest's complement in the centre

Conclusion

The native forests of the Wollongong area show distinct differentiation of species due to influences of physical elements. The coastal zone has plants characteristic of seashore atmospheric conditions, sandy soils or brackish lagoon soils. The coastal plain, with lower rainfall than the escarpment and slow draining clayey soils, has species of trees which are most competitive in these conditions and which form communities distinctly different to those on the escarpment. The escarpment, with its orographic effects, has trees stratified according to climatic variables associated with altitude and water movement through the soil. The plateau has a Hawkesbury Sandstone capping over much of its area and this carries characteristic species. Where eroded to expose underlying strata, tall wet sclerophyll forest may grow and sometimes rainforest establishes in the most protected places.

Rainforest occurs where soil moisture is high enough and some protection from drying westerly winds is afforded. Also freedom from bushfires is necessary for rainforest to spread. In the Wollongong area the main situations where rainforest occurs are; along coastal plain creeks, in deep gullies between foothill spurs, at the rear of the escarpment benches, on the talus slope on the escarpment and in gullies formed by westward flowing streams on the plateau.

Trees in Other Roles

TREES AND BIRDS
J. D. Gibson

Birds have evolved numerous adaptations to utilise the many ecological niches in the various habitat types. Trees being the dominant component of so many environments, their importance in the economy of many bird species is not surprising. Each is important to the other in a balanced ecosystem; trees provide essential requirements for birds and derive benefits from the relationship in return.

Birds and Blossoms

The nectar supplied by the blossoms of eucalypts, banksias, grevilleas etc. is an important food resource for many of the district's birds, notably the honeyeaters. Blackbutt, swamp mahogany, bloodwood, scribbly gum and Sydney blue gum are good nectar producing eucalypts. The intensity of flowering is variable from year to year and different species flower in different months thus spreading the nectar supply over much of the year. As a consequence, the principal nectar-feeders are usually found to be nomadic or make regular seasonal movements. Unusually heavy flowering can cause spectacular invasions of certain species.

Honeyeaters do not rely entirely on nectar for their sustenance, insects and pollen are also taken, supplemented in some species by fruits and berries — young in the nest are invariably fed on insects. The distinguishing characteristic of the group, however, is the brush-tipped tongue, a striking adaptation for nectar feeding involving tube-like folds and a frayed tip. With this unique apparatus honey-eating birds are able to imbibe nectar from the open and diffuse eucalypt blossoms by a combined licking/sucking action. A similar tongue modification appears in the hummingbirds *(Trochilidae)* of America and the sunbirds *(Nectariniidae)* of Africa enabling them also to exploit the nectar of flowering plants.

Of the eighteen or so honeyeaters that are known from the area, the following six are most commonly observed. Eastern spinebill *(Acanthorhynchus tenuirostris)* is common in gardens and forest country where a suitable shrub layer exists, often probing blossoms while briefly hovering in front of them. Yellow-faced honeyeater *(Lichenostomus chrysops)* inhabits eucalypt forests. The resident population of this species is augmented by migrating flocks travelling northward in April/May and southward in August/September. Lewin's Honeyeater *(Meliphaga lewinii)*, the only rainforest honeyeater may also be found in wet sclerophyll forests and nearby gardens. Its diet also includes fruit and berries. New Holland honeyeater *(Phylidonyris novaehollandiae)* favours banksias and melaleucas while little wattlebird *(Anthochaera chrysoptera)* and red wattlebird *(A. carunculata)* which are both large nomadic honeyeaters follow blossoming eucalypts and banksias, especially *Banksia ericifolia*.

Several species of honey-eating parrots share in the Australian nectar harvest, these are the lorikeets which first crush the blossoms in their bills then lick up the nectar and pollen with their brush-tipped tongues. Noisy and gregarious they are not, however, very numerous or well-known in this area. The commonest is the little lorikeet *(Glossopsitta pusilla)*. In earlier days nomadic movements of lorikeets on a large scale were a feature of the district, probably when food trees in coastal dune forests provided an abundant seasonal attraction.

Blossom feeders provide an efficient means of pollination by transferring the pollen grains accidentally adhering to their head parts, from tree to tree. Whereas insects and wind are the principal pollinating agents considered on a world basis, many Australian eucalypts, banksias etc. depend on honeyeaters and lorikeets to perform this function.

Seed Dispersal

Trees depend on various means for the dispersal of their seeds such as wind, water and birds. Grain-eating (graminivorous) birds get protein from the seeds themselves while fruit-eating (frugivorous) birds seek the pulpy flesh in which the seeds are encased. Seeds consumed by fruit-eaters are later regurgitated with other indigestible matter or pass through the alimentary canal and are voided intact, often with their hard covering softened sufficiently to increase the chances of germination. One wonders how seeds which are too heavy to be spread by the wind can germinate at a higher elevation than the parent tree. It is quite possible that the distribution of such trees would slowly contract to ever lower elevations if it was not for the assistance of fruit and seed-eating birds.

Trees in tropical climates are capable of providing a diet of various fruits throughout the year which is why specialist fruit-eating birds are mainly to be found in those areas. Fruit-eaters of temperate regions, as in this district, must either have the ability to forage over considerable distances or accept alternative foods when fruit is scarce. Topknot pigeons *(Lopholaimus antarcticus)* especially seek the fruit

Fig. 4.1 Topknot pigeon feeding on fruits of the cabbage palm.
Photo: E. McNamara

of our large native figs *(Ficus sp.)* and later the still viable seeds are voided, often in places remote from the parent tree. Other arboreal fruit-eaters which play their part in the dispersal of seeds are the white-headed pigeon *(Columba leucomela)*, pied currawong *(Strepera graculina)*, satin bowerbird *(Ptilonorhynchus violaceus)*, green figbird *(Sphecotheres viridis)*, olive-backed oriole *(Oriolus sagittatus)*, king parrot *(Alisterus scapularis)*, silvereye *(Zosterops lateralis)* and red-whiskered bulbul *(Pycnonotus jocosus)*. Typical of the many trees whose seeds are mainly spread by birds are pittosporum, white cedar, bangalow and cabbage-tree palms, lillypilly and, regretfully, the camphor laurel and privet, these two being introduced "weed" species whose proliferation is degrading our native forests in some areas.

Insect Suppression

The importance of birds in the control of insects injurious to trees is difficult to assess though observation of the almost ceaseless activity of many species in this area leads one to conclude that their role must be significant. Birds often tend to congregate where insect outbreaks provide abundant food thus they apply pressure on insect life in proportion to insect abundance.

Because of their active life, high temperature and small size, birds in general require proportionally more food than other animals. Small insectivorous birds like the warblers and thornbills because of their high metabolic rate are constantly engaged in gleaning the vegetation for insect prey. Spotted pardalotes *(Pardalotus punctatus)* are typical of the leaf gleaners. Weighing only a few grams they are easily supported by the leaves amongst which they forage for small insects especially "lerp-insects" *(Psyllidae)* which can be very damaging to some eucalypt species if infestations are heavy in successive years.

In their tireless foraging, the various thornbills and warblers are assisted by other mainly or exclusively insectivorous groups such as the whistlers, flycatchers, thrushes, cuckoos, cuckoo-shrikes, frogmouths, dollarbirds, bee-eaters and woodswallows, the last three catching their prey on the wing. Treecreepers and sittellas specialise in searching the trunks and branches for insects concealed in the crevices while currawongs and cockatoos occasionally adopt the same procedure. Shrike-tits have a powerful short beak with which they prise off pieces of bark to reveal the insects underneath. The combined efforts of all the above must add up to a measure of control over thrips, leaf-miners, scale insects, spiders, caterpillars, beetles etc. and thus reduce the debilitating effect that these animals can have on trees in general.

Yellow-tailed black cockatoos *(Calyptorhynchus funereus)* are particularly fond of the wood-boring larvae of longicorn beetles. When they locate an infested tree, by hearing the grubs at work, the birds methodically strip away the bark and outer growth layers until the prey is exposed. Because of their wary nature the cockatoos are seldom seen at this task but trees damaged in this typical way are testimony to the fact and it is generally conceded that destruction of infested trees contributes to the overall health of the forest.

Outside the breeding season, different species of insectivorous birds often band together and move through forested areas in mixed feeding flocks. It has been proposed, and seems logical, that the foraging potential of individuals or small parties of one species is enhanced by this interspecific association, each bird exploiting its own particular part of the food spectrum and benefitting from the general disturbance of quiescent insects by other group members.

Other essential avian requirements provided by trees include nesting sites, nesting material, song perches, vantage points for hunting and shelter for roosting and resting.

From consideration of the above comments it is fairly obvious that the course of evolutionary development has made trees and birds to a certain extent mutually dependent. Loss of tree species from an area inevitably means a loss of bird species and a consequent impoverishment of the natural environment.

LOCAL TREES IN THE GARDEN

In the forests of Illawarra there lies a huge number of plant species as yet largely untapped for their use in parks and gardens. The trees alone number over 100 and cover a wide range of form, colour, foliage texture, flowers and fruits. Some of the trees such as flame tree *(Brachychiton acerifolium)*, lillypilly *(Acmena smithii)* and spotted gum *(Eucalyptus maculata)* have been used successfully to enhance gardens for years. Many remain to be brought out into cultivation.

The large number and diversity of trees ensure that there are species suitable for most situations in gardens. The descriptions of the trees later in this book will give some idea of the conditions each species grows under naturally and hence what might be expected of them under cultivation. Most of the urban development in Wollongong is from the hind dune zone, across the coastal plain and up into the foothills of the escarpment. There has been some residential growth on the lower bench of the northern part of the area, but the upper bench, the steeper escarpment slopes and the plateau have little need for cultivation of trees.

The seaside always presents a problem for tree growers. The windy, salty environment not only restricts the number of species which grow there naturally, but once the natural tree cover has been removed, the establishment of trees facing the full onslaught of the elements becomes more difficult by one hundredfold. Tree selection for this area must be confined to such species as coast banksia *(Banksia integrifolia)*, coast tea tree *(Leptospermum laevigatum)*, and where the water table is high or the ground wet, swamp she-oak *(Casuarina glauca)* and *Melaleuca* species. Where a situation is exposed to the full force of wind off the sea, trees must be planted densely (i.e. 1-2m apart in groups) and the tree planting supplemented by dense shrub planting of such species as coast rosemary *(Westringia fruticosa)*.

By far the greatest demand for trees as ornamentals exists on the coastal plain. Here the soil conditions are often clayey and slow draining. This proves extremely difficult for many "Australian Native" plants introduced from such places as Western Australia. In fact, the failures, after attempting to grow Western Australian plants in conditions so alien to them, were partly responsible for the reputation some years back, of native plants being difficult to grow. For trees which form the large and basic elements of a domestic landscape, those indigenous to the coastal plain of Illawarra offer some reliable, fast growing and handsome alternatives. Forest red gum *(Eucalyptus tereticornis)* is probably the most reliable of these, but grey ironbark *(Eucalyptus paniculata)*, small leaved stringybark *(Eucalyptus eugenioides)* and woollybutt *(Eucalyptus longifolia)* are also reliable and worth growing. Intermediate forms of *Eucalyptus botryoides* and *Eucalyptus saligna* form adaptable and successful trees, but they are not as good for ornamental purposes as those previously named, because of their susceptibility to lerps. This sap sucking insect causes brown, dead patches on the leaves increasing in number through the summer, and by about June, the trees are completely brown and unattractive. It is possible for these insects to misshape trees or actually kill them, but this is usually not the case. The use of insecticides against the lerp problem is pointless because of the enormous population of the insects over the whole Wollongong area. Insecticides also penalise the bird population, which is the major predator of lerps. Melaleucas are another group of trees which have representatives indigenous to the Wollongong coastal plain, and which form attractive ornamental trees. In fact, the melaleucas and *Callistemon salignus* are particularly suited to domestic gardens because of their small size.

Apart from those trees indigenous to the coastal plain, many other trees native to Wollongong make good ornamental subjects. The tall elegant trees of deep mountain soils such as coast white box *(Eucalyptys quadrangulata)* and gully gum *(Eucalyptus smithii)* will grow on the coastal plain although they do not attain the same proportions under cultivation. Another large group of plants rather neglected as garden specimens are the rainforest trees. Most of this group are beautiful, often with large and shiny leaves crowded into a dense crown. Under cultivation they grow into small or medium sized trees. Unfortunately, there is not a lot known about the use of these as ornamentals, and the great variety of shapes, sizes, environmental requirements and establishment procedures generally does not make them easy to grow. Even so, many can be grown readily, and for a keen gardener, with patience and the desire to try new and different techniques, rainforest trees offer great rewards.

The greatest value of Wollongong's native trees in horticulture, is the range of foliage colours and textures, and variety of forms, but showy flowers are not

Fig. 4.2 Red ash *(Alphitonia excelsa)* growing as street trees.

completely absent. Swamp mahogany *(Eucalyptus robusta)* produces flowers "en masse" and native hibiscus *(Hibiscus heterophyllus)* with its 100mm wide white and red throated flowers is an attractive and easily grown plant. *Eucryphia moorei*, which is related to the Tasmanian leatherwood *(Eucryphia lucida)* is a particularly attractive plant, including its showy flowers. Of course, for flower display, there are the well known subjects of flame tree, banksias and wattles.

For displays of interesting and coloured fruit there is no shortage among trees of the Wollongong area. The currently best known of these are New South Wales Christmas bush *(Ceratopetalum gummiferum)*, and the closely related coachwood *(Ceratopetalum apetalum),* brush cherry *(Syzygium paniculatum)* and lillypilly *(Acmena smithii).* There are, however, many more with *Emmenosperma alphitonioides* showing a mass of orange across its crown during fruiting, the bright yellow composite fruit of native mulberry *(Hedycarya angustifolia)*, the white fruits of *Schizomeria ovata* and *Acronychia oblongifolia*, and the shiny black fruits of black apple *(Planchonella australis)*, native laurel *(Cryptocarya glaucescens)* and celerywood *(Polyscias elegans).*

Apart from domestic gardens, there are also trees suitable for open spaces, public parks etc. Moreton Bay fig *(Ficus macrophylla)* has been widely used in the Illawarra district and can be seen on many old dairy farms and in parks. Some of the larger eucalypts can also be used to great effect to match the scale of large areas.

The potential of the trees which grow naturally in Wollongong should not be overlooked. In their own right they are handsome plants, and as supplements to an otherwise exotic garden, they can be invaluable. It is pleasing to see greater use currently being made of these trees; and the character of the surrounding bushland becoming a part of suburban scenery.

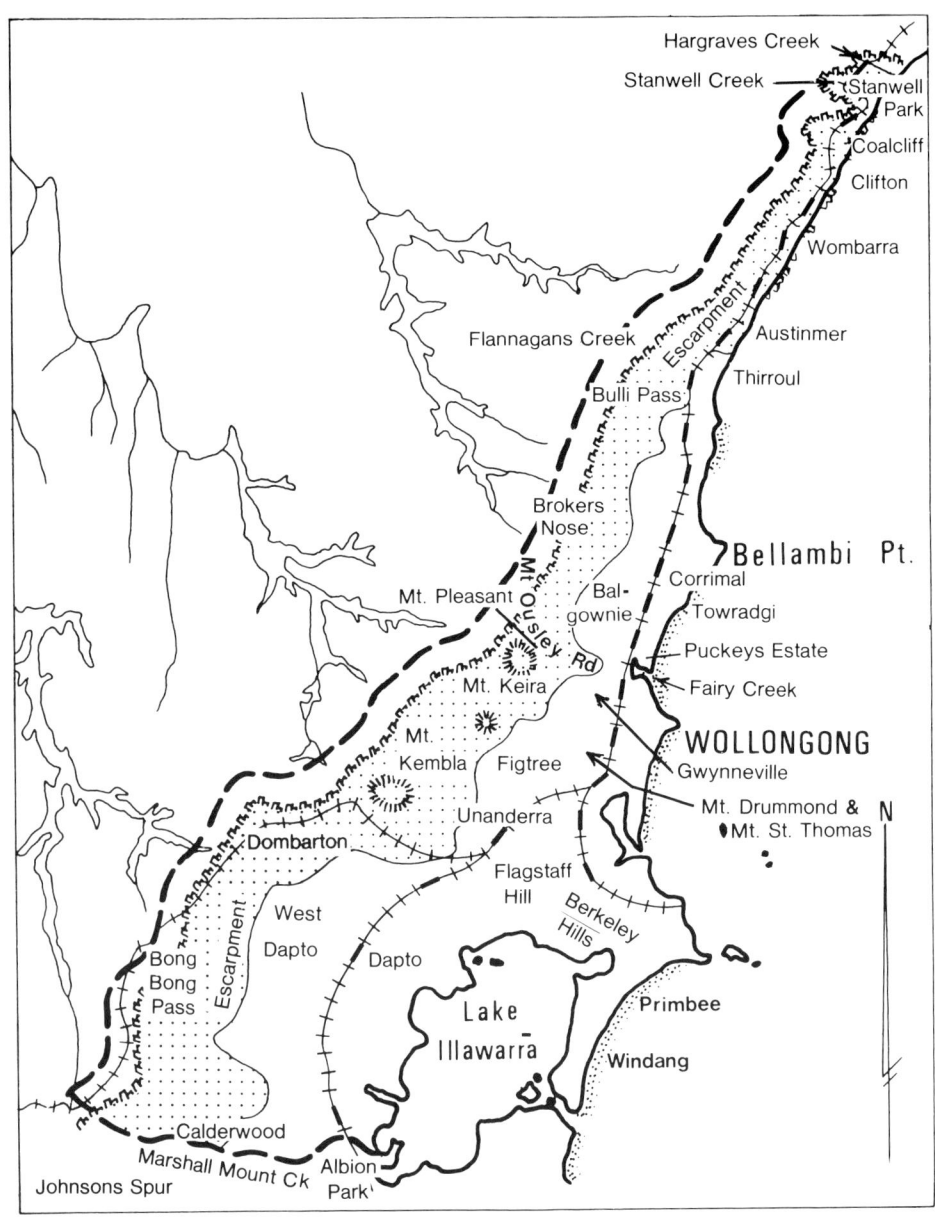

Fig. 5.1 Reference map for descriptions.

Wollongong's Native Trees

DESCRIPTIONS

In a limited area such as that covered in this book identification of trees is a relatively simple matter especially when armed with a list of species which are present. Having established that a species occurs in the area the list of trees in community groups and the distribution maps will further limit the number of possibilities. Of course some discrepancies may be found in the exact limits of some of the species since it is impossible to check every single tree in the area. However, the maps reflect general trends, and deviations between the distributions drawn and reality should arise only in minor detail. Further information on species distribution from interested readers would be welcomed and included in any later editions of this book.

The general notes for each species are intended to give a quick reference to the overall habit, size and habitat. Following this, the more detailed morphological details should enable the reader to ascertain the identity of a tree.

Photographs are included as a guide but it must be remembered that it is impossible to cover the natural variation of all characters of a species so that "typical" characters have been photographed where possible. In some cases large differences may be found between living specimens and the photographs. The staff used for measurement reference in overall tree photographs is one metre long and divided into 100mm black or white subdivisions.

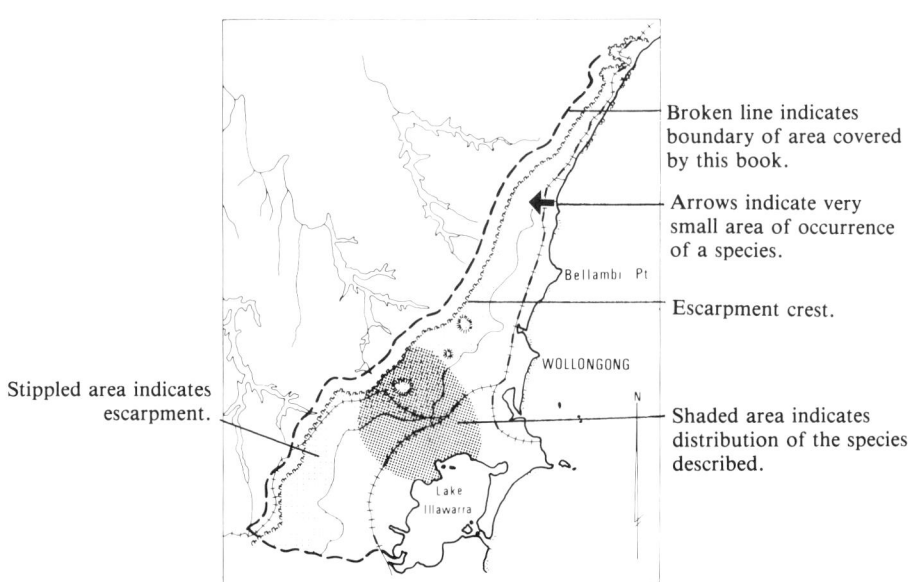

Abarema sapindoides (A. Cunn.) Kosterm.

Snow wood or stink wood
Mimosaceae

Snow wood is one of the few representatives of the mimosa family which grow in rainforest in the Wollongong area. It is uncommon and mostly seen as a spindly plant one to three metres tall. Sometimes, however, it reaches 10m tall and forms an attractive tree with fine textured foliage. The unusual bipinnate leaves are the most distinctive feature of this tree while its common name is derived from the unpleasant smell of the freshly cut wood.

Bark: Grey.

Leaves: Bipinnate up to about 400mm long; the primary axis (rhachis) has a number of pairs of secondary axes bearing leaflets; the Y that the end pair of secondary axes forms with the rhachis is distinctive in this species. Leaflets — irregularly alternate, elliptical, rhomboidal; sometimes with a point and sometimes with an oblique base, 15mm to 75mm long, 10mm to 30mm wide.

Inflorescence: Globular umbels.

Flowers: Greenish, about 4mm long.

Fruit: A legume twisted in a circle, reddish inside.

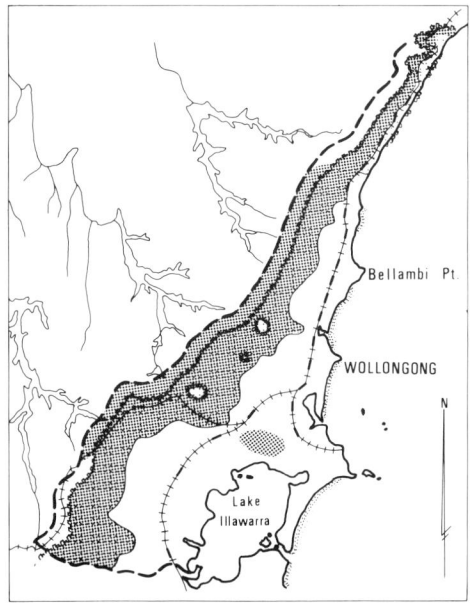

A single leaf.

Tree in rainforest.
A person can be seen,
rather indistinctly,
standing to the right of
the base of the tree, to
give some idea of size.

Acacia binervata DC.
Two-veined hickory
Mimosaceae

Acacia binervata is the most common wattle in the Wollongong area. It occurs right across the coastal plain, up the escarpment slopes and on the plateau. It does not appear in rainforest but reaches its best development on the edges. As with many wattles, *A. binervata* is quick to regenerate on cleared or disturbed ground and dense thickets of this species may be found preceding regenerating forest.

Two-veined hickory forms a large rounded shrub when growing out in the open but on the edges of rainforest it forms a handsome dense foliaged tree about 10m tall. As an understorey plant in eucalypt forest it tends to grow with a more open crown.

The phyllodes of this wattle are quite distinctive having two obvious parallel veins and sometimes a third vein.

Bark: Dark brown, rough.

Phyllodes: Alternate, rhomboid; elliptical or lanceolate with two or sometimes three parallel veins; 70mm to 120mm long, 10mm to 50mm wide; marginal gland below middle of phyllode.

Inflorescence: Panicles with terminal groups in balls, about 20 fls in each ball. Balls 8mm to 12mm diameter.

Flowers: Pale yellow. Flowers October.

Fruit: An oblong pod about 12mm wide; flat, thin and straight. Fruits December.

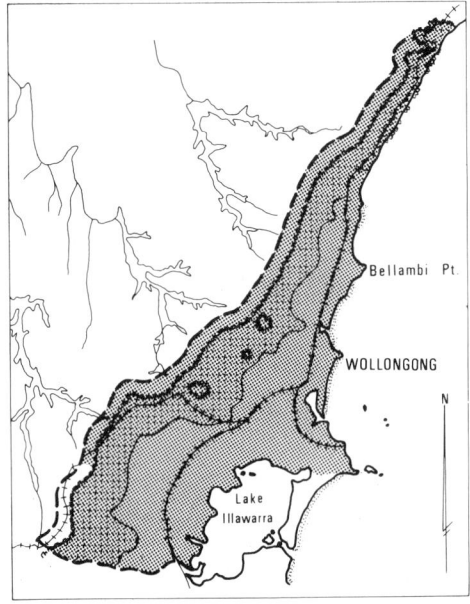

TOP LEFT: Tree. TOP RIGHT: Fruit. MIDDLE RIGHT: Bark. BOTTOM LEFT: Phyllodes. BOTTOM RIGHT: Flowers.

Acacia maidenii F. Muell.
Maiden's wattle
Mimosaceae

This wattle is most easily identified by its long narrow phyllodes and when in flower, by its spike inflorescence instead of balls. It is a common wattle on the edge of rainforest and also in much of the sclerophyll forest growing throughout the area except on the Hawkesbury Sandstone.

Maiden's wattle grows to about 20m tall but is most often found about 6m tall with a rounded crown. The bright green crown of this tree is quite conspicuous against surrounding foliage.

Bark: Grey, fibrous.

Phyllodes: Alternate, long and narrow, several longitudinal veins, curved, 50mm to 160mm long, 6mm to 15mm wide, tapering at each end.

Inflorescence: One, two or three spike clusters in forks of phyllodes. Spikes 20mm to 30mm long.

Flowers: Pale yellow. Flowers January-June.

Fruit: A legume 50mm to 150mm long, much twisted, 5-6mm wide.

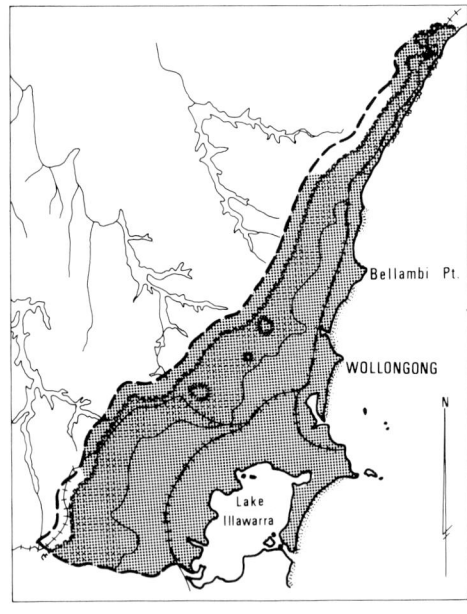

TOP LEFT: Phyllodes and flowers. TOP RIGHT: Tree. BOTTOM LEFT: Bark. BOTTOM RIGHT: Fruit.

Acacia mearnsii De Wild.
(formerly incorrectly known as *A. Mollissima*)

Black wattle
Green wattle
Mimosaceae

This species is the easiest of the wattles to identify in the Wollongong area. It is the only fern leaved (bipinnate) wattle in the area which reaches tree proportions. It is a common feature of Berkeley/Flagstaff Hills and coastal plain at Dapto and Yallah but occurs over the whole coastal plain and onto the lower slopes of the escarpment. It also occurs on the plateau on favourable sites. Like most wattles *Acacia mearnsii* can be found in dense thickets where it has recolonised cleared land.

Black wattle grows to about 10m tall in this area but is more commonly seen as a mature tree 5-6m high. It is a rapid grower.

Bark: Brown, hard, rough. Young bark green. Smaller stems velvety pubescent.

Leaves: Alternate, bipinnate, 70mm to 150mm long, 50mm to 100mm wide. Leaflets: 1.0mm to 3mm long, hairless above, pubescent below. Numerous glands along rhachis.

Inflorescence: Panicles in forks of outer leaves and terminal at ends of branches.

Flowers: In ball clusters, pale yellow. Flowers October-December.

Fruit: A pod, brown-black, 40mm to 90mm long, 4mm to 8mm wide. More or less segmented.

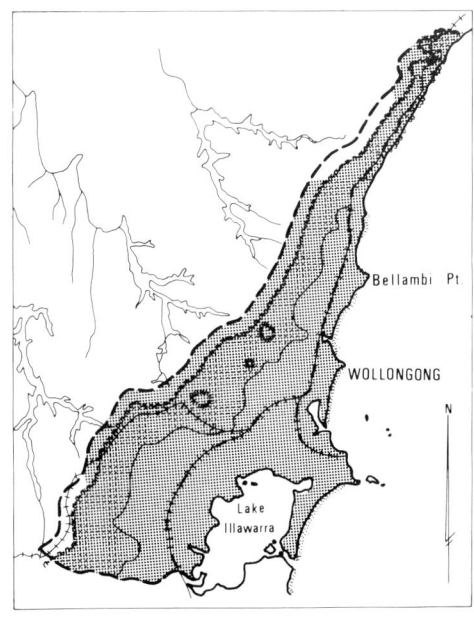

Trees.

Leaves.

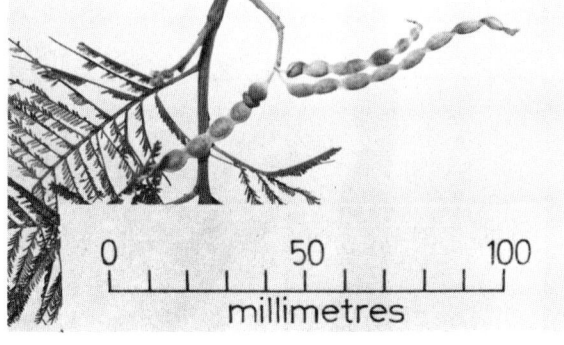

Fruit.

Acacia melanoxylon R. Br.

Blackwood

Mimosaceae

Blackwood is not as widely distributed in Wollongong as the other three tree wattles. It has a marked preference for richer and moister soils and can be found commonly in the foothills of the escarpment in sclerophyll forest, on the edges of and sometimes in rainforest where it attains a height of over 20m.

Bark: Grey, fibrous.

Phyllodes: Alternate, sickle shaped, dark greyish green, 70mm to 120mm long, 9mm to 17mm wide, thick with several longitudinal veins.

Inflorescence: Panicles in upper axils or terminal on branches.

Flowers: In ball clusters, pale yellow. Flowers August-November.

Fruit: A legume, curved or twisted, 80mm to 100mm long, 5mm to 8mm wide. Funicle twice encircling seed.

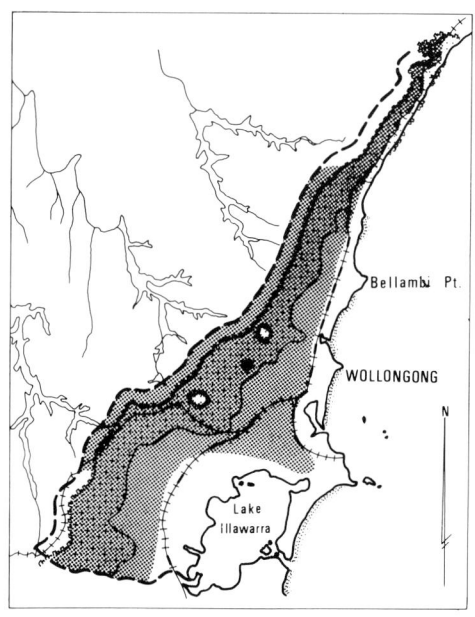

TOP LEFT: Bark. MIDDLE LEFT: Fruit and leaves. TOP RIGHT: Tree. BOTTOM LEFT: Juvenile leaves. BOTTOM RIGHT: Phyllodes with flower buds.

Acmena smithii (Poir.) Merrill et Perry

syn. *Eugenia smithii* Poir.

Lillypilly

Myrtaceae

Lillypilly is one of the commonest trees in the rainforest of this area. It is an adaptable species and grows in the rainforest of the plateau gullies, escarpment slopes, coastal plain, and on the sea cliffs where conditions are favourable. It is one of the few rainforest trees which extend into Victoria.

Within the area included in this book *Acmena smithii* grows to about 20m in good rainforest but in more exposed situations it is smaller and under the severe conditions of the sea cliff vegetation it is found as a shrub often 1m to 2m high. It is one of the five common species of the simple rainforest on the talus slope immediately beneath the cliff line of the escarpment.

Lillypilly has been immortalised by May Gibbs in her book *Snugglepot and Cuddlepie*, and because of its handsome foliage and distinctive fruit has been grown widely as an ornamental plant.

Care must be taken to distinguish this species from *Backhousia myrtifolia* and *Syzygium australe* if only leaves are available.

Bark: The bark of this tree is a reddish brown, flaky to almost powdery. The colour makes the trunk of this tree easy to identify in the rainforest.

Leaves: Oppositely arranged, ovate to elliptical, drawn out to a point at the apex. The upper surface is dark glossy green and the underside paler. 35mm to 100mm long, 30mm to 60mm wide. (Sometimes very large, up to 150mm long and 100mm wide.)

Inflorescence: Axillary panicles; shorter or sometimes longer than leaves.

Flowers: Petals white-pink; stamens numerous and white about 3mm long. Flowers summer.

Fruit: White to pale purple; globular 8mm to 15mm diam. with a flat crown. Fruits autumn and winter.

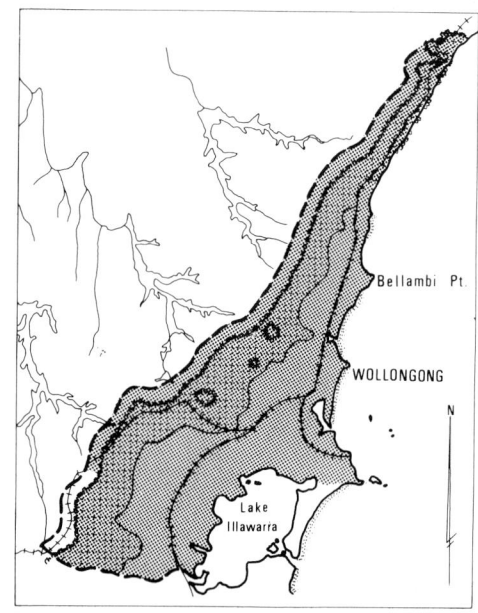

Tree.

Fruit.

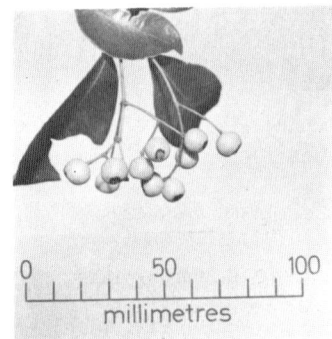

Leaves. Leaf laid across stem shows underside.

Acronychia oblongifolia (A. Cunn ex Hook) Endl. ex Heyn.

syn. *A. laevis* Forst et f.

Rutaceae

Acronychia oblongifolia is rather uncommon in the Wollongong area. It reaches its best development at about 12m tall in rainforest but sometimes grows in tall moist eucalypt forest where it is a smaller tree or a bushy shrub. It is most common around the Mt. Keira area both on the escarpment and the plateau where strata below Hawkesbury Sandstone are exposed.

The most distinctive feature of this tree is the articulation of the leaves. At the base of the leaf blade there is a bump which serves to orientate the leaf to light and is also possibly an evolutionary left-over where more leaflets once originated. The leaf blade is often found kinked at a different angle to the leaf stalk.

Bark: Brown or grey.

Leaves: Opposite or alternate, stalked; blade articulates on petiole, oblanceolate; with a rounded end or short point; 60mm to 100mm long, 20mm to 40mm wide; numerous oil dots present in leaves.

Inflorescence: Loose cymes in forks of leaves.

Flowers: Calyx 4 lobed, petals 4, white or yellowish. Flower about 7mm across. Flowers late summer.

Fruit: Globular, slightly lobed. White, yellow or greenish, 6mm to 12mm diam. Fruits summer.

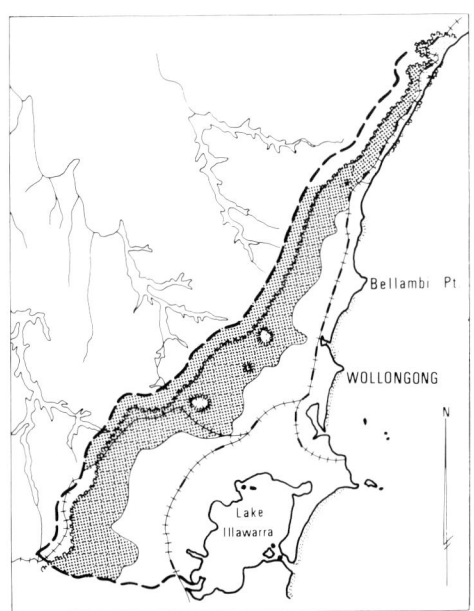

Leaves and fruit.

Alectryon subcinereus (A. Gray) Radlk.

syn. *Nephelium tomentosum* F. Muell.

Native quince

Sapindaceae

Native quince when growing in the open forms a broad, dense crowned tree about 5 metres tall. In rainforest it may grow up to about 8m tall but is often seen as a small understorey bush. It is rarely found outside rainforest although it may grow at the edges, at least in the Wollongong area.

The most distinctive feature is the compound leaves with lumps at the base of the leaflets.

Bark: Grey.

Leaves: Alternate, pinnate with 4 to 6 leaflets. Leaflets — Shortly stalked with lumps where petiolules attach to the rhachis, oblong-elliptical to lanceolate, 40mm to 100mm long, dull green. Venation prominent on undersurface; margins sometimes toothed. The two terminal leaflets are often larger than others on the same leaf.

Inflorescence: Loose panicles.

Flowers: 3-4mm across. Flowers August to September.

Fruit: 8mm to 10mm diam. with 2 or 3 distinct obtuse lobes, opening to expose black seed and bright red, fleshy, edible aril.

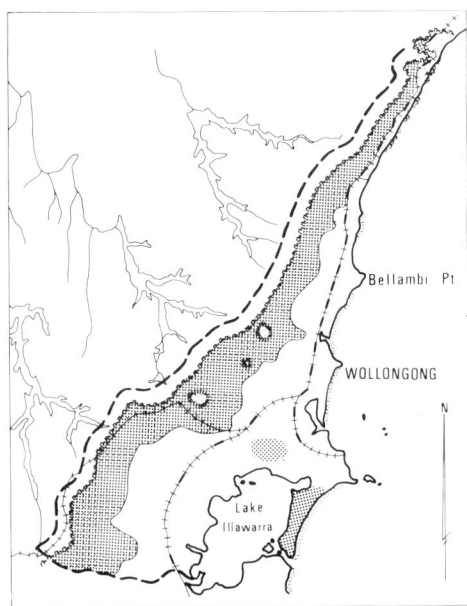

Tree.

Leaf.

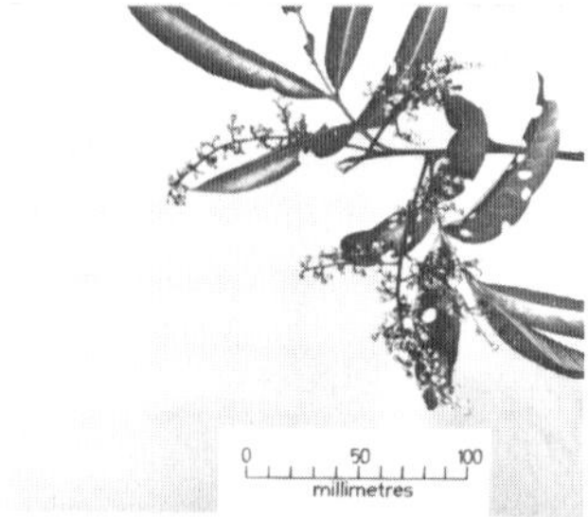

TOP: Flowers.
BOTTOM: Fruit.

Allocasuarina littoralis (Salisb.) L. Johnson

syn. *Casuarina littoralis* Salisb.
   C. suberosa Otto et Dietr.

Black she-oak

Casuarinaceae

This tree is probably the most widespread of *Allocasuarina* in the Wollongong area. It appears on the plateau, scattered across the escarpment and coastal plain and in the dune system near the sea. There are some very good specimens of the black she-oak atop Mount Kembla where it grows up to a height of about 10m. Usually, however, it is found as a small tree 3m to 6m tall. In exposed situations such as at the crest of the escarpment it is only a shrub about 1m high.

Bark: Varies from hard, dark brown or black bark to grey-brown, and fissured.

Leaves: Whorls of 6-8. Branchlets slender and erect.

Inflorescence: Male spikes slender and weak.

Fruit: Cones truncate, cylindrical, 10mm to 40mm long, 10mm to 20mm across, brown.

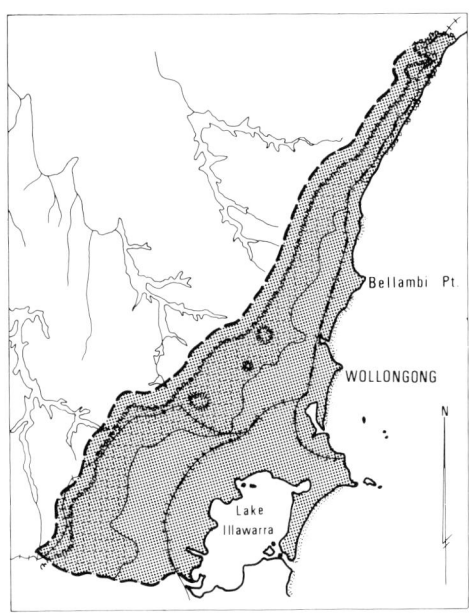

ABOVE: Fruit.
TOP RIGHT: Tree.

Branchlets and fruit.

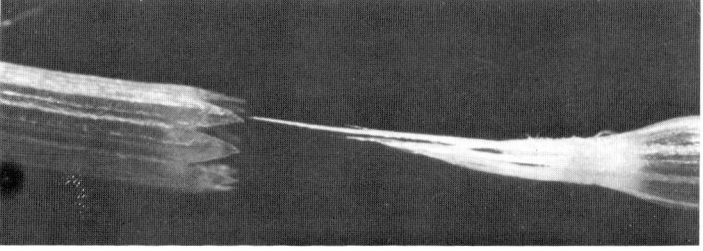

Branchlet parted to show scale leaves.

Allocasuarina torulosa (Ait.) L. Johnson
syn. *Casuarina torulosa* Ait.
Forest oak
Casuarinaceae

Allocasuarina torulosa may be found on the coastal plain although it is rather uncommon there and confined to richer and well drained soils. However, on the escarpment slopes, particularly north of Mt. Keira, this species becomes much more common, usually growing as an understorey to blackbutt *(Eucalyptus pilularis)*.

Forest oak is a beautiful tree with very fine and pendulous branchlets which turn a reddish purple colour in the cooler months. It is only of medium height, growing to about 10m tall. In cultivation this tree prefers good conditions and may be slow to become established.

Bark: Deeply furrowed corky bark, rather spongy on small branches, red-brown or grey.

Leaves: Leaves arranged in whorls of 4 or 5. Branchlets fine and usually quadrangular or 4-angled, turning reddish under poor conditions or in cooler months.

Inflorescence: Male spikes slender, 2-4cm long.

Fruit: Cones stalked, globular, 15mm to 25mm diameter, flat topped, reddish brown in colour.

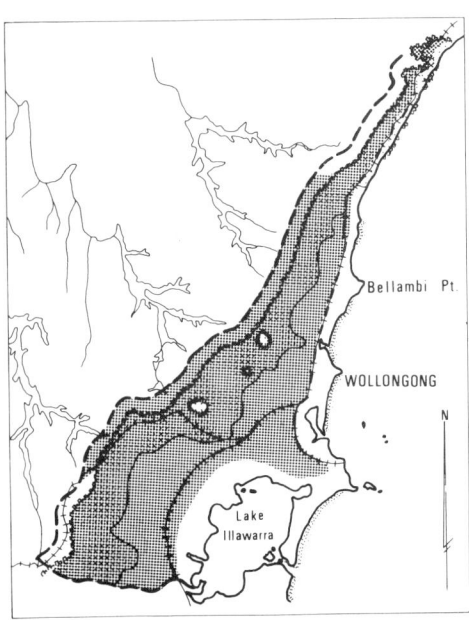

TOP LEFT: Branchlets and male flowers. TOP RIGHT: Tree. BOTTOM LEFT: Bark (pencil indicates scale). BOTTOM CENTRE: Fruit. BOTTOM RIGHT: Branchlet parted to show scale leaves.

Allocasuarina verticillata (Lamk.) L. Johnson
syn. *Casuarina stricta* Ait.

Drooping she-oak

Casuarinaceae

Allocasuarina verticillata only occurs on the sea cliffs north of Coledale. Because of the testing environment it does not attain a height of more than about 3m. Although *Casuarina glauca* also grows on the sea cliffs, *A. verticillata* can be distinguished from it by its drooping, rather coarse branchlets and large fruit. The distributions of these two species are complementary with *C. glauca* being more common on sea cliffs south of Coledale and *A. verticillata* being more common to the north.

Bark: Dark brown, fissured.

Leaves: Whorls of about 11. Branchlets rather thick and coarse.

Inflorescence: Male spikes about 50mm long, dense when young.

Fruit: Large at 25mm diameter, globular, reddish brown. Valves with a small pointed protruberance.

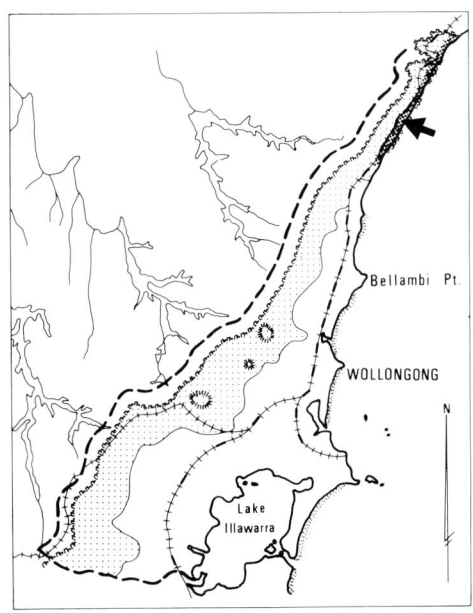

Trees on cliffs.

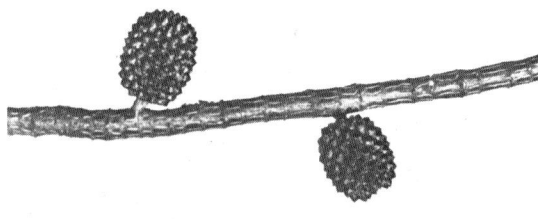

Fruit.

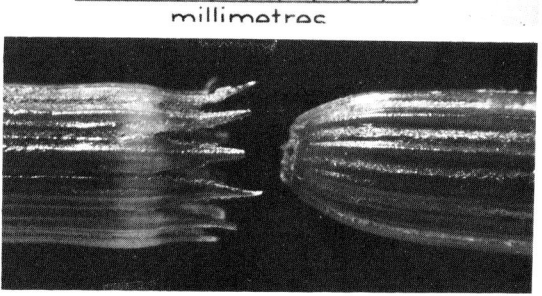

Branchlet parted at node to show scale leaves.

Alphitonia excelsa (Fenzl) Benth.
Red ash
Rhamnaceae

Red ash occurs in rainforest, on the edges of rainforest and in wet sclerophyll forest. It is found most commonly on the lower half of the escarpment where it may attain a height of 20m and is also found on the coastal plain, usually 6-10m tall.

Alphitonia excelsa is a tree easily distinguished by the dark green upper surface of the leaves and white underside, so that when the leaves become upturned in the breeze the whole crown takes on a grey or white appearance. The light grey bark and wrinkles on the sides and top of the branch joints help in placing the identity of this tree.

It is probably the woolly undersurface of the leaf similar to coast banksia which endows this species with the ability to withstand seaside conditions because red ash is common in the hind dune community of Puckeys Estate.

This species makes an ideal ornamental tree with its attractive leaves, massed flower display and abundant black fruits.

Bark: Grey, smooth, the lower trunk fissured in old specimens. The young branches are covered with short brown hairs.

Leaves: Alternate, elliptical to lanceolate. 70mm to 120mm long, 20mm to 40mm wide, dark glossy green on top, paler on undersurface.

Inflorescence: Terminal cymes in upper axils; trees usually flower in profusion.

Flowers: 5mm diam. greenish white, 5 petals. Flowers January to March.

Fruit: Globular, stalked, black, 6mm to 10mm diam. Fruits in winter and spring.

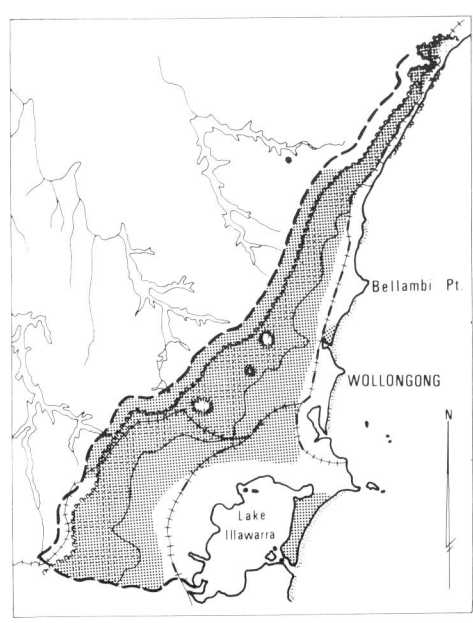

TOP LEFT: Bark. TOP RIGHT: Tree. BOTTOM LEFT: Fruit. BOTTOM RIGHT: Leaves and flowers.

Angophora costata (Gaertn.) Druce
syn. *A. lanceolata* Cav.

Sydney red gum
Smooth barked apple
Myrtaceae

The angophoras are often mistaken for eucalypts in the bush and although they are closely related there are a few features which separate these two genera. The adult leaves are oppositely arranged instead of alternate as are eucalypts. Also the flower buds are covered in the unopened state by 5 small calyx lobes or scales instead of an operculum or bud cap.

As a tree, *Angophora costata* has great character in all its forms; as a young tree, as an old weathered tree, as a twisted, gnarled tree growing on a difficult site, and as a tall well formed forest tree.

In the Wollongong area the smooth barked apple is confined to the northern part of the area on the plateau west of Clifton, Coalcliff and Stanwell Park. A few stray trees have found their way onto the eastern escarpment slopes. This tree is mostly found in this area growing about 15m tall. The smooth red to grey, sometimes mottled bark, together with the twisted nature of the branches make this red gum easily recognised in the bush.

Bark: Smooth throughout, falling off in irregular patches leaving the new bark an orange-red colour. The bark is sometimes red-grey mottled.

Leaves: Juvenile — opposite, stalkless or shortly stalked, pale green. Adult — opposite with short stalks, lanceolate 70mm to 120mm long, 20mm to 25mm wide. Young leaves are bright red.

Inflorescence: 3 flowered cymes in heads at ends of branches. Buds — shortly stalked, egg shaped 10mm to 12mm long, 10mm across.

Flowers: Ridged calyx tube with 5 calyx lobes and 5 petals. Numerous white stamens. Flowers spring-early summer.

Fruit: Bell shaped 10mm to 14mm long, 10mm to 14mm across with 5 main ribs, 5 small teeth on rim, valves enclosed.

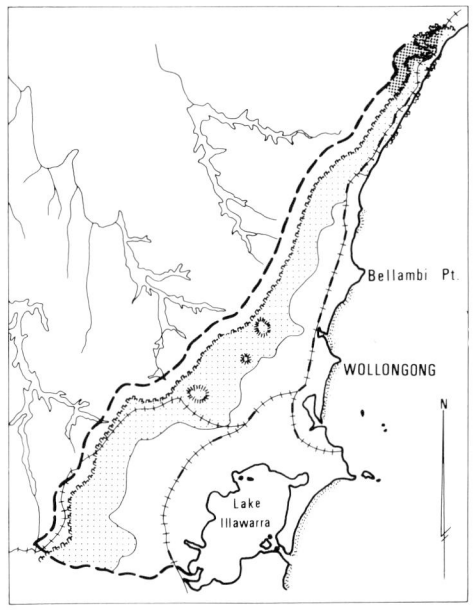

Fruit.

Tree.

Leaves.

Angophora floribunda (Sm.) Sweet
syn. *A. intermedia* DC

Rough barked apple

Myrtaceae

In the Wollongong area this species is found on the coastal plain south of Unanderra. It does not extend into the escarpment foothills. It occurs on undulating country such as at West Dapto and is usually found in association with *Eucalyptus tereticornis, E. longifolia, E. globoidea, Melaleuca styphelioides* and *M. decora*.

Rough barked apple is found up to about 20m tall and has characteristic twisting, turning branching habit. As the common name implies it has fibrous rough bark.

Bark: Shortly fibrous, grey or brownish, persistent to the small branches.

Leaves: Juvenile — opposite, stalked, narrow ovate to oblong, 50mm to 80mm long, 20mm to 30mm wide, branchlets bristly. Adults — opposite, stalked, narrow ovate, lanceolate or oblong, conspicuous oil glands, 50mm to 120mm long, 15mm to 30mm wide.

Inflorescence: Terminal panicles made up of 2 to 7 flowered umbels. Buds — egg shaped. 10mm to 14mm long, about 10mm across with bristles on stalks.

Flowers: 5 calyx lobes across unopened end, 5 small teeth, 5 petals, numerous white stamens. Good nectar producer. Flowers spring to early summer.

Fruit: Egg shaped capsule, with five main ribs, five teeth, enclosed valves and rather thin walls.

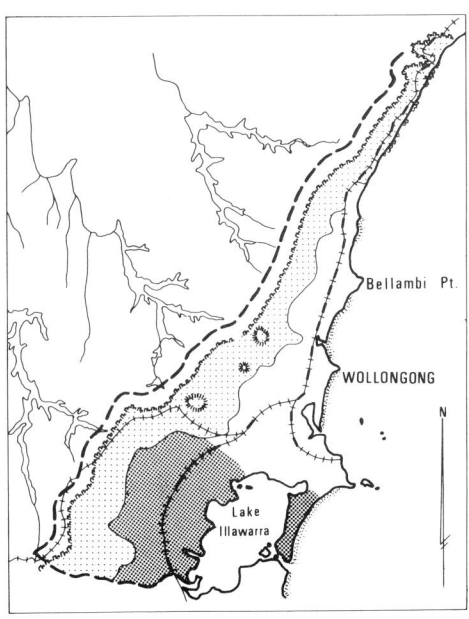

Tree.

Fruit.

Leaves.

Archontophoenix cunninghamiana (H. Wendl.) H. Wendl et Drude

Bangalow palm
Piccabeen palm (Queensland)
Palmae

Of the two species of palm in the Wollongong area bangalow palm is quite the more uncommon. It may be found as individual specimens sometimes miles apart or occasionally occurring in dense stands of many trees. However, its general status is uncommon and rarely is it seen unless one ventures right into the escarpment rainforest. Dapto Creek gully immediately south of Mount Kembla holds many of these palms tucked up in the headwaters. At Bulli Pass and in the rainforest of Wombarra also quite a large number can be found.

When growing in groups bangalow palm is often found to be growing in saturated ground, however, the saturation is due to creeks or other **moving** water. Often it grows in association with the cabbage palm, but otherwise it is a tree of rainforest alone.

This palm is indeed a beautiful tree, up to about 15m tall with a stem diameter of up to 400mm. It is easily distinguished from the cabbage palm, the only other palm in the area, by its pinnately divided leaves, the smooth leaf sheath just below the crown and the silvery white and drooping paniculate inflorescence arising from immediately below the leaf sheaths. It also has a spreading rather than globular crown.

Bark: The outside of the trunk is smooth, with annular ridges and grey in colour.

Leaves: Dark green, 3m to 4m long, up to one metre wide and pinnately divided. At the base each leaf rachis broadens out to a sheath which wraps around the upper part of the stem for about one metre.

Inflorescence: The inflorescence projects from the main trunk immediately below the leaf sheaths. It is a silvery-grey, dense, panicle which droops and is about 500mm long.

Flowers: Small, pale lilac.

Fruit: Red globular, 12mm in diameter.

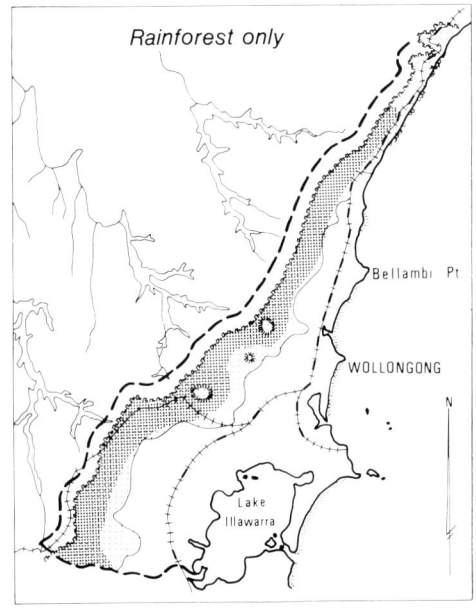

TOP: A gully containing both cabbage palm *(Livistona australis)* and bungalow palm *(Archontophoenix cunninghamiana)*. BOTTOM LEFT: Tree. BOTTOM RIGHT: Leaves and inflorescence.

Avicennia marina (Forsk.) Vierh. var. *australasica* (Walp.) Moldenke

syn. *A. officinalis* L. (also widely known as *A. marina* var. *resinifera* (Forst. f.) Bakh.

Grey mangrove

Verbenaceae

A little to the south of the area covered by this book, grey mangrove grows in profusion along the Minnamurra River but in the Wollongong area it only occurs as specimens here and there and in small groups. In fact, Fairy Creek at North Wollongong is the only small estuary open to the sea frequently enough to support mangroves.

Mangroves usually grow within the tidal reaches of estuaries but occasionally may be found beyond. There is no mistaking this tree with its root projections (pneumatophores) sticking up above the mud at low tide. Grey mangrove grows to about 7m in Wollongong and forms a rather spreading tree with laurel-like leaves having a whitish undersurface.

Bark: Grey, rough, fissured.

Leaves: Opposite, ovate to lanceolate, glossy on upper surface, whitish beneath, 50mm to 80mm long, 30mm to 60mm wide. Veins yellowish.

Inflorescence: Small cymes, in forks of upper leaves or terminal panicles.

Fruit: A compressed capsule about 30mm diameter. The single large seed germinates before fruit drops. The large, 20mm across, green embryo can be seen washed up on mudflats. Fruits December.

Pneumatophores: Are vertical projections of the roots which stick up above the mud during low tide and are used by the roots for gas exchange with the air since the roots themselves are continually underwater (or mud).

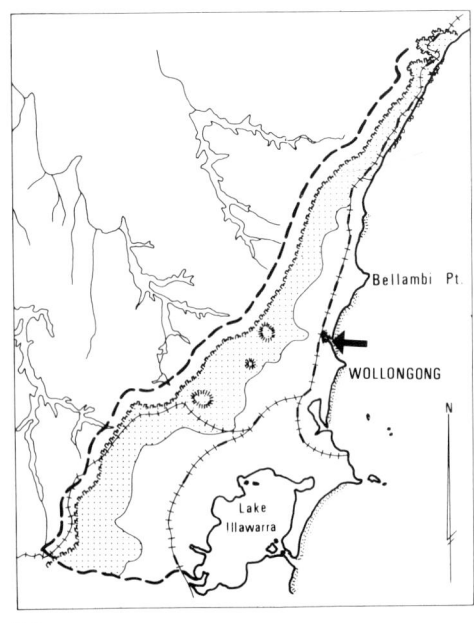

Tree.

Pneumatophores.

Leaves.

Backhousia myrtifolia Hook. f. et Harv.

Ironwood, grey myrtle

Myrtaceae

Backhousia myrtifolia is a common tree of the edges of rainforest and along the banks of watercourses on the coastal plain. It is a rather hardy tree even though it tends to grow in or near rainforest and can be found in rainforest occupying drier sites as well as on seacliffs. This tree sometimes forms dense thickets where it has regenerated after clearing of previous forest.

This species can be seen as a shrub only a metre high in some situations such as seacliff communities but in good rainforest it can grow up to 15m tall with a stem diameter of 400m. However, it usually grows to about 6m tall with a bushy habit.

Grey myrtle is a pretty tree and flowers profusely. It is a tree well worth considering as an ornamental.

Bark: Light grey, brown or fawn coloured, short grained and sometimes flaky.

Leaves: Opposite, shortly stalked, ovate with a drawn out point, 30mm to 70mm long, 20mm to 40mm wide. Sometimes young leaves and shoots are hairy. Lateral venation is close and parallel.

Inflorescence: Small cymes.

Flowers: Greenish or whitish, calyx tube and sepals form main part of flower, petals only half as long as sepals. Stamens numerous about 10mm long. Flower about 12mm across. Flowers November to December.

Fruit: Dry, enlarged calyx enclosing seeds. Calyx lobes or sepals persistent.

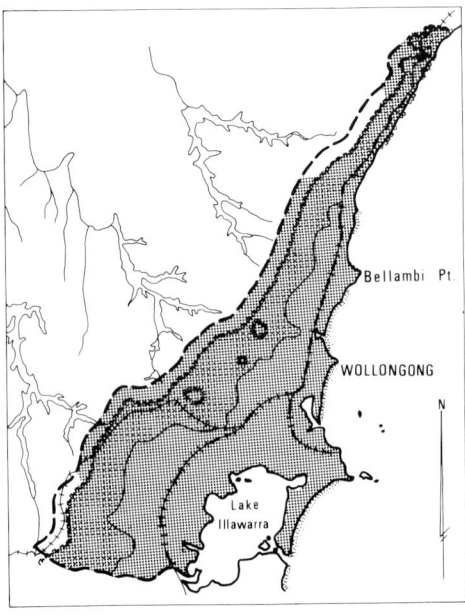

Tree.

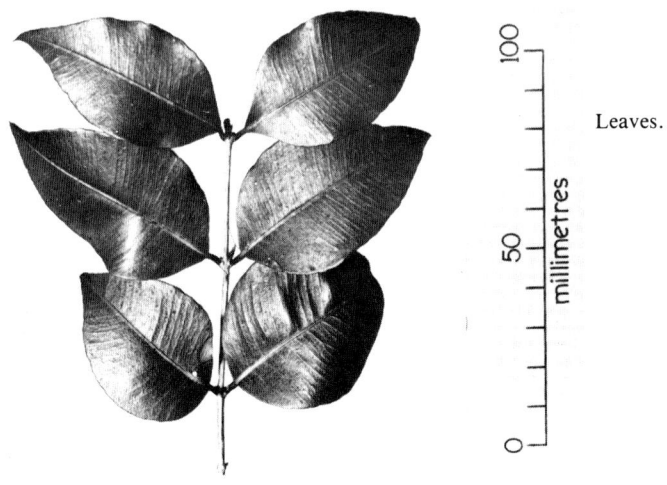

Leaves.

Baloghia lucida Endl.
Brush bloodwood
Euphorbiaceae

The bark of this tree is rather easy to recognise in the rainforest because of the dark coloured, rough, raised areas scattered on an otherwise smooth light grey-fawn bark. Also if the bark is cut it exudes a dark red sap or clear at first then turning red; hence the common name.

Baloghia lucida does not grow to a large size but is usually found as a small tree about 6m tall in rainforest, with a stem diameter of 150mm. It is not common, only found here and there in the escarpment rainforest. Further south in the Jamberoo-Saddleback area it is far more common.

Bark: Grey or fawn-brown, scattered with knobbly raised pustules.

Leaves: Opposite, stalked, hairless, elliptical, lanceolate or obovate in shape, tapering gradually at the base and abruptly at the apex, but the apex has a short blunt point or mucro (drip tip) 60mm to 150mm long, 30mm to 50mm wide.

Inflorescence: Racemes on the end of branches male and females parts in separate flowers.

Flowers: Male flowers with numerous stamens joined at the base and on a lobed disc. Female flowers on a lobed disc also, three ovaries three styles, each style divided into two.

Fruit: Hard, globular 12mm to 20mm diameter.

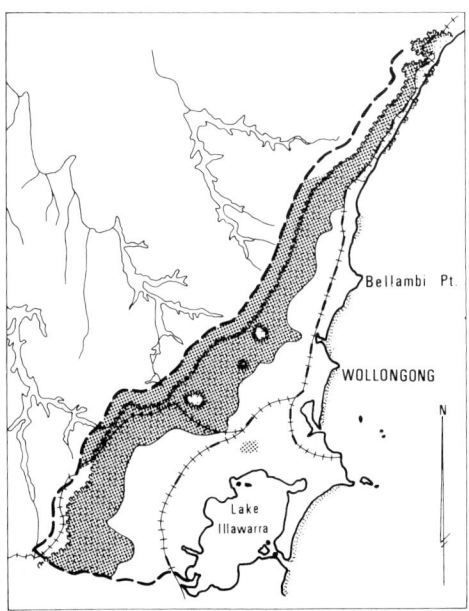

Leaves.

Bark.

Banksia integrifolia L.f.
Coast banksia
Proteaceae

Coast banksia occurs along the entire coastline of the Wollongong area. Being quite resistant to and probably most competitive in this environment it is confined to within a few hundred yards of the beaches except at Clifton and further north where it extends up the mountain slopes and onto the plateau. It grows in association with other seaside resistant plants such as *Eucalyptus botryoides* and *Leptospermum laevigatum*.

This banksia is a tree of great character in all its weather beaten poses. It grows up to about 10m tall and under good conditions has a rounded crown which partly covers the trunk. In more exposed situations it becomes shaped by the elements and is often straggling, bent or leaning. When in flower the bright yellow flower spikes give it an added attraction. With the old inflorescences less conspicuous than old man banksias, *(Banksia serrata)*, coast banksia does not have as gnarled an appearance and carries itself more elegantly against the backdrop of the sea.

Bark: Grey and rough.

Leaves: Juvenile leaves — alternate, coarsely serrate margin variable in shape and size but about 80mm long and 30mm wide. Adult leaves — alternate, entire margin or irregularly toothed, oblanceolate, 50mm to 100mm long, 10mm to 30mm wide. The upper surface is smooth and green, the underside is white.

Inflorescence: Dense spike (bottlebrush-like), 70mm to 100mm long, 70mm diameter.

Flowers: Yellow, the thin stigmas giving the inflorescence a bristly appearance.

Fruit: The valves of the fruit are thin and often only a few follicles ripen on each inflorescence.

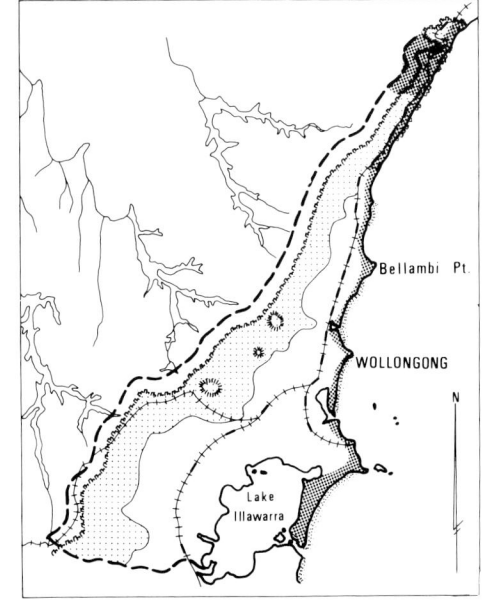

Tree.

Flower spike.

Fruit.

Leaves. Leaf aside shows undersurface of a juvenile leaf.

Banksia serrata L.f.

Red honeysuckle
Old man banksia
Proteaceae

The name of the genus *Banksia* is taken after Sir Joseph Banks who discovered this species at Botany Bay in 1770. *Banksia serrata* is a large shrub or small tree not growing as big in the Wollongong area as other areas. Its height is up to 7m and the tree is best distinguished by its gnarled and usually crooked habit. The inflorescences bearing fruit are persistent and on weathering the "Banksia men" add to the gnarled appearance.

Red honeysuckle in the Wollongong area is confined strictly to the sandy soils of the plateau and the hind dunes.

Bark: Grey, brown where outer bark is broken off, very rugged and knobbly, thick.

Leaves: Oblanceolate, or narrow with a rounded end. 80mm to 160mm long, 20mm to 40mm wide. The leaf margin is coarsely serrate, saw-like. The young leaves are hairy but the older leaves glabrous above and sometimes hairy beneath.

Inflorescence: A dense oblong-cylindrical spike, bottlebrush like.

Flowers: Dove grey, to yellow, heavy nectar producers. Flowers January to March.

Fruit: Woody follicles with thick valves embedded in the furry inflorescence stem.

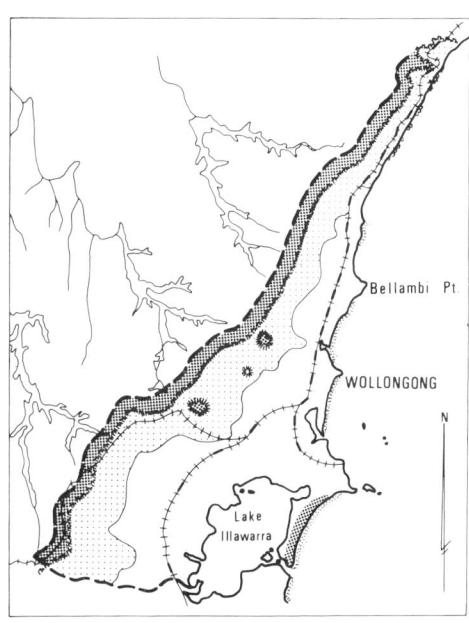

Flower spike and leaves.

Bark.

Tree.

Brachychiton acerifolium (A. Cunn. ex Don) F. Muell.

Flame tree
Illawarra flame tree
Sterculiaceae

When the flame tree has a good flowering year the brilliant red shows up against the dark green foliage of the escarpment rainforest. The massed flowers of a whole tree can be seen clearly from the coastal plain with the habit of the tree facilitating this by the losing of its leaves at flowering time in late November.

This tree has been grown frequently as an ornamental but the lack of acknowledgement that it is a rainforest tree and likes sheltered conditions, has been the cause of many a failure to thrive.

Under natural conditions in the rainforest it is found up to 20m tall with a main stem diameter of about 600mm. Though deciduous, it is very variable in the time and extent of its loss of leaves as well as having a sporadic flowering cycle. It may take over ten years to first flower; then afterwards is very irregular with sometimes only part of the tree flowering.

Illawarra flame tree can be found in most rainforest communities on the escarpment as well as the western side of the coastal plain. It displays heterophylly with its leaves varying from a lanceolate shape to a deeply dissected shape.

Bark: Smooth to wrinkled or fissured, brown.

Leaves: Palmately lobed with varying degrees of dissection, to elliptical lanceolate with an entire margin or some irregular bumps. Leaves up to 200mm long and wide, dark glossy green on top.

Inflorescence: Panicles in the leaf forks. Inflorescence stalks red, flowers red.

Flowers: Bell shaped, bright red, 20mm long, unisexual or polygamous. Flowers December to January.

Fruit: Pod-like follicle, 100mm long, 40mm wide, triangular in cross section opening along one side to expose numerous yellow covered oval seeds.

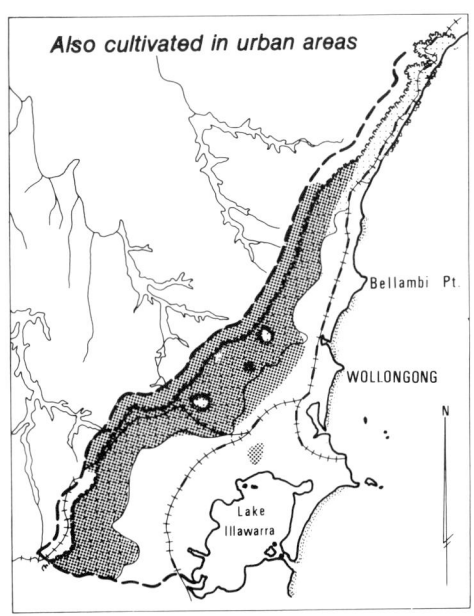
Also cultivated in urban areas

TOP LEFT: Flower. TOP RIGHT: Tree. MIDDLE LEFT: Leaf from young tree. BOTTOM LEFT: Leaves. BOTTOM RIGHT: Fruit.

Brachychiton populneum R. Br.
Kurrajong
Sterculiaceae

This is a tree with a rather sporadic natural distribution and is also grown as an ornamental making it difficult to determine its overall distribution. Excluding those trees growing in urban areas this species has been recorded at Austinmer, a very old specimen pointed out by Mr. J. Wilton, at Mt. Brown recorded by Mr. K. Mills and a number of other sightings at West Dapto. There are probably more "natural" trees of this species in the Wollongong area although the sporadic distribution of kurrajong is normal along the coastal strip.

Bark: Grey or brown, somewhat wrinkled.

Leaves: Alternate, stalked, thin, dark green and glossy on upper surface. Juvenile leaves — 3 to 5 lobed, 40mm to 80mm long. Adult — ovate to lanceolate or may be three lobed, 30mm to 80mm long.

Inflorescence: Panicles in forks of leaves.

Flowers: Pale, yellow or reddish inside, 7mm to 12mm long. Flowers summer.

Fruit: A pod-like follicle up to 80mm long. Seeds embedded in a loose hairy covering.

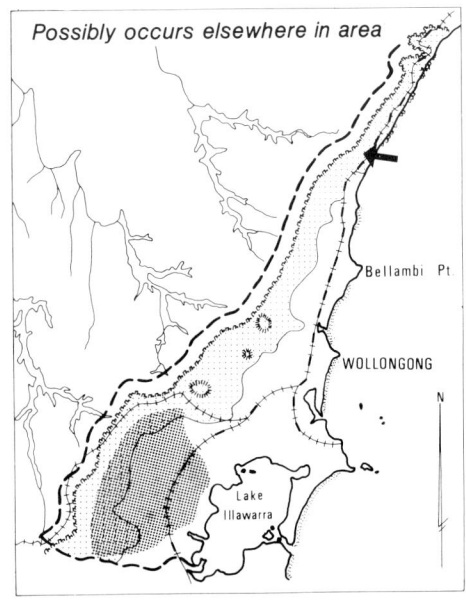

Leaves.

Fruit.

Callicoma serratifolia Andr.
Black wattle
Cunoniaceae

The leaves of this species are the most distinctive feature with saw edged serrations along the margin, white undersurface and clear regular venation. It is often found in gullies in sandstone country in the Sydney region where it grows as a twiggy, slender shrub or small tree and is noted for its use by early settlers in wattle and daub houses. In the Wollongong area it grows on the plateau in the moist gullies, along with other rainforest species. On the eastern side of the escarpment it can be found as a tree of climax rainforest and in fact it reaches about 15m in height along Flannagans Creek headwaters at Austinmer with a stem diameter of over 300mm. Here it grows in association with *Ceratopetalum apetalum*, coachwood.

Bark: Brown or dark brown, somewhat rough.

Leaves: Opposite, lanceolate in outline with a coarsely serrated margin, 50mm to 120mm long, 15mm to 50mm wide. The upper surface is glabrous but the regular lateral veins are quite obvious. The undersurface is densely hairy with white or brown hairs and the regular, parallel lateral veins are raised and quite visible.

Inflorescence: Globular heads of pale yellow flowers (rather wattle-like) on single stalk, in clusters on one stalk or a number of single stalks in the fork of the leaves. Globular heads 10mm to 20mm diameter.

Flowers: Individual flowers, stamens 10mm long in calyx. Flowers October.

Fruit: Two hairy carpels 3mm long.

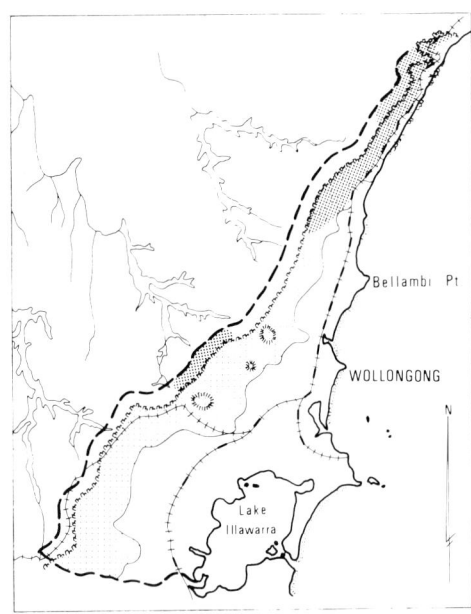

Leaves and flowers.

Callistemon salignus (Sm.) DC.
Pink tips
Myrtaceae

Pink tips is a rather showy little tree. It has been grown as an ornamental quite extensively and for some time. The new foliage of this species is vivid pink, soft and downy and when in flower the creamy white bottlebrushes show another face of this tree.

Callistemon salignus grows to about 8m tall and may be found growing on the coastal plain and foothills of the escarpment. It is often found in association with *Melaleuca decora* and *Melaleuca styphelioides* where soil drainage is somewhat slow. It is the only paper bark tree in the Wollongong area which is not a melaleuca.

Bark: Whitish to light brown, papery and thick.

Leaves: Alternate, lanceolate, 60mm to 100mm long, 7mm to 10mm wide. Young shoots, silvery pink.

Inflorescence: Spike 30mm to 80mm long (Bottlebrush).

Flowers: Staminate, creamy-white. Flowers spring.

Fruit: Woody capsule 5mm diameter.

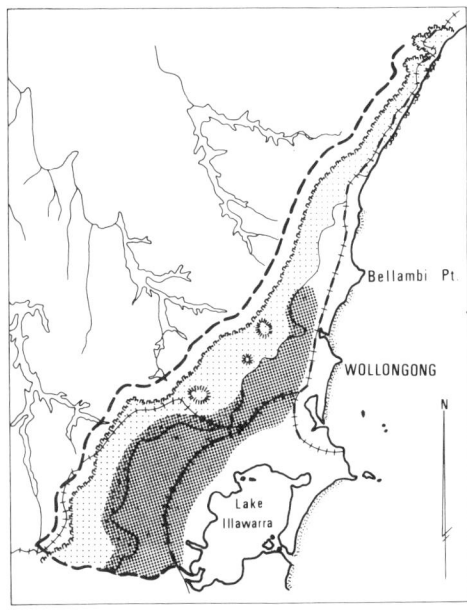

TOP LEFT: Bark. TOP RIGHT: Tree. MIDDLE LEFT: Fruit. BOTTOM LEFT: Flowers.
BOTTOM RIGHT: Leaves.

THE FAMILY CASUARINACEAE

In the area covered by this book there are two species of *Casuarina* and five species of *Allocasuarina*. However, two of these *Allocasuarina paludosa* and *A. distyla* are shrubs, leaving five which reach tree proportions. The following few pages and those under *Allocasuarina* contain brief descriptions of the respective species but it is also worth noting some of the general distinguishing features of the family to which they belong.

The Casuarinaceae family is characterised by the stems (branchlets) being segmented and the leaves reduced to ridges along the stem projecting as "teeth" at the node. The leaves are arranged in whorls around the branchlets.

The internodes are green and carry out the process of photosynthesis. Between the ridges on the stem lie the pores for gas exchange (stoma). These features enable casuarinas to lose water from their aerial parts at a very slow rate which means that they can withstand very dry, difficult conditions. Hence they are found along the seashore, on cliffs and with their feet in salty water. In the dry, inland desert oak *Allocasuarina decaisneana* grows in arid conditions. Roots of the casuarinas support nitrogen fixing bacteria, another feature giving them self-sufficiency in difficult soil conditions. The flowers in this family are either male or female and sometimes have different sexes on different trees (dioecious). The male flowers are borne at the branchlet nodes at the ends of the branchlets and are very small. When massed they can give a tree a brown or reddish appearance. The female flowers are borne on older wood on short lateral branches. Sometimes they appear on thick and very much older wood.

The genus Casuarina is distributed in Australia and Indo Malaya and is represented in the Wollongong area by *Casuarina cunninghamiana* and *C. glauca*. *Allocasuarina* which is entirely Australian comprises the other species of this family in the Wollongong area.

Casuarina cunninghamiana Miq.
River oak
Casuarinaceae

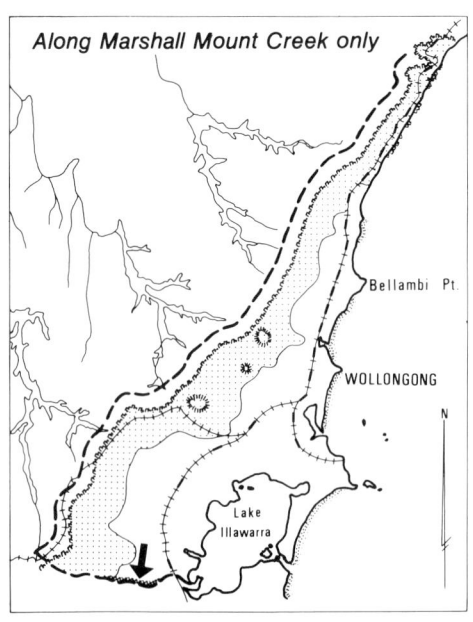

Within the area covered by this book river oak only occurs along the southern boundary on the banks of Marshall Mount Creek. It plays a role in stabilising banks of streams and is rarely found far from this habitat. *Casuarina cunninghamiana* grows to a large tree but along Marshall Mount Creek it is found to be about 20m tall. The branchlets are not as dark green as other species in the area but the crown is usually very dense.

Leaves: Arranged in whorls of 8-10. Branchlets are slender and more or less erect. The branchlets are crowded.

Inflorescence: Male spikes are dense, brown.

Fruit: Cones are small, 8mm in diameter, grey and globular.

TOP: Trees along Marshall Mount Ck. BOTTOM LEFT: Tree on creek bank. MIDDLE RIGHT: Fruit. BOTTOM RIGHT: Branchlet parted at node to show scale leaves.

Casuarina glauca Sieb. et Spreng.

Swamp oak
Swamp she-oak
Casuarinaceae

This species ranges from a stunted shrub, sometimes only 200mm high living on windswept headlands, to a lofty tree 20m tall growing in forest formation in low lying lagoon communities. It is quite a familiar feature of Lake Illawarra foreshores and Stewart Park at North Wollongong. Oak Flats owes its name to this tree. As well as along the coastline zone, swamp oak can be found in poorly drained depressions on the coastal plain and extending inland along creeks such as Allans and Mullet Creeks.

Swamp oak is generally a narrow tree unlike the wide spreading river oak. The branchlets are mostly erect and are rather thick (about 1mm in diameter). In severely stressed specimens on the sea cliffs the branchlets may be as thick as 4mm.

Bark: Grey, cracked and flaky; sometimes the trunk is slightly fluted in older trees.

Leaves: Leaves arranged in whorls of 12-16. Branchlets are thick and ridged.

Inflorescence: Male spikes dense, brown, 10mm to 30mm long.

Fruit: Cones globular to cylindrical about 12mm diameter, grey in colour.

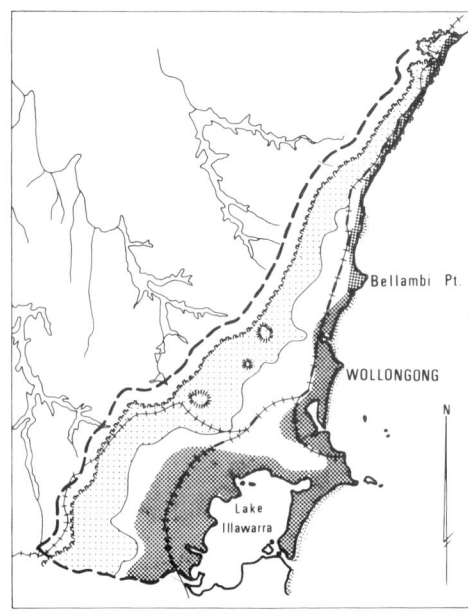

TOP: Trees. ABOVE: Fruit.
MIDDLE RIGHT: Branchlets.
RIGHT: Branchlet parted at node
     to show scale leaves.

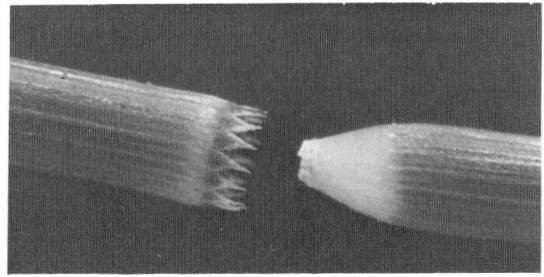

Ceratopetalum apetalum D. Don
Coachwood
Leatherjacket
Cunoniaceae

Even though this tree is one of the most common trees in the rainforest of the upper half of the escarpment, it is rather uncommon in rainforest below the lower Narrabeen Series bench and does not occur on the coastal plain at all. It often dominates the simple rainforest of the talus slopes and in this situation may be found up to 30m tall with a stem diameter of 600mm. The abundance of this tree on the talus slope can be gauged at Christmas time when the calyces of the flowers turn red, like its relative the NSW Christmas bush, and from the coastal plain the escarpment can be seen to display the reddish brown colour of coachwood. Earlier in springtime the white flowers stand out conspicuously as showy white patches on the escarpment.

The timber of coachwood, as the name implies, is of commercial value and many parts of the area have been logged.

Within the rainforest the main stems of coachwood are clearly distinguished by their smooth dove grey bark and the fine circumferential ridges around the stem. The trunks are often covered with whitish lichens but the smoothness is still apparent.

Coachwood competes well in soils of low nutrient status where adequate moisture is available and can be found alongside creeks on the Hawkesbury Sandstone as well as on the lower, more fertile Narrabeen Series.

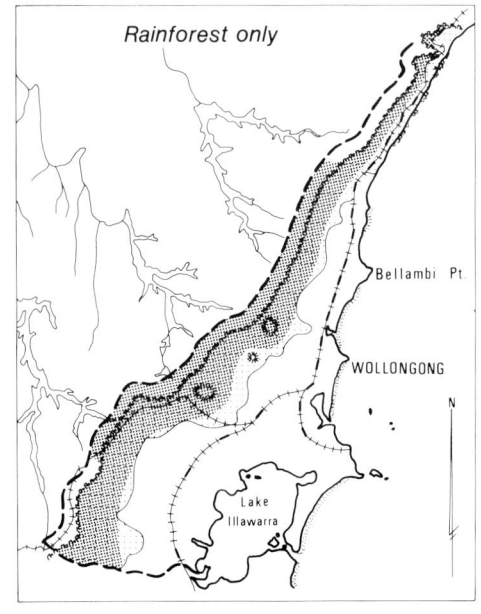

Rainforest only

Bark: Grey, smooth with fine circumferential ridges; sometimes in old trees lower bark may be fissured. Bark is fragrant when broken.

Leaves: Opposite, compound leaf with one leaflet but appears as a simple leaf with the leaf blade able to articulate on the leaf stalk (swollen area at junction of leaf stalk and leaf blade). Leaves 80mm to 180mm long, 20mm to 50mm wide, serrated margin, acuminate tip, elliptical to lanceolate.

Inflorescence: Axillary cymes.

Flowers: Petals absent, after flowering calyx enlarges with fruit and turns red.

Fruit: Egg shaped about 3mm across, but surrounded by enlarged calyx lobes which are about 12mm long. Fruits December to January.

TOP LEFT: Flowers. TOP RIGHT: Tree. MIDDLE LEFT: Fruit. BOTTOM LEFT: Bark. BOTTOM RIGHT: Leaves.

Ceratopetalum gummiferum Sm.
NSW Christmas bush
Cunoniaceae

This tree has been widely cultivated in east coast gardens and the showy red calyces at Christmas time make it easy to recognise. NSW Christmas bush can be found up to a tree 10m tall but in the area included in this book it occurs naturally only as a shrub or small tree up to about 5m tall, on the plateau west of Clifton, Coalcliff and Stanwell Park.

Bark: Grey, somewhat rough.

Leaves: Opposite, trifoliolate. Leaflets — up to 70mm long and up to 15mm wide, lanceolate, finely serrated margins, blunt serrations.

Inflorescence: Cymose panicles, loosely trichotomous.

Flowers: 6mm across, white, Sepals 2mm long but after flowering enlarge to 12mm long and turn red.

Fruit: A capsule, with red calyx and calyx lobes. Fruits December to January.

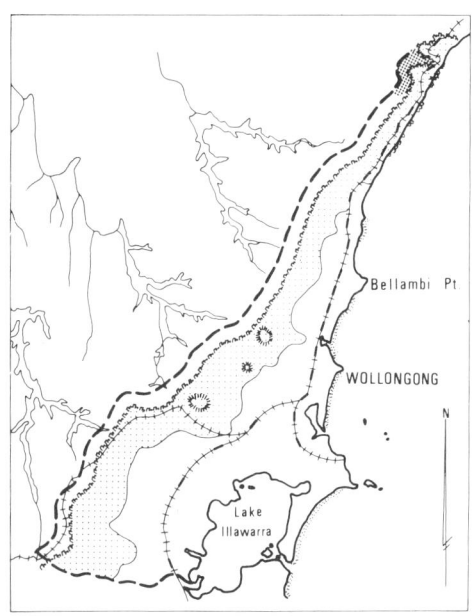

Leaves and flowers.

Choricarpia leptopetala (F. Muell.) Domin.

Myrtaceae

This tree is only found in the Wollongong area at Stanwell Park where it grows on what could be considered coastal plain. In fact Stanwell Park is the southernmost limit of its distribution with the range extending north to the Brisbane River.

Choricarpia leptopetala grows into a tree about 10m tall, having a rather rounded shrubby appearance when young. It is a handsome tree with yellowish white ball inflorescences and strongly aromatic foliage.

Bark: Brown.

Leaves: Opposite, shortly stalked, broadly lanceolate to elliptical, drawn out to a long point, paler on underside 50mm to 100mm long, 15mm to 50mm wide. Young branches and underside of leaves scurfy. Leaves aromatic when crushed.

Inflorescence: Compact globular heads about 15mm in diameter on stalks about 30mm long.

Flowers: Floral tubes 2-3mm long, separate from each other, sepals and petals 4 or 5, cream coloured, as are the numerous stamens which are about 7mm long. Flowers spring.

Fruit: The globular heads are conspicuously brown before ripening. Individual fruit are capsules.

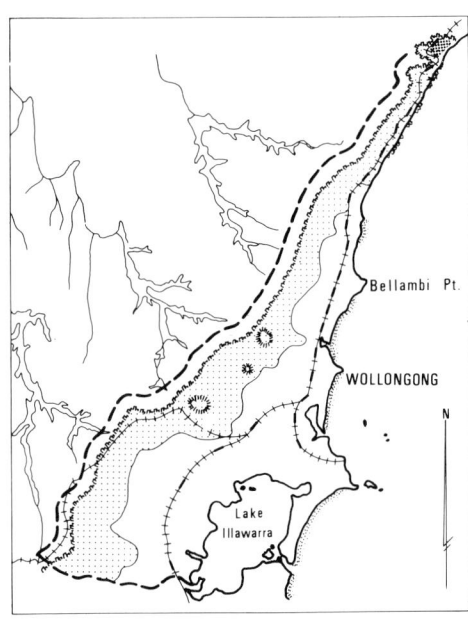

Trees.

Flowers.

Leaves.

Citronella moorei (F. Muell. ex Benth.) Howard

Churnwood

Icacinaceae

Churnwood is one of the rainforest giants. It is most commonly seen as a fluted tree trunk disappearing up through the canopy. Even with little to be seen other than the main stem it is still relatively easy to identify. The main trunk is often leaning or bent; buttressing and fluting are a conspicuous part of the lower stem and the bark displays longitudinal fissures, particularly on the outer part of the flutes.

This tree attains a height of 30m or more and has a stem diameter of over 1m at a height of 1m from the ground. Being a typical rainforest tree its crown is dense and dark green. *Citronella moorei* only occurs in climax rainforest associated with the escarpment, although there is one specimen in Mangerton Park, Mangerton. The southern limit of its Australian distribution is recorded as the Shoalhaven district.

Bark: Grey with longitudinal fissures. Rather corky in appearance.

Leaves: Ovate to broadly lanceolate, alternately arranged, stalked, 35mm to 100mm long (sometimes 150mm or longer), 20mm to 50mm wide. Dark green and shining above, paler beneath, leaf apex drawn out into a point. Young twigs green.

Inflorescence: Narrow axillary panicle, up to 100mm long, bearing many sessile flowers about 5mm long. Flowers September.

Fruit: Egg shaped, black, up to 25mm long. Fruits summer-autumn.

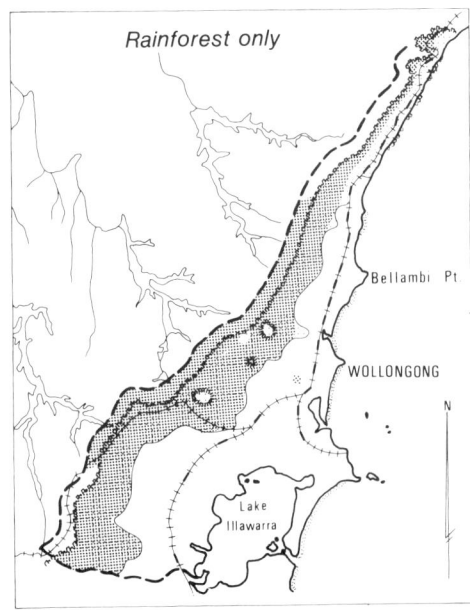

Leaves.

Trunk of tree showing fissures and flutes. The tree trunks in the background are of red cedars.

Claoxylon australe Baill.
Euphorbiaceae

Mostly found as a shrub, this species may attain a spindly tree habit up to 4m high. It is found throughout the Wollongong area in rainforest and sometimes moist eucalypt forest. The leaves are either covered with fine short hairs or are hairless. When hairless this species may be mistaken for *Croton verreauxii*; however, *Claoxylon australe* generally has wider, more oval leaves than the lanceolate leaves of the *Croton*.

Leaves: Spirally arranged, stalked; obovate, lanceolate or elliptical; 60mm to 120mm long, 30mm to 60mm wide; sometimes hairy; two small stipules on leaf stalk at base of leaf blade.

Inflorescence: Axillary racemes shorter than the leaves.

Flowers: 3 calyx segments, 2mm long; no petals; stamens numerous.

Fruit: Globular, 3 lobed, 6mm diameter.

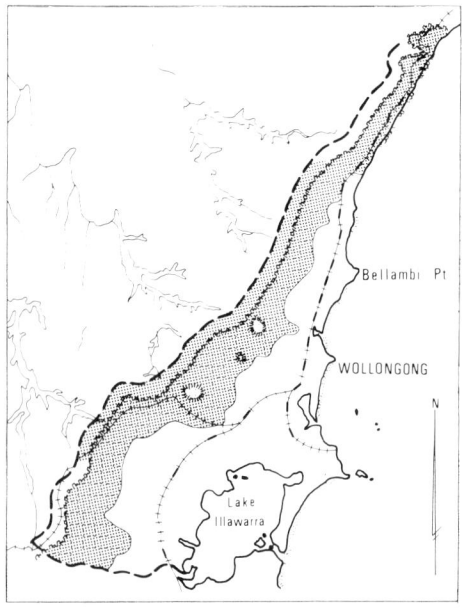

Leaves.

Clerodendrum tomentosum R. Br.
Native clerodendrum
Verbenaceae

Mostly occurring as a shrub the native clerodendrum sometimes reaches 4m tall. It is a showy plant with dark dull green leaves with a hairy covering and often with purple petioles and twigs. The flowers are white and sometimes massed. When the fruit develops, the bright red swollen calyx and the black seeds form another ornamental dimension.

Clerodendrum tomentosum is to be found in almost every plant community in the Wollongong area, from the hind dunes to the rainforest. It is most common as an understorey plant in wet sclerophyll forest and on the edges of rainforest.

Bark: Brown or grey with smaller stems bearing raised lenticels.

Leaves: Opposite; ovate to elliptical, entire; 50mm to 110mm long, 25mm to 50mm wide; often velvety-pubescent, sometimes glabrous; often the petioles and undersurface of midrib are purplish.

Inflorescence: Compact, terminal corymbs, or loose cymes in forks of outer leaves.

Flowers: Showy white, up to 40mm long including stamens, 20mm across. 5 calyx lobes. Flowers October and November.

Fruit: Black shiny drupes sitting atop the calyx which becomes swollen and bright red at fruiting stage.

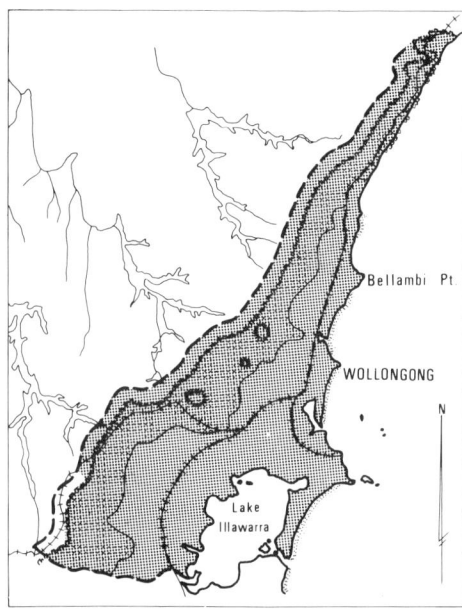

Leaves and flowers of *Clerodendrum tomentosum*.

Commersonia fraseri J. Gay

Brown kurrajong
Sterculiaceae

Brown kurrajong is widespread throughout the Wollongong area. It is most conspicuous in areas of regeneration after disturbance and is also quite prominent at the edges of rainforest. Otherwise it is scattered over the whole area. Its root suckering behaviour is responsible for forming massed stands which when in flower stand out conspicuously white, particularly on the foothills where forest is taking over what was previously pasture land.

This species grows most often as a tall shrub 2m to 4m tall but occasionally forms a tree-like habit to about 5m in height.

Bark: Brown, with hairy young branches.

Leaves: Young leaves are somewhat large and rounded with pointed lobes or a dentate margin, and also a soft hairy covering. Older leaves are ovate to broad lanceolate with a long point; 60mm to 150mm long, 40mm to 100mm wide; white tomentose on underside; pointed lobes, or dentate margin.

Inflorescence: Loose panicles.

Flowers: White, often massed on plant; 8mm to 10mm diameter. Calyx lobes 4mm long. Staminodes as long as the petals. Flowers in spring.

Fruit: A capsule about 20mm diameter.

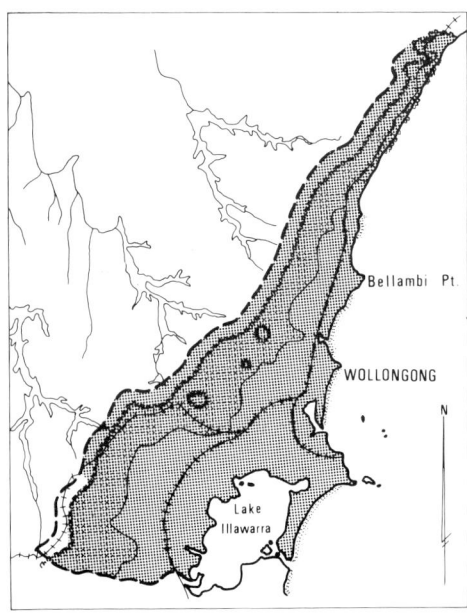

TOP: Trees forming dense thicket.
MIDDLE LEFT: Juvenile leaves.
MIDDLE RIGHT: Adult leaves.
BOTTOM RIGHT: Flowers.

Croton verreauxii Baill.
Native cascarilla
Euphorbiaceae

This species is most conspicuous during winter and spring months when some or all of the older leaves turn bright orange in colour. Native cascarilla is normally not a very large plant, only attaining 4m in height under exceptional conditions. It is usually found in or on the edge of rainforest as a shrub about 2m to 3m tall although it does grow in wet sclerophyll forest.

Leaves: Alternate, stalked, lanceolate; 40mm to 120mm long, 15mm to 30mm wide; shallow blunt serrations along margin, two small glands at base of leaf blade. Older leaves turn bright orange before falling.

Inflorescence: Terminal raceme up to 100mm long.

Flowers: Male flowers mainly on upper part of raceme. Glands alternating with hairy petals. Stamens 11. Female — ovary 3 locular. Both male and female — 5 sepals and 4 petals. Flowers November-December.

Fruit: 3 celled.

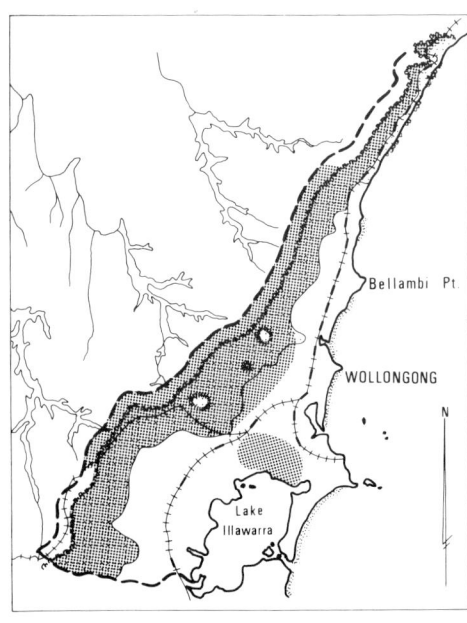

Junction of leaf blade
and stalk showing stipules.

Leaves.

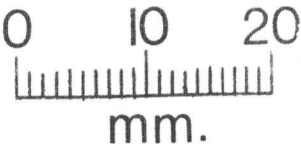

Flowers.

Fruit.

Cryptocarya glaucescens R. Br.
Native laurel
Lauraceae

This tree is one of the most common rainforest trees, especially on the talus slopes of the escarpment. The best identifying features are the leaves' white midrib which can be seen many metres away, and bluish undersurface.

The native laurel can be found as a fair sized tree up to about 20m tall. When growing in the open like many rainforest trees it forms a dense, rounded crown. This tree is confined to the rainforest of the escarpment.

Bark: Dark grey to blackish, slightly rough.

Leaves: Alternate, elliptic, dark glossy green on top, paler and with a bluish covering beneath; 60mm to 120mm long, 30mm to 50mm wide; midrib white or yellowish.

Inflorescence: Terminal panicles.

Flowers: 3mm long.

Fruit: Black, with a characteristic shape, one horizontal axis longer than the other and longer than the vertical 20mm x 12mm x 12mm.

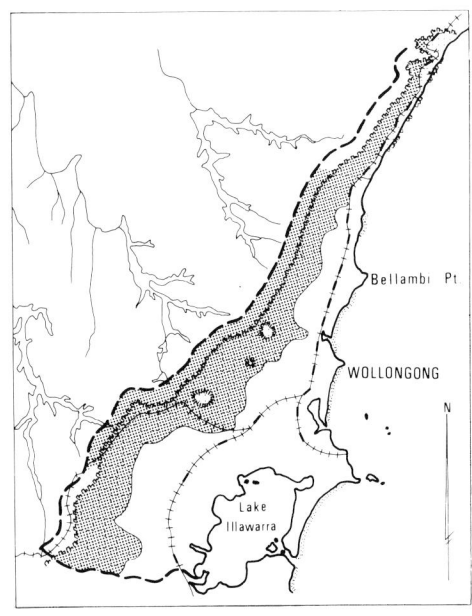

Leaves.

Flowers.

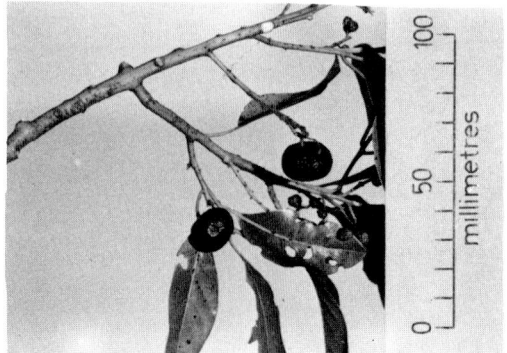

Fruit.

Cryptocarya microneura Meissn.
Murrogun
Lauraceae

This cryptocarya is very similar to *Cryptocarya glaucescens*. The main differences are: *Cryptocarya microneura* does not have a bluish undersurface of the leaf, the lateral veins are more distinct and widely spaced, the fruit is globular and not transversely elongated as with *Cryptocarya glaucescens*.

In the area covered by this book murrogun is not as common as the native laurel. However, it is widely spread along the length of the escarpment in rainforest and sometimes in the moister eucalypt forest. It tends to be more common in the northern suburbs. This tree grows to about 15m tall with an attractive dense crown of dark green laurel leaves. The white midribs of the leaves are clearly visible from the ground and are a useful identifying feature for the laurels.

Bark: Grey, slightly rough.

Leaves: Alternate, stalked, oblanceolate or elliptical, accuminate, 60mm to 120mm long, 20mm to 40mm wide. Conspicuous white midrib and 5 to 7 lateral veins clearly visible on both surfaces.

Inflorescence: Terminal or axillary panicles.

Flowers: Small, 3mm long.

Fruit: Globular, black, 8mm to 12mm diameter somewhat pointed at ends. Fruits winter.

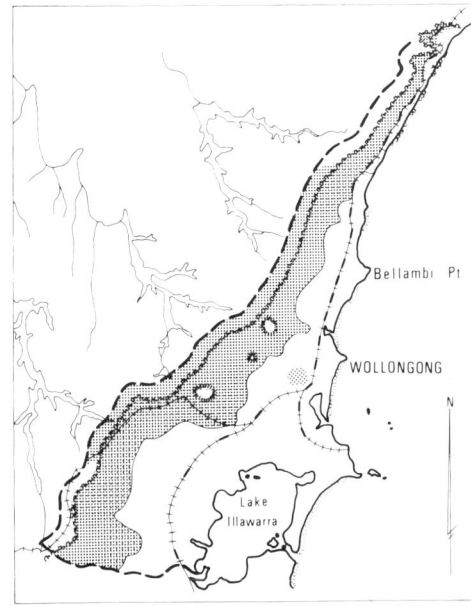

Leaves.

TREE FERNS

There are four species of tree fern occurring in the Wollongong area. They are: rough tree fern *(Cyathea australis)*, prickly tree fern *(Cyathea leichhardtiana)*, soft tree fern *(Dicksonia antarctica)* and *Cyathea cooperi*.

The common names of the first three species gives a clue to their identification; that of touch. The degree of roughness refers to the main rhachis or stem of the frond which bears prickles, blunt bumps or are smooth. *Cyathea cooperi* may be confused with *Dicksonia antarctica* in terms of their fronds but *Cyathea cooperi* has distinctive, oval, more or less smooth scars on its trunk which leave no question as to its identity.

Cyathea australis (R. Br.) Domin.

Rough tree fern

Cyatheaceae

This species is the most adaptable and widespread of the tree ferns in the Wollongong area. It can be found across the coastal plain and throughout the escarpment and plateau in sheltered eucalypt or rainforest. It can best be distinguished by the short prickles and the glossy brown scales at the base of the frond stalk (stipe).

Rough tree fern is usually found up to about 6m tall but may be taller. It is often grown as an ornamental.

Trunk: Up to 1m thick at base but 150mm to 200mm towards the middle and upper portions. To over 6m tall. Base of trunk is a mass of wiry roots. The broken stipe bases persistent on trunk.

Fronds: Up to 4m long. Rhachis covered with short obtuse prickles. Scales of the stipe base, brown glossy and thick.

Sori: Round, on under surface of frond at fork of veinlets.

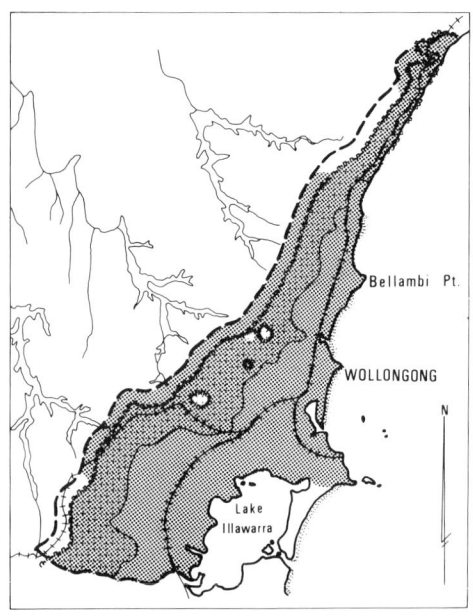

TOP: Upper part of main trunk. BOTTOM RIGHT: Frond bases showing scales. BOTTOM LEFT: Underside of frond showing sori.

Cyathea cooperi (Hook. ex F. Muell.) Dom
Cyatheaceae

The occurrence of this tree fern is based on a single specimen found in rainforest west of Fairy Meadow by Mr. K. Mills. There have also been a number of other reported sightings. All recordings of this species have been on the escarpment in the vicinity of the benches.

This species is most easily distinguished from the other tree ferns in the area by the dense light coloured scales clothing the lower part of the stipe bases and the new unrolling fronds. Also the stipe bases are not persistent on the trunk and where they detach there are left clean oval shaped scars.

Trunk: About 150mm diameter with distinctive oval scars on surface left by stipes.

Fronds: Up to 3m long, soft bright green coloured. White or straw coloured scales clothing young unrolling fronds and stipe bases.

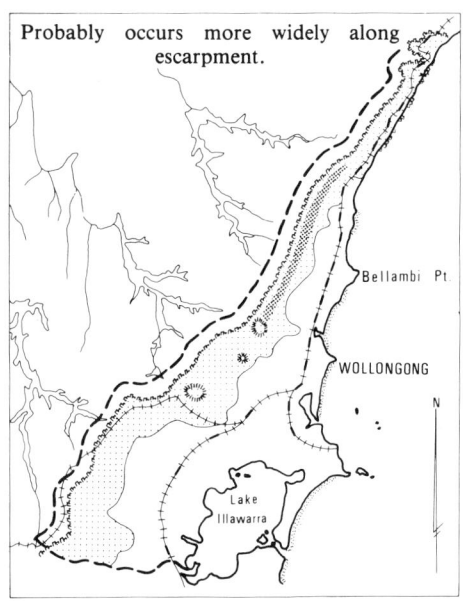

Probably occurs more widely along escarpment.

Close-up of trunk showing oval scars where leaf stalks have fallen off.

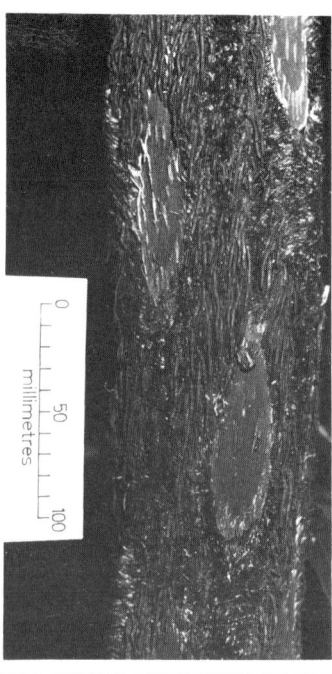

Cyathea cooperi in rainforest.

Upper part of trunk.

Cyathea leichhardtiana (F. Muell.) Copel.

Prickly tree fern

Cyatheaceae

This tree fern is confined to rainforest on the escarpment and is particularly common on the talus slope. It is most easily recognised by its thin trunk (less than 100mm thick) and on close contact with the rhachis of the frond its sharp prickles becomes obvious. Prickly tree fern is not an easy fern to cultivate; it is slow growing and does not take well after transplanting.

Trunk: Up to 7m tall, less than 100mm in diameter, most of the old stipe bases persistent on the trunk.

Fronds: Up to 3m long, dark green and shiny above. Rhachis covered in sharp prickles 1-3mm long. Scales of stipe bases; straw coloured to almost white.

Sori: Round, on undersurface of frond and at junction of veinlets.

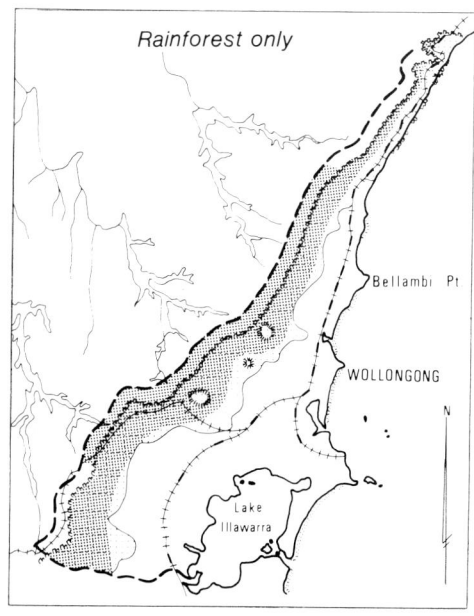

Tree.

FAR LEFT: Stipe base showing scales.

IMMEDIATE LEFT: Close-up of upper part of trunk.

Dendrocnide excelsa (Wedd.) Chew
syn. *Laportea gigas* Wedd.

Giant stinging tree
Urticaceae

There is no mistaking the giant stinging tree when confronted with it in the rainforest. It is set apart by its large leaves (up to 300mm across), whitish bark and stinging hairs on the leaves which on contact with skin deliver a business-like sting. The stinging hairs are easily seen with the naked eye and lie numerously on both sides of the leaf.

This species is a moderately large tree and is found only in rainforest on the escarpment and Berkeley and Flagstaff Hills. It grows up to about 15m high and the stem is often buttressed at the base. Thick white roots of this tree are sometimes conspicuous on the forest floor.

Bark: Grey to creamy coloured with scattered small bumps.

Leaves: Alternate, 80mm to 300mm long, 60mm to 250mm wide; ovate with a cordate base, bright green, covered with stinging hairs.

Inflorescence: Axillary panicles shorter than the leaves.

Flowers: The flowers contain either male or female parts with the sexes on different trees (dioecious). The flowers are small and white.

Fruit: Nuts about 2mm diameter, the stalk of the nuts enlarges to a mauve-coloured fleshy mass. Fruit bears stinging hairs.

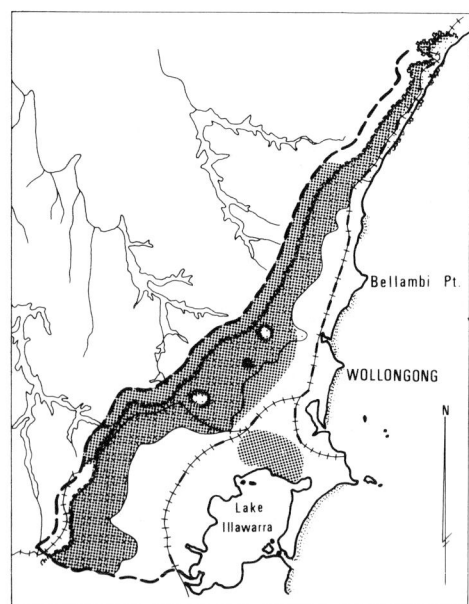

TOP LEFT: Underside of leaf. TOP RIGHT: Tree. MIDDLE LEFT: Top side of leaf showing stinging hairs. BOTTOM LEFT: Leaves. BOTTOM RIGHT: Young tree with large leaves.

Dicksonia antarctica Labill.
Soft tree fern
Cyatheaceae

As the common name suggests this species lacks the prickles that the two other tree ferns in the Wollongong area possess. The rhachis is always quite smooth. Other identifying features of *Dicksonia antarctica* are the stiff brown hairs in place of the scales at the base of the stipes and the large number of fronds which often unroll up to 30 at a time.

Soft tree fern is distributed throughout the Wollongong area in rainforest and eucalypt forest but always in moist places. It is commonly found along watercourses. It often grows quite large with a thick trunk (300mm) and up to 5m tall. The trunk often supports epiphytes, mainly other ferns.

Trunk: Up to 400mm diameter, 5m tall, persistent stipe bases densely matted with coarse fibrous roots.

Fronds: 1.8m to 4m long, rather harsh, dark green above, paler beneath. The fronds unroll in flushes of up to 30 at a time. Rhachis smooth. Stipe bases covered in stiff brown hairs.

Sori: Globular 1-2mm diameter, marginal, terminal on minor veinlets. The leaf margin is reflexed to form a two-lipped cup over the sorus.

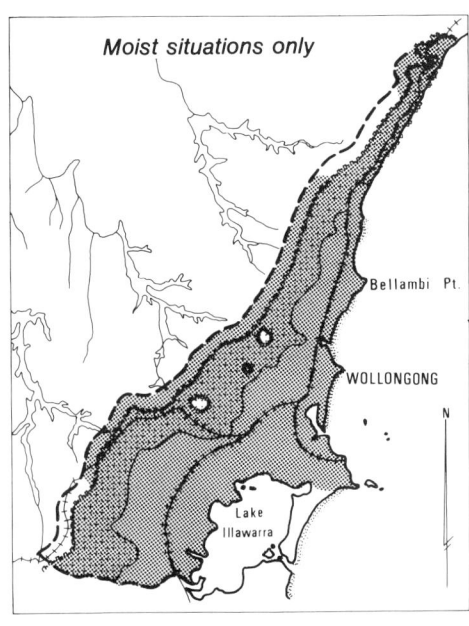
Moist situations only

Tree.

Stipe base.

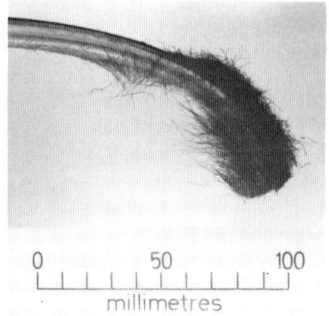

Close-up of upper part of trunk showing fine hairy scales.

Diospyros australis (R. Br.) Hiern
syn. *Cargillia australis* R. Br.

Black plum

Ebenaceae

Diospyros australis is reasonably common throughout rainforests of the Wollongong area but nowhere is it abundant. It grows to a medium sized tree about 10m tall and is most easily picked out in the rainforest canopy by its small oval leaves arranged in two regular rows along the stems. Viewed closely the yellowish undersurface of the leaf is the most distinctive feature.

Leaves: Alternate, shortly stalked, elliptical with a rounded end, dark green on upper surface, yellowish beneath, 30mm to 80mm long, 20mm to 40mm wide.

Fruit: Single in forks of leaves, oval, fleshy up to 20mm long, black, enclosed at base by a cup-shaped 4 or 5 lobed calyx, single seed, about 8mm diameter. Fruits March-April.

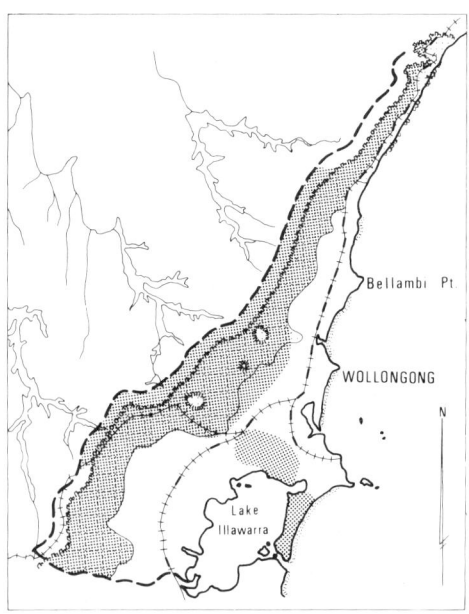

Leaves.

Underside of leaves and fruit.

Diospyros pentamera (Woolls et F. Muell.) F. Muell.

syn. *Cargillia pentamera* Woolls et F. Muell.

Myrtle ebony
Black myrtle
Ebenaceae

Myrtle ebony reaches its largest size on the latite areas of Jamberoo and Kiama, south of the area covered by this book. There, it is relatively common and grows to about 10m tall. However, in the Wollongong area it is rare and has only been observed up to about 4m tall as a rather spindly tree. It is only found in the rainforest of the escarpment in the vicinity of the benches.

Bark: Grey or black.

Leaves: Alternate, shortly stalked, elliptical to narrow rhomboid; 30mm to 60mm long, 12mm to 25mm wide; dark green and dull on upper surface, pale whitish or yellowish underneath.

Inflorescence: Singly or in groups of 3 to 5 along branches.

Flowers: About 3mm long, 5 calyx lobes, 5 corolla lobes.

Fruit: Globular, 12mm diameter 2-5 seeds.

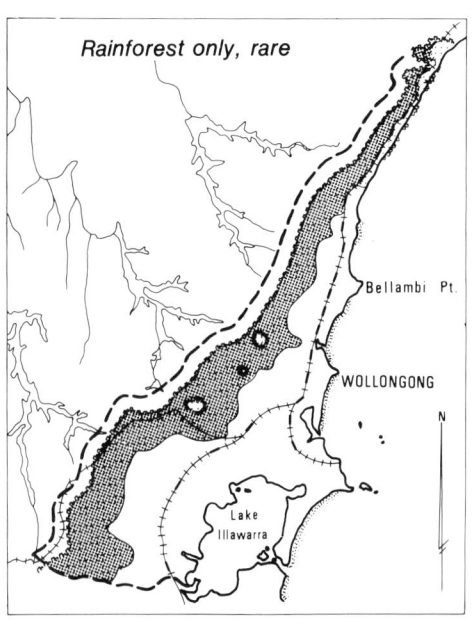

Diploglottis australis (G. Don) Radlk.

syn. *Diploglottis cunninghamii* Hook f.

Native tamarind

Sapindaceae

Especially on young trees, the large (1m long) dark green velvety, pinnate leaves give the crown of this tree a coarse textured appearance and make it easy to pick out in the rainforest. While not a common tree, the native tamarind can be found in most rainforest patches along the escarpment. It grows up to about 20m tall and is sometimes found as a many-stemmed tree.

Bark: Brown to grey with fine circumferential rings like coachwood.

Leaves: Up to 1m long with 8-12 large leaflets 130mm to 200mm long. The whole leaf and small branches are covered with a dense brown tomentum, giving them a velvety feel. Dark green in colour.

Inflorescence: Large (300mm long) panicles in forks of upper leaves.

Flowers: Numerous, calyx 3mm long, petals 3mm long.

Fruit: Yellow, 2 or 3 globular lobes with each measuring over 12mm. Edible. Large seed about 10mm diameter. Fruits January.

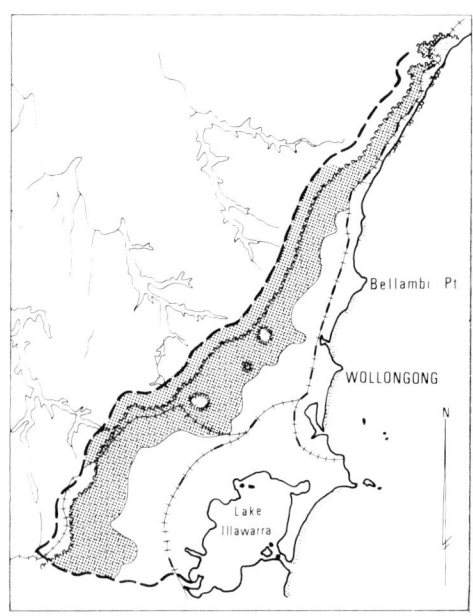

Tree.

BELOW: Leaves.

BELOW: Flowers.

Doryphora sassafras Endl.
Sassafras
Yellow sassafras
Monimiaceae

Sassafras is one of the most common trees of the escarpment rainforest and an easy one to identify. All parts of the tree are highly aromatic and a few leaves crushed and smelled leave no question as to its identity. Also the coarsely serrated leaves and fawn flaky bark, make this tree stand out in the rainforest. Sassafras is a medium to large tree up to 30m tall and with a trunk diameter of up to 1m.

This species occurs in rainforest of the gullies between foothills, on the benches and slopes of the escarpment and in gullies of the plateau. It does not extend out on to the coastal plain except for one place at Mangerton Park, Mangerton.

Bark: Fawn to light brown or sometimes greyish, soft and flaky, tesselated.

Leaves: Opposite; shortly stalked; elliptical in outline but with a coarsely serrated margin; dark, glossy green on top; 60mm to 120mm long, 40mm to 70mm wide; highly aromatic when crushed.

Inflorescence: Clusters of three flowers on short stalks in the leaf forks.

Flowers: To 30mm across, 6 white perianth segments tapering to fine points. The flowers are quite showy massed on the tree. Flowers July.

Fruit: The floral tube or lower part of perianth segments enlarge to form the fruit. When ripe it is brown, 10mm to 20mm long, egg or pear shaped and splits open to reveal the seeds which are about 3mm diameter with a short appendage covered in hairs for wind dispersal. Fruits summer and autumn.

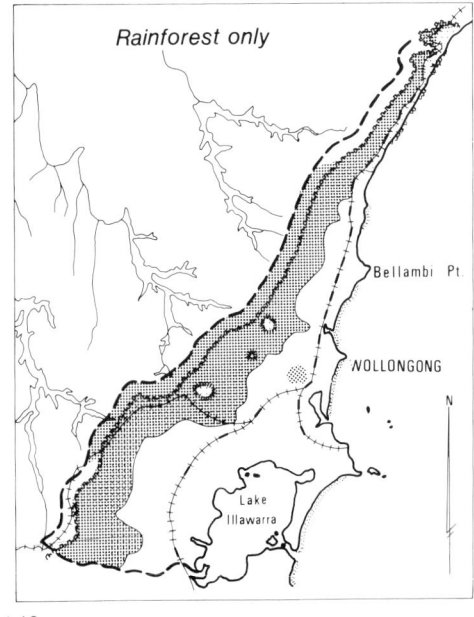

TOP LEFT: Tree. TOP RIGHT: Fruit. MIDDLE RIGHT: Bark. BOTTOM: Leaves.

Duboisia myoporoides R. Br.
Corkwood
Solanaceae

This plant was much sought after for the drugs it contains. Whether it was harvesting for this purpose or just that the tree has a sporadic natural distribution, it certainly occurs today only in limited numbers in the Wollongong area. Within the area covered by this book it has only been observed in the Rixon's Pass area on the plateau and along the Windang peninsula. However, because of its sporadic distribution, it can probably be found elsewhere.

Corkwood usually grows at the edges of rainforest but can occur in wet sclerophyll forest also. It is often only of shrub size but sometimes forms a small tree about 5m tall.

Bark: Brown, fawn or grey with longitudinal fissures, corky on older plants.

Leaves: Alternate, stalked, oblanceolate to obovate, 30mm to 120mm long, 15mm to 30mm wide, rather thin, soft and bright green.

Inflorescence: Loose panicle at end of branches.

Flowers: White, bell shaped, about 6mm long. Flowers spring.

Fruit: Black, globular, about 6mm diameter.

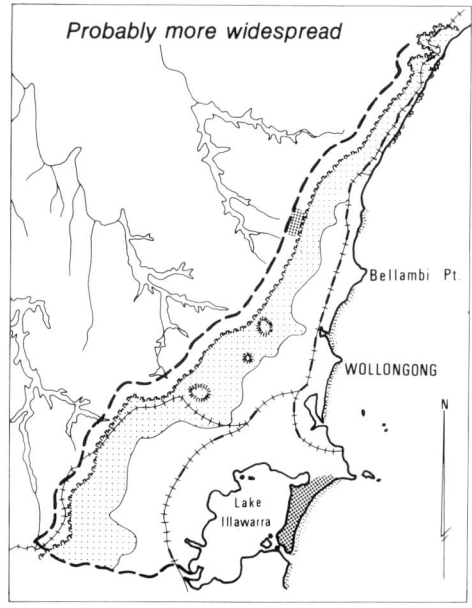

Leaves.

Ehretia acuminata R. Br.
Koda
Ehretiaceae

Another of the few deciduous native trees of the Wollongong area, Koda grows to a tree about 10m tall. It is an inhabitant of the escarpment rainforest and is rather uncommon. The most noteworthy feature of this tree is its deciduous habit, especially in spring when it dons an entirely new dress of bright green, soft leaves. The leaves of Koda are serrated and somewhat thin, resembling cherry tree leaves.

Bark: Grey or brown.

Leaves: Alternate, stalked, serrated; elliptical or egg shaped with a drawn out point (acuminate); 80mm to 150mm long, 40mm to 80mm wide; rather thin, venation prominent on underside. Older leaves dark green, young spring leaves, bright soft green.

Inflorescence: Panicles terminal on branchlets or in forks of leaves.

Flowers: Small, 6mm across, white, strongly scented, 5 calyx lobes, 5 petals and 5 stamens. Flowers September and October.

Fruit: Globular, orange, up to 7mm diameter, a drupe. Fruits autumn and winter.

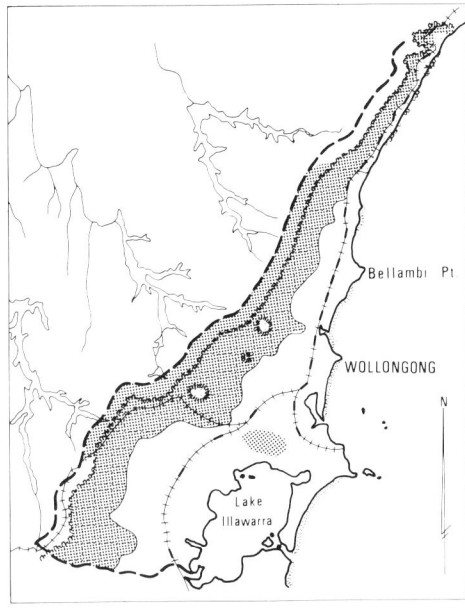

Leaves.

Elaeocarpus kirtonii F. Muell. ex F. M. Bailey

syn. *Elaeocarpus longifolius* C. Moore
E. baeuerlenii Maid. et R. T. Bak.

Pigeonberry ash

Whitewood

Elaeocarpaceae

Unlike blueberry ash, pigeonberry ash is confined to the rainforest of the escarpment. It grows to a medium tree about 15m tall. During spring when the new growth emerges this tree displays vivid pink new growth which stands out in the canopy of the rainforest. The leaves of pigeonberry ash look similar to coachwood with the same sized serrations and a second articulation point at the base of the leaf blade. However, coachwood leaves are usually wider and have a more contoured surface.

Bark: Grey, fairly smooth.

Leaves: Alternate, lanceolate, narrows at both ends, serrated, venation conspicuously reticulate, bump (articulation point) at junction of leaf blade and petiole as well as at the junction of petiole and stem. Leaf blade measures 80mm to 170mm long, 15mm to 40mm wide, rather thick.

Inflorescence: Racemes up to 120mm long, in forks of leaves.

Flowers: 10mm long, white, petals fringed, 5 calyx lobes, 5 petals, 25 or more stamens. Flowers March.

Fruit: Blue, egg shaped, 10mm to 12mm long.

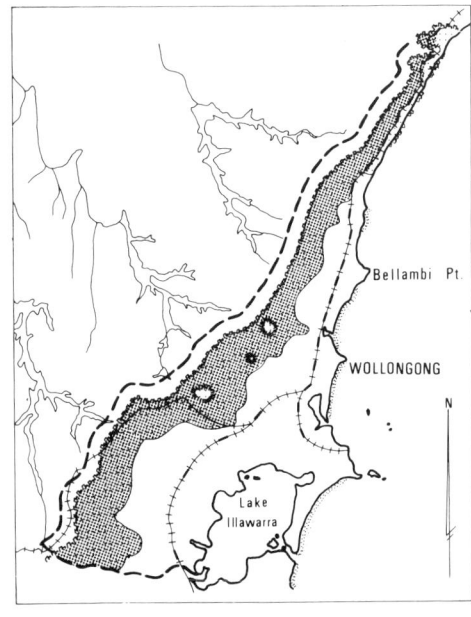

Leaves.

Flowers.

Elaeocarpus reticulatus Sm.

syn. *E. cyaneus* Ait.

Blueberry ash

Elaeocarpaceae

The flowers, which are bell-like with a fringed edge, vary on different plants from rose pink to white, making this tree an ideal ornamental subject. It also carries grey-blue berries in autumn and has attractive foliage.

Blueberry ash does not grow as big in the Wollongong area as it does in some parts of Sydney but it does reach about 4m in height. It is mainly found in sheltered eucalypt forest on the sandstone soil of the plateau but is occasionally seen in the rainforest on the escarpment.

Bark: Grey.

Leaves: Alternate, lanceolate, drawn out to a point, serrated, venation very clearly reticulate, 70mm to 120mm long, blade tapering gradually at base. A slight bump is visible at the junction of the leaf blade and petiole.

Inflorescence: Racemes up to 80mm long in forks of the leaves.

Flowers: White or pink, stalked, bell-shaped, hanging petals fringed. Flower measures about 8mm long and 8mm across. Flowers October-November.

Fruit: Globular, dark blue or grey, about 7mm diameter.

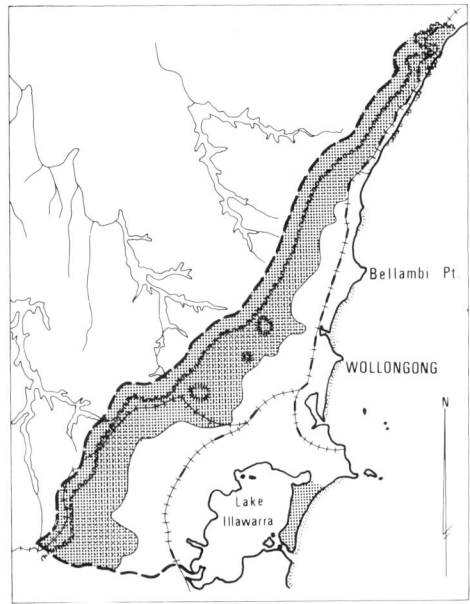

Leaves.

Flowers and fruit.

Elaeodendron australe Vent.
Red-fruited olive plum
Celastraceae

Often seen growing as a shrub but attaining a tree shape and size to 4m tall, red-fruited olive plum is one of the most widespread of the mesophytic species of the Wollongong area. It can be found in both rainforest and sheltered wet sclerophyll forest across the plain and on the escarpment slopes. The bright green and rather thick leaves as well as bright orange-red fruit are the most distinctive features of this plant.

Leaves: Opposite, stalked. The shape of the leaves of this species is rather variable; they may be lanceolate, elliptical, ovate or obovate. The outer half often has blunt serrations but the outline is sometimes entire. The size of the leaf is 50mm to 100mm long, 30mm to 70mm wide. The leaf is often thick, particularly when growing on sea cliffs in the north of the area.

Inflorescence: Axillary or lateral cymes.

Flowers: Greenish, small, petals 2-3mm long.

Fruit: Egg shaped or rounded, about 20mm diameter, bright orange red, with a thin fleshy covering; one large seed.

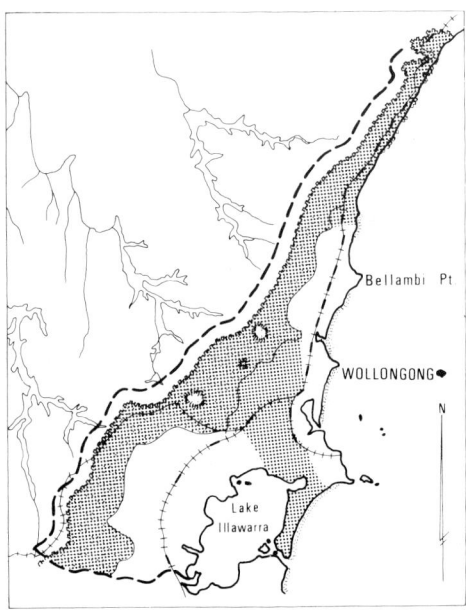

Young street tree.

Leaves and fruit.

Leaves and flowers.

Emmenosperma alphitonioides F. Muell.
Bonewood
Rhamnaceae

Bonewood is an uncommon tree found in rainforest in the Wollongong area. It is most conspicuous when carrying fruit in winter. The bright orange drupes are often massed over the canopy making the tree stand out from afar. The leaves and green twigs of this species can look very similar to churnwood *(Citronella moorei)* but bonewood has opposite leaves whereas churnwood has alternate leaves.

Bonewood is an inhabitant of the rainforest of the escarpment and lower slopes and grows to a medium sized tree about 15m tall usually with a long straight trunk.

Bark: Grey, slightly wrinkled.

Leaves: Opposite, stalked, egg-shaped or elliptical, sometimes narrowed to a blunt point; 30mm to 80mm long, 20mm to 40mm wide, dark glossy green on upper surface. Twigs dark green.

Inflorescence: Terminal or axillary panicles mostly shorter than leaves.

Flowers: Stalked, 5mm diameter, 5 calyx lobes, 5 petals, 5 stamens. Flowers September-October.

Fruit: Bright orange, nearly globular, 5-7mm diameter. Often covering of fruit falls away leaving seed on the end of the fruit stalk. Seed flattened about 3mm across, bright orange. Fruits winter.

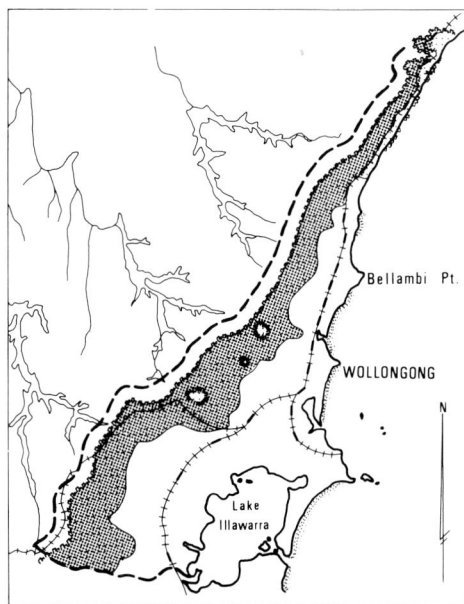

Endiandra sieberi Nees

Corkwood (not to be confused with *Duboisia myoporoides*)
Lauraceae

Endiandra sieberi looks very similar to the two cryptocaryas occurring in Wollongong. However, the leaves do not have the bluish undersurface of *Cryptocarya glaucescens* or the widely spaced conspicuous lateral veins of *Cryptocarya microneura*. *Endiandra sieberi* also has distinctive corky bark but it has the white midrib on the leaves like the other laurels.

This species is not very common in the Wollongong area but grows on the edge of rainforest on the plateau west of Coalcliff and Stanwell Park along the crest of the escarpment and at Windang. It forms a small tree up to about 10m tall.

Bark: Grey-brown corky.

Leaves: Alternate, stalked, narrow elliptical to lanceolate, 50mm to 100mm long, 15mm to 35mm wide, white midrib, entire margin.

Inflorescence: Panicles in forks of leaves.

Flowers: Small, perianth segments 6, stamens 3, alternating with 3 staminodes.

Fruit: A black egg-shaped or globular berry with a thin fleshy outer covering.

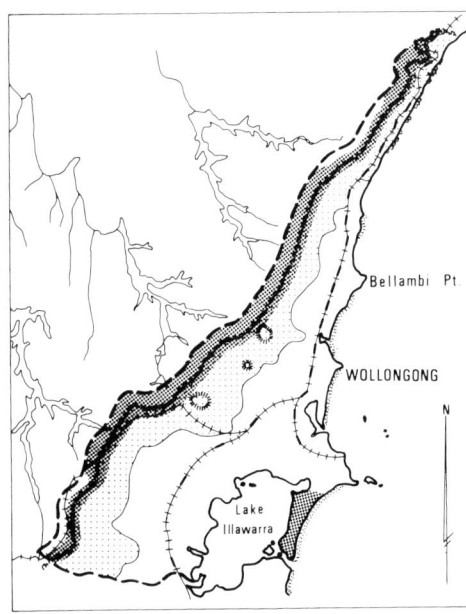

TOP: Leaves. BOTTOM LEFT: Bark. BOTTOM RIGHT: Fruit.

Eucalyptus amplifolia Naudin

Cabbage gum

Myrtaceae

Cabbage gum is not a common tree in the Wollongong area. It occurs in depressions, along watercourses and where drainage is poor and the soil clayey. This tree is easily mistaken for forest red gum *(Eucalyptus tereticornis)* but its preference for lower lying sites as well as the narrower and more numerous buds (11 to more than 20) and smaller fruit help distinguish it from forest red gum. Also as the name implies the juvenile leaves are rather large and coarse and are quite green instead of the slight bluishness of forest red gum leaves.

In the Wollongong area cabbage gum grows to a medium sized eucalypt about 20m tall and has an ascending branch habit similar to *Eucalyptus tereticornis*. Cabbage gum is mostly found growing in association with or adjacent to forest red gum *(Eucalyptus tereticornis)*, small leaved stringybark *(Eucalyptus eugenioides)*, prickly leaved paperbark *(Melaleuca styphelioides)* and *Melaleuca decora*.

Bark: Smooth throughout, white, grey and blue mottled, shed in irregular sized flakes.

Leaves: Juvenile — opposite for 3-4 pairs shortly stalked, broadly ovate to orbicular 70mm to 140mm long, 70mm to 140mm wide, dark green, thick. Branchlets angular. Adult — alternate, stalked, narrow to broadly lanceolate, 100mm to 200mm long, 20mm to 40mm wide.

Inflorescence: 11 to more than 20 flowered umbels. Buds — horn shaped, stalked, 10mm to 15mm long, 3mm to 4mm diameter. Operculum — 3 times longer than calyx tube. Flowers — November-January.

Fruit: Globular, 4mm to 6mm long, 4mm to 7mm wide, with an almost hemispherical disc and strongly exserted incurved valves.

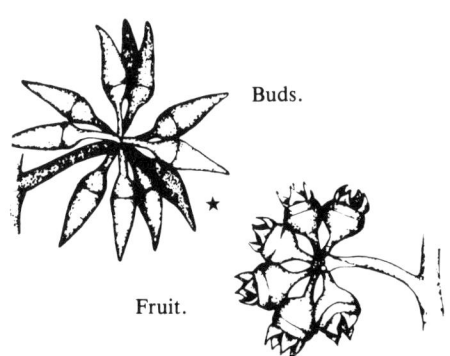

Buds.

Fruit.

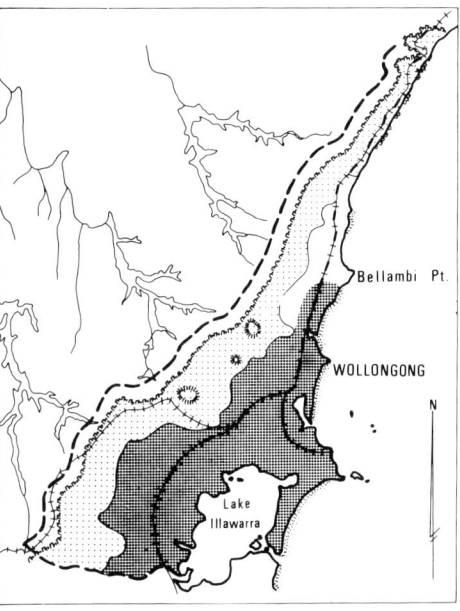

Juvenile leaves.

Fruit.

Adult leaves.

Eucalyptus bosistoana F. Muell.

Coast-grey box

Myrtaceae

Coast-grey box occurs on the undulating parts of the coastal plain in the Dapto/Yallah area. It grows in association with *Eucalyptus tereticornis* which it resembles somewhat. However it is not a common tree and only occurs scattered among other trees.

This species is distinctive by virtue of its dense, dark green and fine textured crown and the stocking of box-like bark at the base of the trunk. It is a handsome tree growing to about 15m tall.

Other species coast-grey box may be associated with, are woollybutt *(Eucalyptus longifolia)*, small leaved stringybark *(Eucalyptus eugenioides)*, *Melaleuca styphelioides* and *Melaleuca decora*.

Bark: Smooth, white or light grey on branches and upper trunk. Finely fibrous or flaky (box-like), fawn or grey on lower trunk.

Leaves: Juvenile — opposite for 4-5 pairs then alternate, stalked, ovate to circular 35mm to 60mm long, 25mm to 60mm wide, thin, pale green. Adult — alternate, stalked, lanceolate with a long point, 80mm to 200mm long, 12mm to 25mm wide, thin, pale green.

Inflorescence: 3-7 flowered umbels in forks of leaves or forming short panicles. Buds — stalked, egg shaped or club shaped, 8mm to 10mm long, about 5mm diameter. Operculum conical as long as calyx tube. Flowers January-March.

Fruit: Stalked, hemispherical to truncated egg shape, about 7mm long, about 7mm wide, valves usually enclosed.

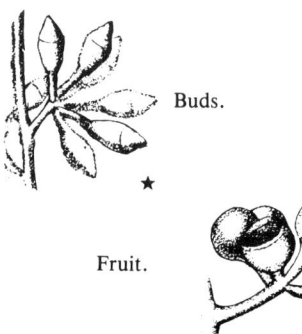

Buds.

Fruit.

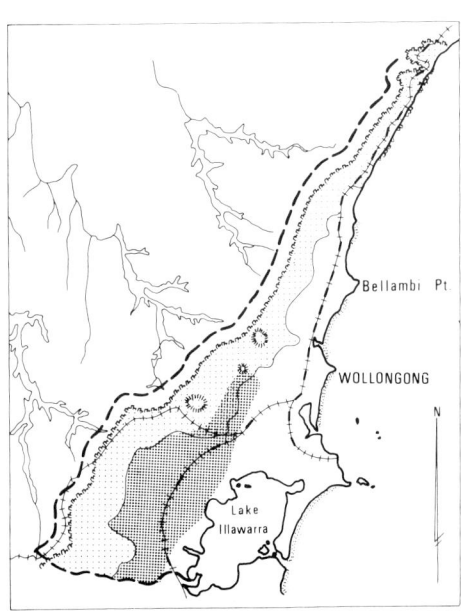

Tree.

Leaves.

Eucalyptus botryoides Sm.
Bangalay
Myrtaceae

The size and habit of this tree are variable with its habitat. The main areas it occupies are the hind dunes, where it grows to a small spreading tree of about 6-10m, and the banks of creeks across the coastal plain and north of Austinmer it extends up the slopes of the escarpment where it can grow into a larger tree up to 20m high.

In some places (e.g. just north of Coalcliff station) it covers the mountain side as a pure stand. It is confined to areas east of the escarpment and less than 300 metres. Bangalay forms a spreading tree with a rather dense crown of leaves and sometimes has, in this area (e.g. Stanwell Park), dead branches projecting from the crown caused by the depredation of lerps, a sap sucking insect on the leaves. *Eucalyptus botryoides* is usually associated with hind dune species such as *Leptospermum laevigatum* and *Banksia integrifolia*, or on creek banks with various rainforest species. On the mountain slopes north of Austinmer it is almost solely associated with blackbutt *(E. pilularis)*.

Bark: Only the smaller branches have smooth bark, the larger branches and main stem are covered with fine, flaky bark. The colour of the flaky bark is grey or brown and the smooth bark varies from cream to blue-grey through the year.

Leaves: Juvenile — opposite for 3-4 pairs, ovate to broadly lanceolate, petiolate; thin and wavy, 50mm to 80mm long, 30mm to 40mm wide, paler on the undersurface. Adult — alternate, petiolate, dark green above, paler beneath, 100mm to 150mm long, 30mm to 60mm wide, broadly lanceolate, tapering to a long fine point. Venation is fine and often obscure, 40°-60° to the midrib.

Inflorescence: Axillary umbels with 6-10 flowers. Peduncles compressed 7mm-10mm long, 4mm-5mm broad. Flower buds sessile, 10mm to 12mm long, 4mm to 6mm wide, cylindrical with two ribs. Operculum hemispherical with a rounded top or short beak. Flowers January-March.

Fruit: Stalkless, cylindrical, 8mm to 10mm long, 6mm to 7mm wide; valves short, enclosed or at rim level.

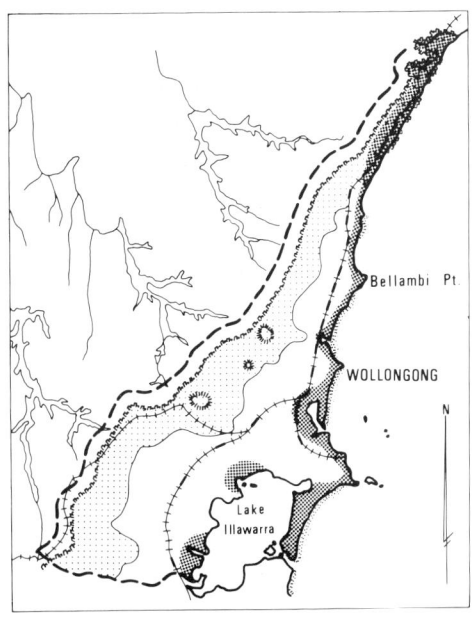

Eucalyptus cypellocarpa L. Johnson
Monkey gum
Mountain grey gum
Myrtaceae

In the Wollongong area this species mainly grows on the plateau in wet sclerophyll forest from Mount Keira to Marshall Mount above 300m. Monkey gum occurs usually on good, deep soils in the area below the Hawkesbury Sandstone and is most commonly associated with yellow stringybark *(E. muellerana)*, gully gum *(E. smithii)* and coast white box *(E. quadrangulata)*. This tree grows up to about 30m and has a clean main stem.

Bark: For most of its height monkey gum has smooth, blue-grey and white mottled bark. A short stocking of flaky bark may persist at the base for a metre or so.

Leaves: Juvenile — opposite for many pairs, stalkless or with a short stalk, broadly lanceolate with a rounded base, may have even a cordate base, 60mm to 80mm long, 25mm to 50mm wide. Covered with a greyish bloom. Adult — alternate, stalked, narrow lanceolate, tapering to a long point, dark glossy green, 100mm to 250mm long, 20mm to 30mm wide, moderately thick. Venation 30° to 45° to the midrib.

Inflorescence: Axillary umbels, with 7 flowers, peduncle compressed 7mm to 20mm long. Buds cylindrical 10mm to 12mm long, 5mm to 6mm across with 2 ribs, operculum conical. Flowers summer.

Fruit: Barrel shaped with short stalk, 8mm to 10mm long, 7mm to 8mm across, 2 ribs.

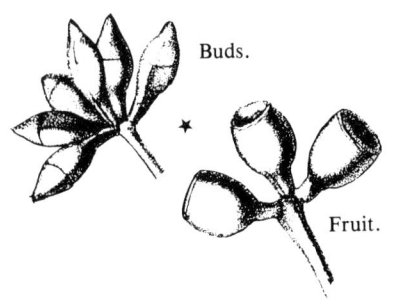
Buds.
Fruit.

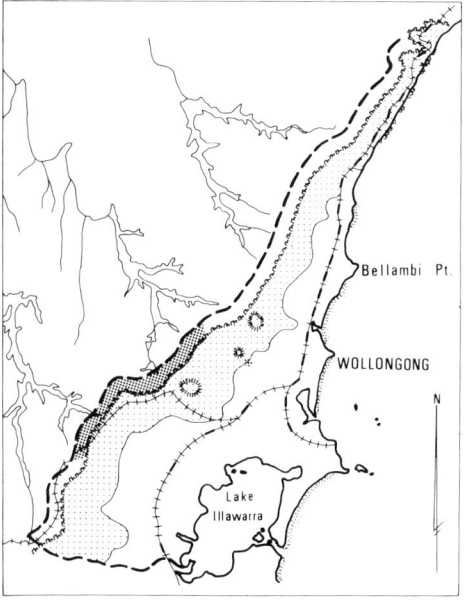

TOP LEFT: Lower trunk showing two types of bark.
TOP RIGHT: Tree.
BOTTOM LEFT: Fruit.
BOTTOM RIGHT: Adult leaves.

Eucalyptus dendromorpha (Blakely) L. Johnson et D. Blaxell

syn. *E. obtusiflora* DC. var. *dendromorpha*

Myrtaceae

There are only two consistently mallee eucalypts in the Wollongong area. They are *Eucalyptus dendromorpha* and Blue Mountains mallee *(Eucalyptus stricta)*. *Eucalyptus dendromorpha* has a very limited distribution in this area occurring on the south and east facing crest of the escarpment on moist slopes above cliffs. Its occurrence along the escarpment is discontinuous and groups of this species are readily seen at Mt. Keira Summit Park and the south facing crest above Austinmer where the escarpment swings toward the sea, but it also grows at West Albion Park, Bong Bong Pass, on top of Mt. Kembla and at Wombarra, all at the crest of escarpment cliffs.

This species is a typical mallee with numerous stems up to about 8m in height and mostly with the foliage carried on the top one-third of the stems. The bark is smooth except for the base of the trunk. The leaves are carried more or less at right angles to the stem.

Bark: Smooth except for some scaly bark at base, white or brown mottled.

Leaves: Seedling — opposite, stalkless, lanceolate. Juvenile — Alternate, stalked, lanceolate, oblique base, 80mm to 120mm long, 2mm to 4mm wide. Intermediate — a gradual transition from juvenile to adult. Adult — alternate, stalked, lanceolate to falcate, oblique base, 70mm to 120mm long, 10mm to 30mm wide. Numerous oil dots in all leaves.

Inflorescence: 4 to 7 flowered umbels. Buds, club shaped, rough with oil glands, 5mm to 10mm long, about 4mm wide.

Fruit: Stalked, ureceolate 8mm to 10mm long, 8mm to 10mm wide, disc moderately wide and inside orifice, valves enclosed.

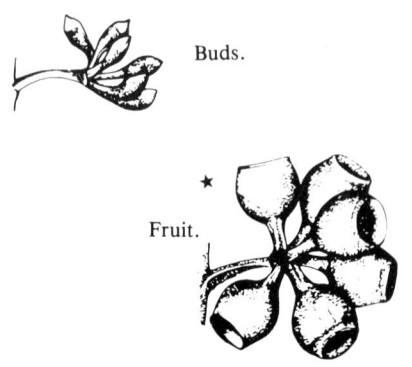
Buds.
Fruit.

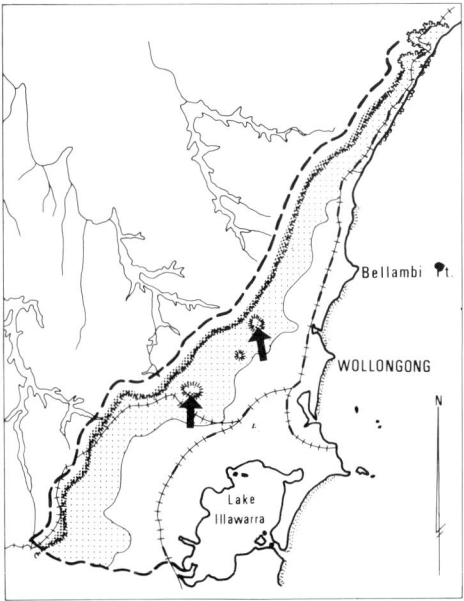

Tree.

Leaves.

Bark.

Eucalyptus elata Dehnh.

syn. *E. andreana* Naudin
E. lindleyana DC.
E. numerosa Maiden

River peppermint

Myrtaceae

River peppermint grows commonly alongside the creeks and rivers flowing westward from the escarpment, where they cut down into strata below the Hawkesbury Sandstone. In the area included in this book, however, it is only to be found on the saddle between Mt. Kembla and the main escarpment and on the plateau in that area above 300m.

This is a beautiful light crowned tree with fine bluish foliage. It looks similar to gully gum *(E, smithii)* but differs in having grey flaky bark at the base instead of brown bark. Also the fruit are distinctly different. River peppermint is usually found in the Wollongong area as a tree 20m to 25m tall but some specimens may be taller. It occurs in association with coast white box *(E. quadrangulata)*, gully gum *(E. smithii)*, Sydney peppermint *(E. piperita)* and mountain grey gum *(E. cypellocarpa)*.

Bark: Grey, flaky and somewhat fissured on lower trunk, smooth and white on upper trunk and branches.

Leaves: Juvenile — opposite, stalkless or sometimes stalked, lanceolate, 40mm to 100mm long, 7mm to 15mm wide, pale green. Internodes very glandular. Adult — alternate, stalked, narrow lanceolate with a long point, 100mm to 200mm long, 10mm to 15mm wide, thin, venation faint, 15°-25° to midrib.

Inflorescence: Umbels in forks of leaves 7 to 40 flowered, peduncles 5-12mm long, terete. Buds; stalked, club shaped 5mm long, 4mm wide. Operculum hemispherical.

Fruit: Stalked, globular to pear shaped, 5-6mm long, 4-5mm wide, valves enclosed.

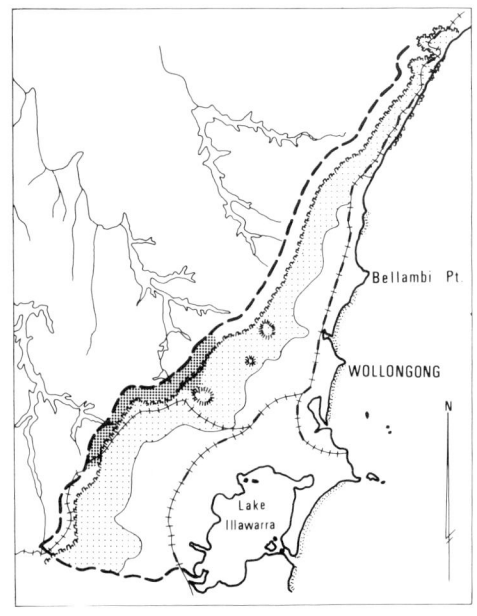

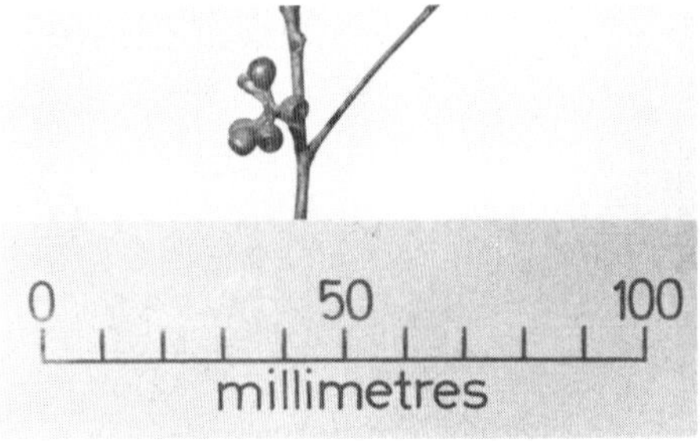

TOP LEFT: Bark.
TOP RIGHT: Tree.
BOTTOM LEFT: Fruit.
BOTTOM RIGHT: Adult leaves.

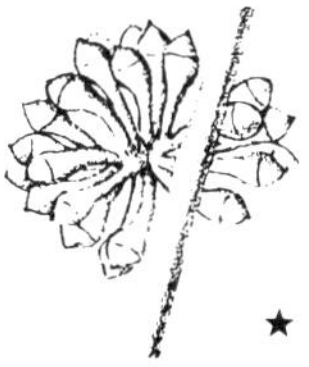

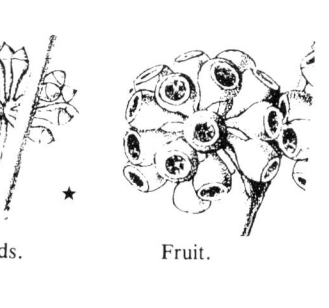

Buds.   Fruit.

Eucalyptus eugenioides Sieb. ex Spreng.

syn *E. wilkinsoniana* R. T. Bak.

Thin leaved stringybark
Myrtaceae

This tree occurs on the coastal plain of the Wollongong area and is very similar to the related species *E. globoidea* but tends to occupy different sites. *E. eugenioides* is a tree which favours hillier country where soil conditions are somewhat drier. This tree may be found in the Dapto and Yallah areas. There is also a fine specimen in the grounds of the Little Flower Church at West Wollongong.

Bark: A typical stringybark, the colour is grey-brown; can be pulled off in strands. The bark is persistent to the small branches.

Leaves: Juvenile — opposite for 5 to 6 pairs, sessile or shortly stalked, elliptical or broadly lanceolate, 30mm to 60mm long, 20mm to 40mm wide, venation 30° to 35° to midrib. The juvenile leaves are softly hairy with stellate hairs. Fragrant when crushed. Intermediate — alternate, stalked, glabrous, broad lanceolate with an oblique base, pale green, 100mm to 150mm long, 25mm to 40mm wide, venation 45° to the midrib. Adult — alternate, stalked, falcate-lanceolate with an oblique base, 80mm to 150mm long, 12mm to 25mm wide, slightly fragrant, venation 20° to 30° to the midrib.

Inflorescence: Axillary umbels, 5 to 12 flowers, peduncle slightly compressed. Buds, 6mm to 8mm long, 4mm wide. Flowers July-September.

Fruit: Globular to hemispherical with short stalks, 5mm to 7mm long, 6mm to 7mm wide.

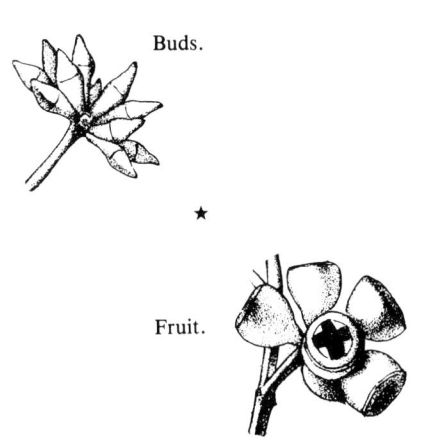

Buds.

Fruit.

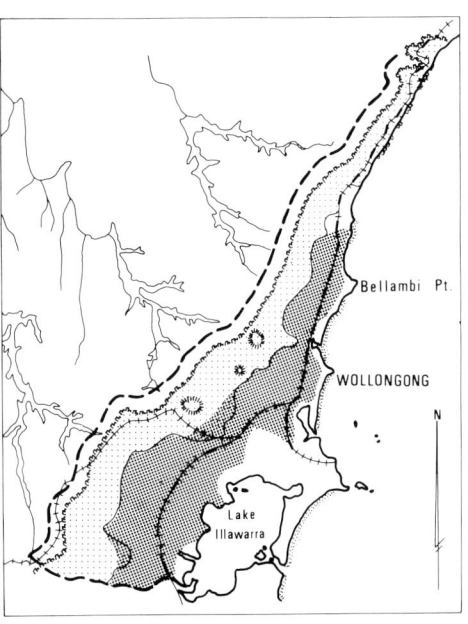

Tree at Little Flower Church, West Wollongong.

Fruit.

Leaves.

171

Eucalyptus globoidea Blakely
White stringybark
Myrtaceae

This stringybark occurs on floodplains and other parts of the coastal plain where soil fertility and water tend to be better. It is closely related to *E. eugenioides* with which it may be easily confused. However, the two species tend to occupy different sites; *E. eugioides* preferring drier hills and slopes. Also *E. globoidea* has generally smaller fruit and thicker, shorter leaves with a more marked colour difference between the top and bottom surfaces of the leaves.

E. globoidea may be found in abundance along Sheafs Rd. at West Dapto.

Bark: Thick, stringy, grey-brown, persistent to small branches.

Leaves: Seedling and juvenile — opposite for several pairs then alternate, stalks short or absent; lanceolate, 15mm to 50mm long, 10mm to 20mm wide, wavy, tufts of fine hairs along midrib and margin. Adult — alternate, stalked, lanceolate, usually oblique 50mm to 130mm long, 15mm to 40mm wide, rather thick, dark green slightly paler on undersurface. Venation 20° to 40° to midrib.

Inflorescence: Umbels in forks of leaves with 7 to 12 flowers. Peduncles cylindrical or slightly angular. Buds; tapering into a short stalk. Operculum conical.

Fruit: Hemispherical to almost spherical, stalkless or with a very short stalk. Disc flat or slightly convex. Valves small, more or less at rim level.

Buds.

Fruit.

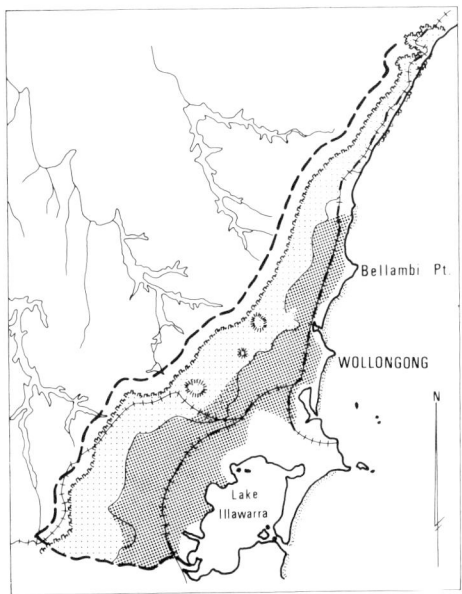

Top: Leaves and buds.
Above: Fruit.
Right: Bark.

Eucalyptus gummifera (Gaertn.) Hochr.

syn. E. corymbosa Sm.

Red bloodwood

Myrtaceae

Red bloodwood grows exclusively on Hawkesbury Sandstone in the area included in this book and because of the poor soil conditions is usually found as a small to medium tree about 6m to 10m high. In some better situations it grows up to about 20m. Because of the frequent burning on the plateau this tree is often found as dense sucker growth or sapling stands about 2m to 3m tall. It is one of the three most common eucalypts on the plateau on Hawkesbury Sandstone.

Bark: Grey to brown, flaky, tesselated, smooth only on smallest branches and twigs.

Leaves: Juvenile — opposite for 3 to 4 pairs, peltate on seedlings not on suckers. Surface bristly. Adult leaves — alternate, stalked, lanceolate, 100mm to 150mm long, 25mm to 50mm broad, much paler on undersurface. Venation fine, regular and 55° to 70° to midrib.

Inflorescence: Terminal corymb, with 4 to 8 flowered umbels. Buds club shaped 12mm long, 10mm wide, pedicels slender, as long as the buds. The flowers are relatively large with white or creamy stamens. This tree flowers well and is conspicuous in flower from January to March.

Fruit: Oval shaped with a short neck at top, 10mm to 20mm long, 10mm to 20mm wide. Valves deeply enclosed.

Wood: The wood of this species is worth noting, it being deep red, very durable in the ground and resistant against termite attack.

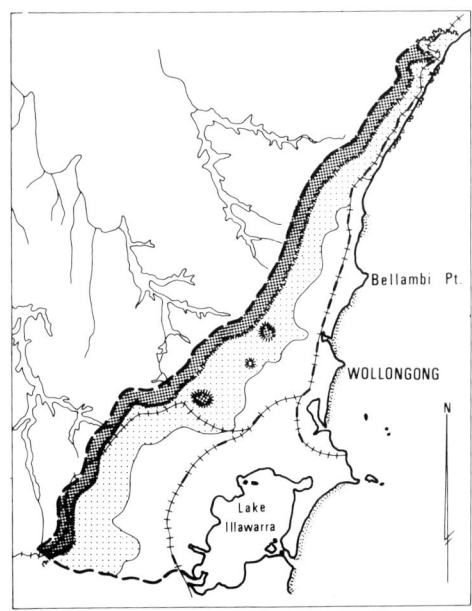

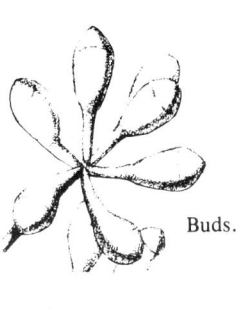
Buds.

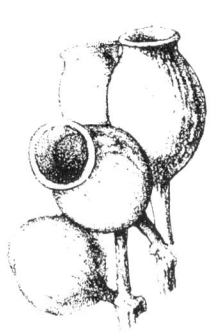
Fruit.

Tree.

Leaves: Topmost leaf shows underside.

Bark.

Eucalyptus ligustrina DC.
Privet leaved stringybark
Myrtaceae

Privet leaved stringybark is confined to the Hawkesbury Sandstone areas of the plateau in the Wollongong area. In fact it has a limited distribution even on the plateau, only occupying high and exposed situations. The main areas where it is to be found are the rocky outcrop of Brokers Nose, West Corrimal and on the plateau west of Dapto.

This eucalypt grows as a shrub, mallee or small tree and can be found as a mature plant less than 1m tall at Brokers Nose. The maximum height of this tree in the Wollongong area is 6m and the crown is dense and bushy with small leaves.

E. ligustrina grows in association with many species but mainly red bloodwood *(E. gummifera)*, silvertop ash *(E. sieberi)*, scribbly gum *(E. racemosa)*, *Banksia sp.*, *Leptospermum sp.* and *Casuarina littoralis.*

Bark: A stringybark, persistent on the larger branches but smooth, falling off in flakes on the smaller branches.

Leaves: The leaves of this tree vary in size as to the maturity of the tree. Seedling — opposite for few pairs stalked, ovate, 12mm to 30mm long, 5mm to 10mm wide. Juvenile — alternate, stalkless, ovate, 25mm to 35mm long, 10mm to 20mm wide with stellate hairs. Intermediate — alternate stalkless, or shortly stalked, oblong to oblong lanceolate, 20mm to 40mm long, 10mm to 20mm wide, thick and glossy, with a short beak, often seen because of their persistence. Adult — alternate, stalked, lanceolate, slightly falcate, 50mm to 80mm long, 10mm to 20mm wide.

Inflorescence: 5-10 flowered umbels in forks of leaves. Buds — club shaped 4mm to 6mm long, 3mm or 4mm wide, operculum hemispherical. Flowers May-June.

Fruit: Globular, sessile, crowded, valves deeply inserted.

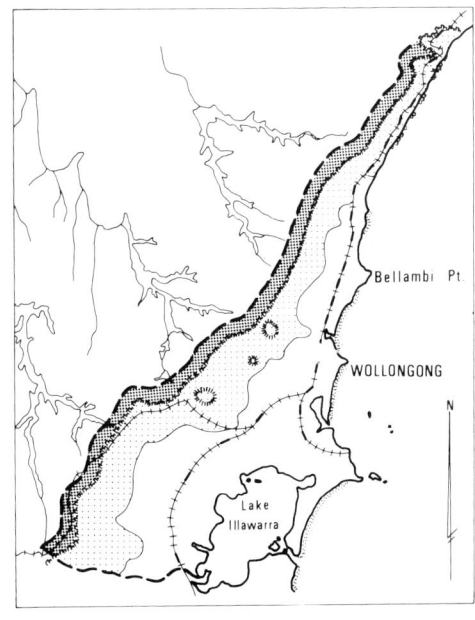

Tree.

Bark.

Leaves.

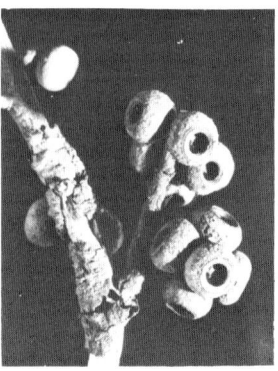
Fruit.

Buds.

★

Fruit.

Eucalyptus longifolia Link et Otto.
Woollybutt
Myrtaceae

Woollybutt is confined to the coastal plain. It is found on the drier undulating parts and on poorly drained but not swampy floodplains. It can be found from Corrimal in the north to Albion Park in the south.

In the Wollongong area woollybutt does not grow to a large tree, as it does further down the coast, but is a medium sized tree up to about 15m with its usual straggly crown and "woolly" trunk.

Bark: Grey, rough, irregularly flaky and cracked.

Leaves: Juvenile — opposite for 3 or 4 pairs then alternate, stalked, ovate, oblong-lanceolate, about 100mm long and 80mm wide. Adult — alternate, stalked, lanceolate — sickle shaped hanging, grey-green 140mm to 220mm long, 20mm to 50mm wide, moderately thick. Venation distinct 35° to 50° to midrib.

Inflorescence: Umbels in forks of leaves. Usually 3 flowered, bent downwards. Buds egg shaped to narrowing at both ends, including operculum, white with pinkish tinge, 15mm to 30mm long, 8mm to 12mm wide. Flowers October-November.

Fruit: Stalked, bell shaped with a wide and angled disc. 15mm to 20mm long, 10mm to 15mm wide.

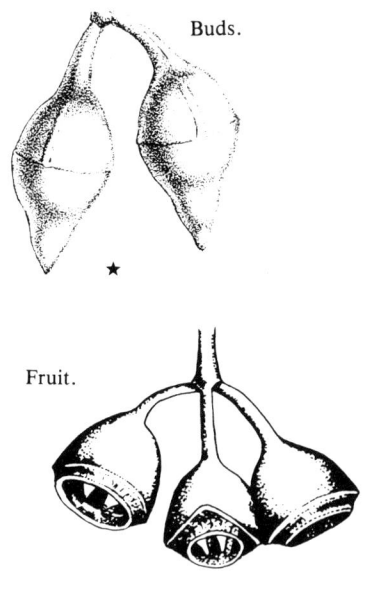

Buds.

Fruit.

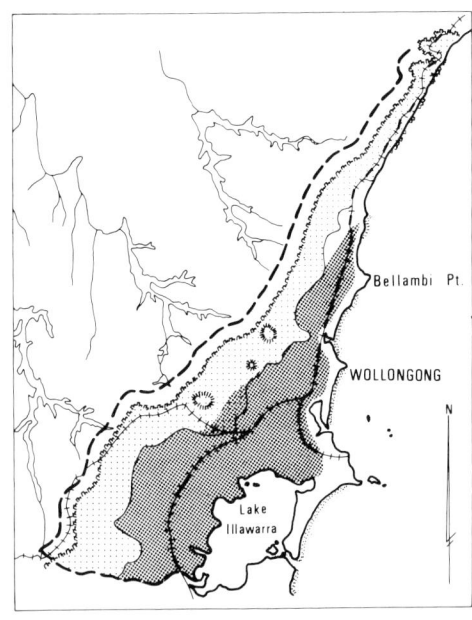

Tree.

Bark.

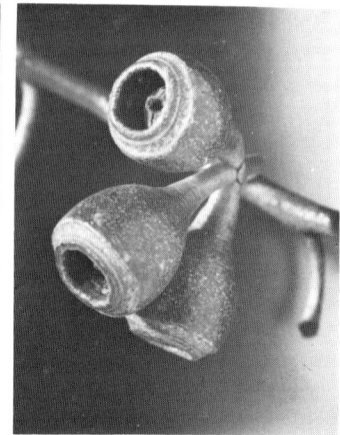

Fruit.

Leaves.

Eucalyptus maculata Hook

Spotted gum

Myrtaceae

Spotted gum is unmistakeable in the Wollongong area. It is the only shaft like tree with smooth bark from top to bottom with grey to pink irregular spots scattered over the trunk. It is also limited in distribution to the volcanic sandstone of the Mt. St. Thomas-Mt. Drummond area with a small patch at Corrimal a few acres in extent. At Mt. St. Thomas where it occurs it dominates the scene.

In this area it does not reach the same proportions as in the far South Coast forest but it can be found up to 20 odd metres high. Spotted gum is a handsome tree and is commonly grown as an ornamental.

Bark: Smooth, base to small branches, white, pink to blue grey irregularly mottled. Shed in patches. Scattered dimples on trunk.

Leaves: Juvenile — alternate, stalked, peltate for several leaves, otherwise ovate to lanceolate, undulate, 80mm to 150mm long, 25mm to 60mm wide. Adult — alternate, stalked, narrow to broad lanceolate, 100mm to 200mm long, 25mm to 60mm wide. Venation 35° to 50° to midrib. Flowers July-August.

Inflorescence: Terminal corymb of 3 to 5 flowered umbels; buds egg shaped, stalked, 10mm to 12mm long, about 7mm across. Operculum with pointed top.

Fruit: Stalked, urn shaped to egg shaped, 12mm to 18mm long, 10mm to 15mm wide.

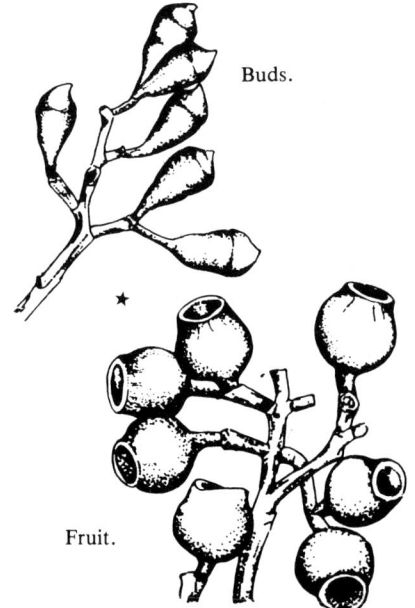

Buds.

Fruit.

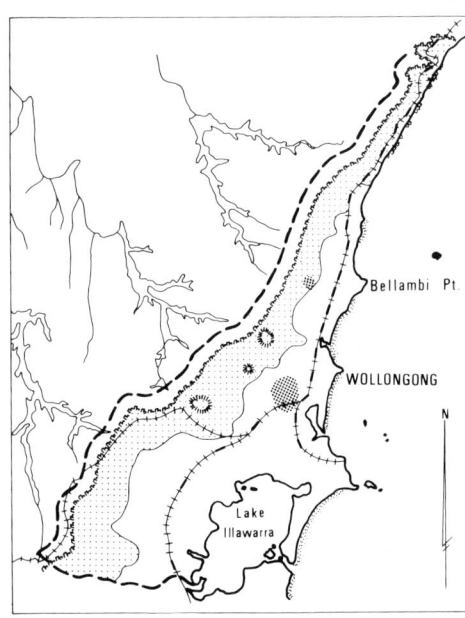

Bark.

Trees.

Leaves.

Buds.

Eucalyptus muellerana Howitt
Yellow stringybark
Myrtaceae

This species only occurs on the better soils in tall wet sclerophyll forest on the escarpment and plateau from Mt. Kembla southwards but above 250m altitude. It is not a common tree and usually does not form pure stands. It is scattered in association with such species as gully gum *(E. smithii)*, coast white box *(E. quadrangulata)* and mountain grey gum *(E. cypellocarpa)*. This tree, like others of tall wet sclerophyll forest, only occurs on the plateau where strata below the Hawkesbury Sandstone are exposed.

Yellow stringybark is described by Blakely as a "massive tree" and certainly there are some large specimens in the Wollongong area. It may be found over 40m tall and frequently has a thick heavy trunk. The crown is dense, dark green and held high.

Bark: Brown, stringy but much finer than a typical stringybark, persistent to the small branches.

Leaves: Juvenile — opposite for 12 or more pairs then alternate, stalked, lanceolate, paler beneath, 30mm to 100mm long, 10mm to 30mm wide. Intermediate — broad lanceolate, 80mm to 100mm long, 20mm to 30mm wide. Adult — alternate, stalked, thick, narrow to broad lanceolate, 100mm to 150mm long, 20mm to 30mm wide. Shiny, oblique base.

Inflorescence: 7-12 flowered umbels in forks of leaves. Buds; stalked, club shaped, 7mm to 8mm long, 5mm or 6mm wide. Operculum hemispherical. Flowers December-February.

Fruit: Stalked, globular, to cut-off pear shaped, 8mm to 10mm long and wide. Valves small, usually enclosed.

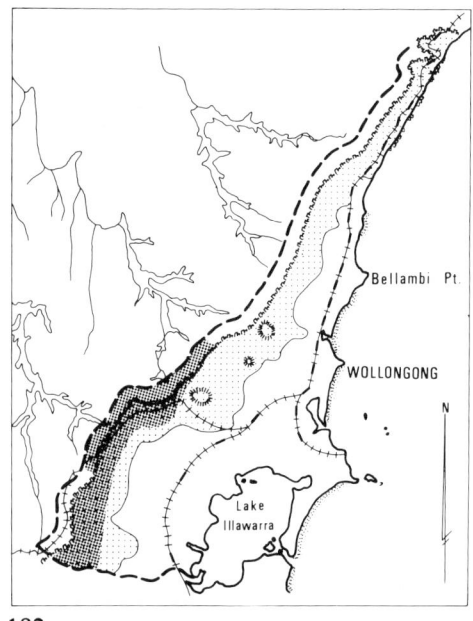

Bark. Tree.

Buds.

★

Fruit.

Leaves.

183

Eucalyptus paniculata Sm.
Grey ironbark
Myrtaceae

Grey ironbark is a common tree in the remains of the coastal plain forest north of Berkeley Hills and grows in tall wet sclerophyll forest to about 300m altitude on the escarpment north of Mt. Keira. It reaches its best development on the escarpment where it grows to 30m or more. On the coastal plain it is usually seen as a medium sized tree 10m to 15m tall. On the escarpment it is nearly always found in association with blackbutt *(E. pilularis)* and turpentine *(Syncarpia glomulifera)*, but on the coastal plain associated species are blackbutt *(E. pilularis)*, forest red gum *(E. tereticornis)*, woollybutt *(E. longifolia)*, small leaved stringybark *(E. eugenioides)*, *Melaleuca styphelioides* and *M. decora*.

Grey ironbark can be seen readily at Phil Adam Park at Corrimal East and Wiseman park, Gwynneville.

Bark: Grey or sometimes black, rough and deeply furrowed, persistent to small branches. Often impregnated with kino.

Leaves: Juvenile — opposite for 3 to 4 pairs then alternate, stalked, ovate to broad lanceolate, 30mm to 60mm long, 15mm to 40mm wide. Adult — alternate, stalked, narrow to broad lanceolate, 70mm to 150mm long, 12mm to 40mm wide, slightly paler on undersurface.

Inflorescence: Panicles at ends of branches with umbels 3-9 flowered. Buds ovate to rhomboid stalked, 10mm long, 5mm wide. Operculum conical. Flowers May-November.

Fruit: Stalked, hemispherical or pear shaped, 6mm to 10mm long, 5mm to 8mm wide, valves exserted or enclosed.

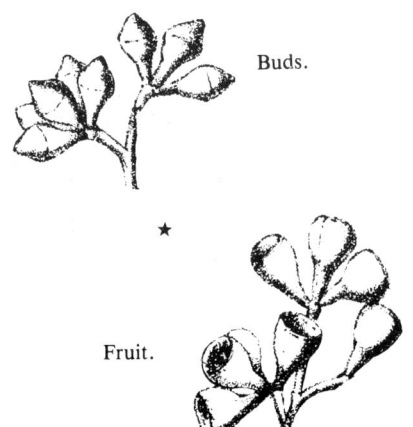

Buds.

Fruit.

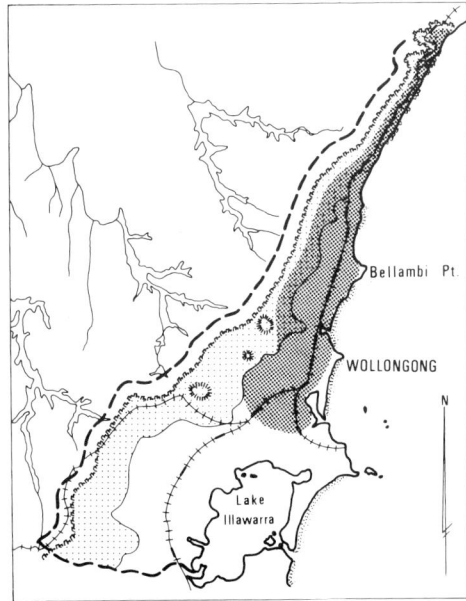

Tree in full flower.

Bark.

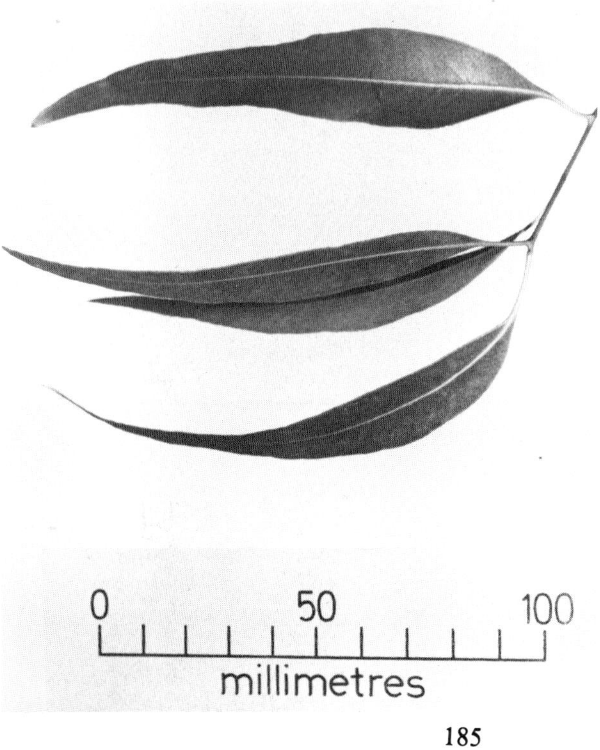

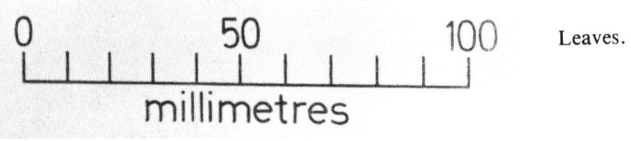

Leaves.

Eucalyptus pilularis Sm.
Blackbutt
Myrtaceae

Blackbutt is one of the commonest and most widespread eucalypts in the Wollongong area. There is, however, a greater concentration of this species north of the city where it grows to a tall tree on the plateau, escarpment, foothill spurs and coastal plain. South of Mt. Keira this species does not occur on the upper two-thirds of the escarpment; other species such as gully gum *(Eucalyptus smithii)* and coast white box *(Eucalyptus quadrangulata)* take over. Blackbutt does occur, however, along the base of the escarpment in the section south of Mt. Keira and also grows on favourable sites across the coastal plain at West Dapto. An unusual occurrence is on the sand dunes in the Windang-Primbee area where it grows to about 8m tall and has distinctive flat-topped and compressed fruit.

Blackbutt grows to a large tree over 30m tall with an ascending branching habit, although some older trees can have an enormous spread. The best forests of this species can be found along the foothills in the northern half of the area included in this book.

As the common name implies the flaky bark on the lower part of the trunk is often blackened from bushfires. Blackbutt is a handsome tree with a tufted dark green crown and smooth white upper branches which turn grey just before it sheds its bark about January. The timber is a good general purpose hardwood. Consequently blackbutt was the target for much of the logging for hardwood in the early days.

Bark: Grey to fire blackened stringy bark on lower trunk. Smooth white to cream or grey on the upper trunk and remaining branches.

Leaves: Juvenile — stalkless, stem clasping, opposite for several pairs then alternate, oblong to lanceolate, 30mm to 100mm long, 10mm to 30mm wide. Adult — alternate, stalked, thick, lanceolate, glossy on both sides, 80mm to 120mm long, 20mm to 40mm wide. Venation 30° to 45° to midrib.

Inflorescence: Umbels in forks of leaves 6-12 flowered. Inflorescence stalk angular or flattened. Buds 8mm to 12mm long, 5mm to 6mm wide with a conical operculum.

Fruit: Stalked, hemispherical to nearly globular, 9mm to 12mm long and wide, valves deeply enclosed. Maiden in his *Critical Revision of the Genus Eucalyptus* states that a form with truncated fruit is to be found at Dapto. These can most readily be found at Windang Beach.

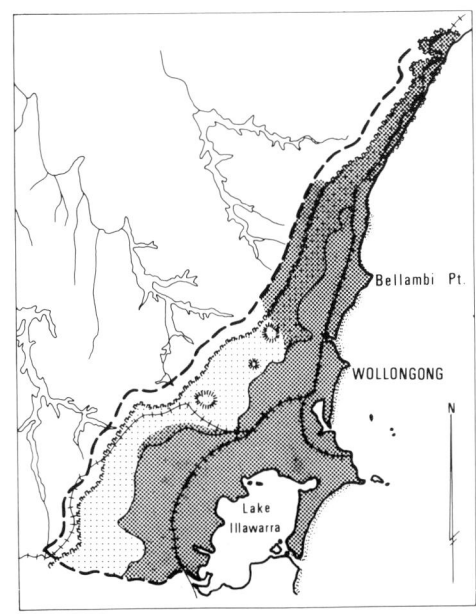

Tree.

Bark.

Fruit.

Leaves.

Buds. Fruit.

Eucalyptus piperita Sm.
Sydney peppermint
Myrtaceae

Sydney peppermint mainly occurs on Hawkesbury Sandstone of the plateau. It does, however, grow on the sides of gullies of streams which flow west across the plateau. East of the escarpment crest it may be found at the very top of the escarpment on Hawkesbury Sandstone where eastward streams have their beginnings. It also occurs in one small area on the Narrabeen Series and Coal Measures, just above the township of Mt. Kembla. Otherwise it can be found in mixed eucalypt forest on the plateau in association with silvertop ash *(E. sieberi)*, red bloodwood *(E. gummifera)*, scribbly gum *(E. racemosa/haemastoma)* and sometimes with blackbutt *(E. pilularis)*.

It is a tree which prefers a little shelter and is usually below the top of rock outcrops. Sydney peppermint grows from a medium to large tree of about 30m tall but the most prominent dimension is the huge girth of the trunk in old age, which may be 7 or so metres. Often also this species has a leaning habit and many rounded bumps on the trunk. The peppermint smell of the leaves when crushed and the oblique base of the leaves are other useful identifying features.

Eucalyptus urceolaris is included as a subspecies of *Eucalyptus piperita*. In some cases trees of the latter species may be found with fruits tending towards the subspecies *urceolaris* and these may represent variation of *Eucalyptus piperita* or an intermediate form.

Bark: Grey, shortly fibrous, persistent to small branches.

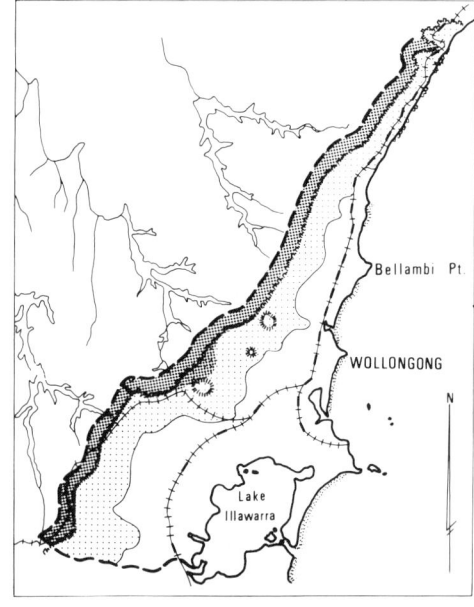

Leaves: Juvenile — opposite for 6-12 pairs shortly stalked to stem-clasping. Oblong to broadly lanceolate pale on lower surface, 90mm to 100mm long, 10mm to 30mm wide. Adult — alternate, stalked, narrow lanceolate, curved, mostly with an oblique base, 60mm to 120mm long, 10mm to 25mm wide. Strongly aromatic (peppermint).

Inflorescence: 6-15 flowered umbels, peduncles slightly compressed. Buds; cylindrical, stalked, pointed 7mm long, 4mm wide. Operculum conical, as long as calyx. Flowers November-February.

Fruit: Stalked, urn shaped, egg shaped to almost globular, thin with narrow disc, 6mm to 8mm long, 5mm to 6mm wide. Valves deeply enclosed.

Eucalyptus quadrangulata Deane et Maiden

White topped box
Coast white box
Myrtaceae

Coast white box is a beautiful tall tree and another tree of the good class of wet sclerophyll forest associated with the escarpment and plateau. It forms a tall straight tree sometimes higher than 30m with box-like bark to the small branches. The crown is rather open and the long narrow leaves give the crown a rather fine textured appearance.

It is only found on clay soils below the Hawkesbury Sandstone in the Wollongong area and its distribution is discontinuous with it being found at Stanwell Park and again from Austinmer to Marshall Mount Creek. It continues to the south of the area included in this book. At Austinmer and Thirroul it only occurs from the upper bench to just below the Hawkesbury Sandstone; but southward it extends lower and lower until at Figtree it can be found in the gullies which run out from the escarpment. At West Dapto it may be found in pure stands on the lower half, as well as being scattered over the rest of the escarpment.

This tree occurs on the plateau but only on the sides of gullies below the Hawkesbury Sandstone in wet sclerophyll forest.

Coast white box, if growing in association with other species, is usually found with blackbutt *(E. pilularis)*, gully gum *(E. smithii)*, and yellow stringybark *(Eucalyptus muellerana)*.

The most distinctive features of this species for identification purposes are the two-toned grey, mottled, box-like bark and the scalloped edge of the leaves caused by marginal oil glands.

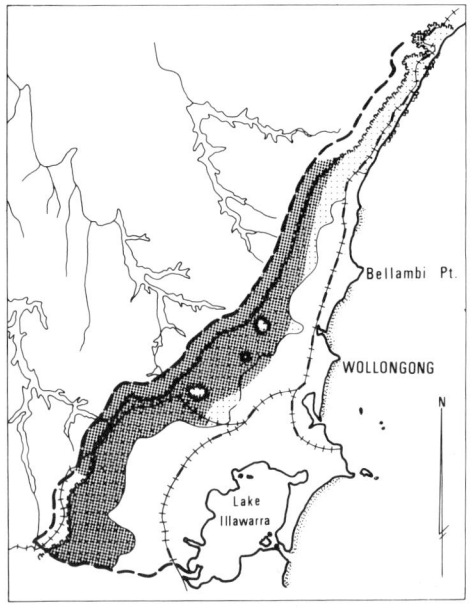

Bark: Two coloured grey, box like (i.e. finely fibrous) persistent to the small branches.

Leaves: Juvenile — opposite for many pairs, narrow lanceolate, stem clasping, stalkless 80mm to 130mm long, 15mm to 30mm wide, light green above paler beneath. Internodes quadrangular. Adult — alternate, stalked, narrow lanceolate, 100mm to 200mm long, 10mm to 20mm wide. The edges of the leaves are more or less irregularly scalloped due to raised marginal glands. Venation just visible and 45° to midrib.

Inflorescence: Umbels in forks of leaves, 4-8 flowered, peduncles about 12mm long. Buds stalkless, club shaped, 7mm long, 3 or 4mm across. Operculum hemispherical. Flowers February-March.

Fruit: Top shaped, or bell shaped, pedicel absent or very short. Valves exserted.

Leaves.

Bark.

Tree.

Fruit.

Buds.

Fruit.

Eucalyptus racemosa Cav.- *Eucalyptus haemastoma* S.M.*

syn. *E. micrantha* DC.

Scribbly gum
Snappy gum
Myrtaceae

This tree is only found in the Wollongong area on the poorer soils of the Hawkesbury Sandstone. It is often found in association with *Eucalyptus sieberi, E. gummifera* and *E. piperita* or may be found in pure stands on its own.

Scribbly gum is a distinctive tree with white, smooth bark right to the ground. The bark is usually marked with scribbles caused by larvae of the scribbly gum moth *Ogmograptus scribula* Meyr which burrow underneath the live bark; their scribbles becoming exposed when the bark falls off. Apart from its bark characteristics this tree can be distinguished by its often crooked habit. It only grows up to about 10m in the Wollongong area even though on good sites elsewhere scribbly gums may attain a height of 20m.

Bark: Smooth throughout, mottled white and/or bluish grey, shed in flakes. Often marked with scribbles from insect larvae.

Leaves: Juvenile — opposite for 3 or 4 pairs then alternate, shortly stalked oblong to lanceolate, 10mm to 30mm long, 5mm to 15mm wide. Adult — alternate, stalked narrow lanceolate, curved, thick, dull slatey green on both sides, 70mm to 140mm long, 10mm to 20mm wide. Venation 15°-40° to midrib.

Inflorescence: Umbels in the forks of the leaves or sometimes terminal 6-20 flowered. Slender round peduncle. Buds club shaped, stalked 4mm to 5mm long, 3mm to 4mm wide. Operculum hemispherical, shorter than calyx tube. Flowers September-March.

Fruit: Stalked, pear shaped, 4mm to 6mm long, 4mm to 6mm wide, valves small at or below rim level.

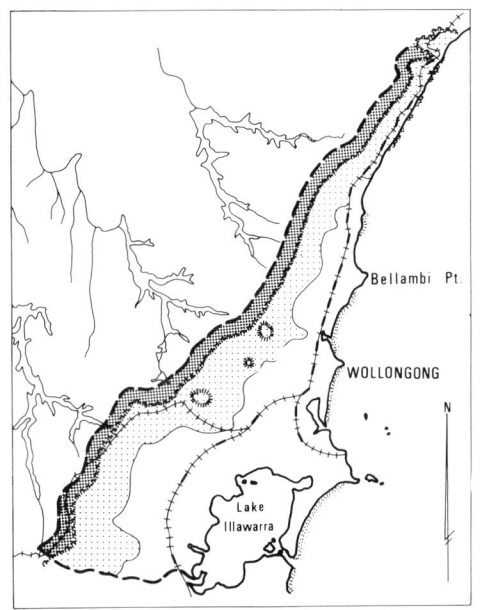

*Note: The scribbly gum group consists of a number of closely related and sometimes integrading species. The scribbly gum in the Wollongong area is as closely related to *E. haemastoma* as it is to *E. racemosa*. It has the smaller fruit of *E. racemosa* but does not have the narrow juvenile leaves typical of *E. racemosa*. The presence of an intermediate form between two species such as this, is not an unusual occurrence in the eucalypts.

Tree.
Buds.
Fruit.
Bark.
Leaves.

Eucalyptus robusta Sm.
syn. *E. multiflora* Poir.

Swamp mahogany
Myrtaceae

As its common name suggests, swamp mahogany grows in rather wet, swampy conditions.

The distribution of this species in the Wollongong area is from the hind dune plant community across the coastal plain at West Dapto to the foot of the escarpment. Of course, where it is found is usually an indication that soil moisture is usually high, whether from a high water table or slow draining soil. Because of residential development, this tree is rather uncommon and is usually found as single specimens here and there. There is one major concentration of trees, however, in the hind dune area at Windang and Primbee where although the soil is sandy, the water table is within a metre or so of the soil surface.

Swamp mahogany is a medium sized tree whose habit in this area varies from a thin stemmed tree in dense thickets (at Windang in sandy soil) to a rather heavy tree about 15m tall with thick trunk and coarse textured crown.

The brown furrowed bark and large leaves are the most distinctive features of this tree. If in association with other trees, it is usually with *E. botryoides, E. tereticornis* or coastal species such as *Melaleuca sp., Leptospermum laevigatum* and *Casuarina glauca.*

Bark: Brown, thick, flaky, often furrowed on older trees.

Leaves: Juvenile — opposite for 3 to 5 pairs then alternate. Broadly lanceolate 80mm to 120mm long, 50mm to 70mm wide, rather thick. Adult — alternate, stalked, broadly lanceolate with a long point, thick and shiny above, paler beneath, 100mm to 200mm long, 40mm to 80mm wide, venation fine, almost parallel, 50°-60° to midrib. Distinct intramarginal vein.

Inflorescence: 5-10 flowered umbels in forks of leaves, peduncles strap shaped. Buds pear shaped with a large blunt point, 10mm to 20mm long, 7mm to 10mm diameter. Operculum at least as long as calyx tube. Flowers white rather large and showy. Flowers September-November.

Fruit: Stalked, cylindrical to urn shaped, 12mm to 15mm long, 10mm to 12mm across, valves usually enclosed.

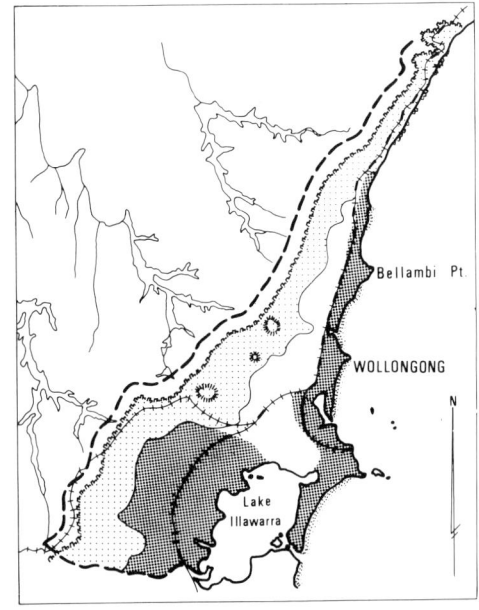

Tree.

Bark.

Leaves.

Buds.

Fruit.

Eucalyptus saligna Sm.
Sydney blue gum
Myrtaceae

Where Sydney blue gum grows in its pure form in the Wollongong area, i.e. where it does not hybridize with *E. botryoides*, it forms a beautiful shaft like tree with bluish grey bark and a small stocking of rough bark at the base. It is only where forest conditions are good, such as the rainforest-sclerophyll forest intermediate zone, where this tree grows in its pure form and reaches its best development. This happens along the escarpment, along coastal creeks and on the plateau where better and more clayey soils form and strata under the Hawkesbury Sandstone are exposed. Pure forms in the Wollongong area are uncommon and care must be taken in identifying this species.

This tree is susceptible to a lerp insect and is rarely seen, without the characteristic damage, which does however serve as an identifying feature. The damage consists of roughly rectangular, brown dead spots on the leaves, 5mm to 10mm wide and 10mm to 20mm long which as the summer progresses, coalesce.

E. saligna grows up to about 35 metres tall and is found in association with blackbutt *(E.pilularis)*, turpentine *(Syncarpia glomulifera)*, coast white box *(E. quadrangulata)*, gully gum *(E. smithii)* and other eucalypts and rainforest species of wet sclerophyll forest.

Bark: Smooth and blue-grey shedding to leave a creamy bark underneath. A small stocking of flaky bark at base of trunk.

Leaves: Juvenile — opposite for 3-4 pairs then alternate, shortly stalked, lanceolate, 30mm to 60mm long, 20mm to 30mm wide, thin undulate. Adult — alternate, stalked, lanceolate drawn out to a point, 100mm to 200mm long, 15mm to 50mm wide. Leaves often showing lerp damage (see above).

Inflorescence: 4-9 flowered umbels on flattened stalks in forks of leaves. Buds, calyx tube cylindrical. Operculum; hemispherical with a short beak. Flowers January-March.

Fruits: Cylindrical or bell shaped, 6mm to 7mm long, 5mm to 6mm wide, stalkless or shortly stalked; valves enclosed or more often exsert.

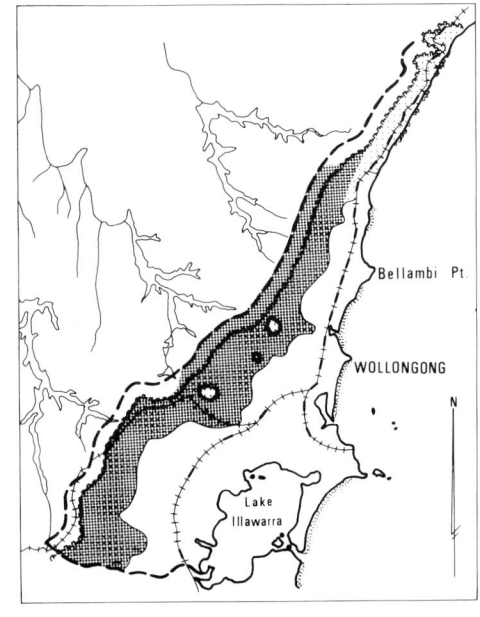

Bark.

Tree.

Fruit.

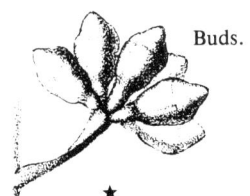

Buds.

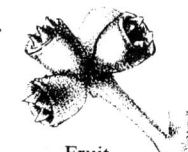

Leaves.

Fruit.

Eucalyptus saliga - Eucalyptus botryoides
Myrtaceae

One of the most common trees to be found in the urban parts and in many other parts of Wollongong is any one of a multitude of hybrids between *Eucalyptus saligna* and *Eucalyptus botryoides*. *Eucalyptus botryoides* typically has rough bark on the trunk and larger branches whereas *Eucalyptus saligna* has smooth bark except for a short stocking at the base of the trunk. The hybrid offspring from these two parents display degrees of flaky bark and other characteristics between the two extremes. There are many places in Wollongong where these hybrids appear to be a natural occurrence, however often they appear in disturbed areas. Disturbance may be due to clearing, fire or urban development.

The natural habitats of the two parent species are widely separated ecologically with *Eucalyptus saligna* preferring deep moist, heavy and rich soils and *Eucalyptus botryoides* tolerating rather poor sandy conditions near the sea. When these two species hybridise the resulting offspring have a greater range of genetic variation. Therefore it is not surprising that, by selection of suitable specimens by the conditions prevailing, the hybrid forms can occupy many sites where either the parents or other species wouldn't thrive.

Apart from the bark characters, leaves, buds and fruit of the intergrade forms show greater variation than the two species. One notable identification feature with *Eucalyptus botryoides*, *Eucalyptus saligna* and all the intermediate forms is the ever present (in the Wollongong area at least) damage to the leaves by lerps. The brown roughly rectangular patches at least serve to place these trees in this group.

These trees as with *Eucalyptus saligna* and *Eucalyptus botryoides* flower about January/February.

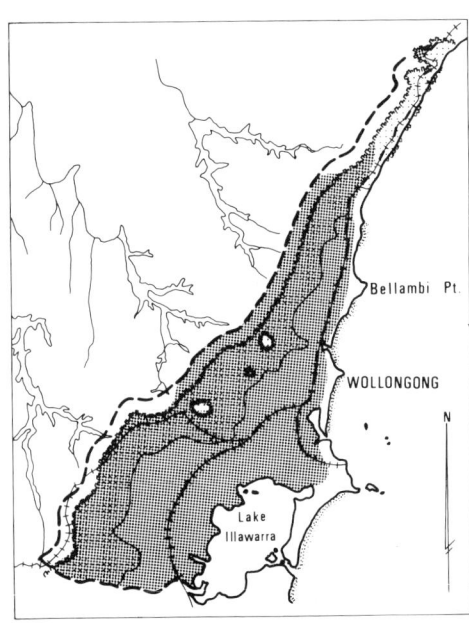

Eucalyptus sieberi L. Johnson

Silvertop ash
Black ash
Myrtaceae

Silvertop ash is a common tree of the Hawkesbury Sandstone areas of the plateau. From Bulli Pass to Stanwell Park near the edge of the escarpment this tree is easily the most common. Again on the plateau on Hawkesbury Sandstone west of Dapto this species dominates.

It grows from a stunted windswept tree in exposed situations to a good sized tree about 25m tall on the sides of gullies.

This species is rather a handsome tree. Its lower bark can vary from deeply fissured like an ironbark to quite stringy in texture but the most constant and distinctive feature is the shiny, sickle shaped grey-green leaves.

Silvertop ash is usually found on the plateau growing in association with one or more of the following: *E. gummifera, E. racemosa, E. piperita*.

Bark: Fibrous or flaky and grey on the lower trunk and larger branches, smooth and white on upper branches. Twigs red.

Leaves: Juvenile — opposite for four pairs, stalkless or shortly stalked. Elliptical to broadly lanceolate, thick, 80mm to 120mm long, 50mm to 70mm broad. Adult — alternate, stalked lanceolate, sickle shaped, 80mm to 180mm long, 15mm to 30mm wide, veins profuse 15° to 30° to midrib.

Inflorescence: Umbels in forks of leaves 5 to 15 flowered. Peduncles about 10mm long. Buds club shaped, shortly stalked, 5 to 7mm long, 4 or 5mm across, operculum hemispherical.

Fruit: Stalked, pear shaped, 8mm to 11mm long, 7mm or 8mm across, disc flat and rather wide, valves at rim level or enclosed.

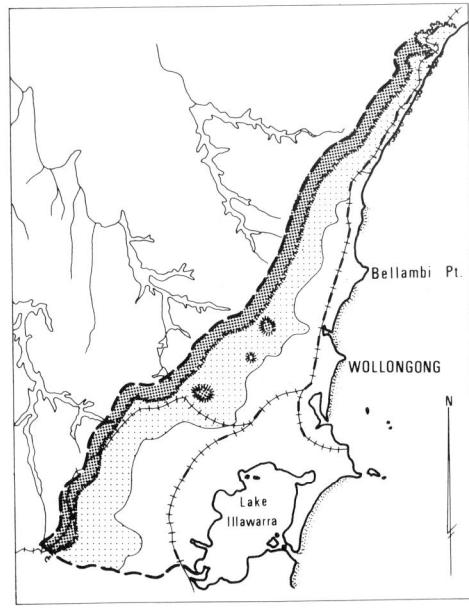

TOP: Trees. MIDDLE LEFT: Bark.
BOTTOM LEFT: Flowers.
MIDDLE BOTTOM RIGHT: Fruit.

Buds.

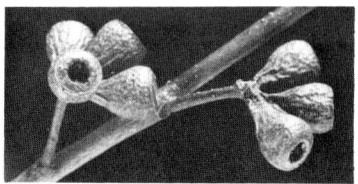

Eucalyptus smithii R. T. Baker
Gully gum
Blackbutt peppermint
Myrtaceae

Gully gum is one of the most handsome of the eucalypts in the Wollongong area. It grows to over 30m and has a long trunk. The crown is well formed and open and the foliage has a fine texture and bluish colour from a distance.

This peppermint occurs in the Wollongong area on the better soils of the plateau, is always found in wet sclerophyll forest, and is common along the escarpment edge above West Dapto. It is nearly always found above 300m altitude with only one or two exceptions near Dombarton at West Dapto. Mount Kembla wears this tree from 350m up to the bottom of the Hawkesbury Sandstone at 500m where *E. sieberi* takes over. This tree does not grow at all on the coastal plain and has not been observed north of Cataract River on the plateau.

Gully gum is usually found associated with monkey gum *(E. cypellocarpa)*, yellow stringybark *(E. muellerana)*, Sydney blue gum *(E. saligna)*, in wet sclerophyll forest.

Bark: White and smooth on upper trunk and branches falling in long strips and sometimes hanging over branches. The lower trunk is covered with hard, dark brown, rough bark.

Leaves: Juvenile — opposite for many pairs, stalkless, lanceolate, 30mm to 70mm long, 15mm to 25mm wide. Venation 30° to 40° to the midrib. Intermediate — lanceolate, shortly stalked, 75mm to 125mm long, 15mm to 20mm wide. Adult — alternate, stalked,, narrow lanceolate, 80mm to 180mm long, 10mm to 20mm wide, same colour both sides of leaf. Venation 20° to 40° to the midrib.

Inflorescence: Axillary umbels with 5 to 9 flowers, peduncle compressed. Buds, stalked, oval, 6mm long, 4mm wide. Flowers January-March.

Fruits: Stalked, ovoid, 5mm to 9mm long, 4mm to 8mm across. Valves large and protruding, to nearly as long as the calyx tube.

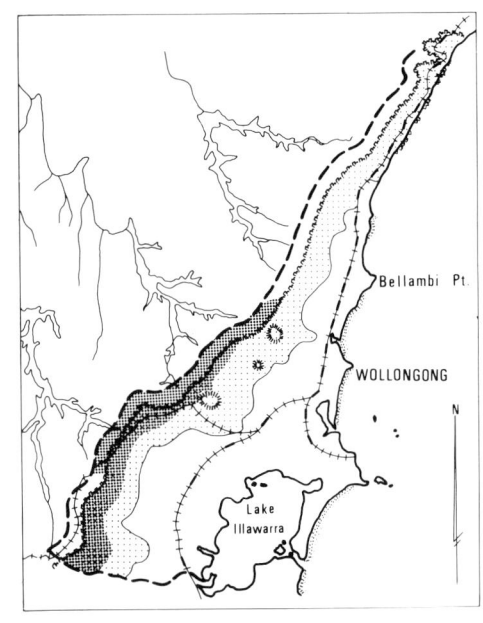

Tree.

Rough bark on lower trunk.

Leaves.

Buds.

★

Fruit.

Eucalyptus stricta Sieb. ex Spreng.
Blue Mountains mallee
Myrtaceae

A true and consistent mallee which grows on the poorer parts of the Hawkesbury Sandstone on the plateau in the Wollongong area. It is not a common plant but is scattered over the plateau area in often shallow soils overlying flat rock areas. It generally grows from 1m to 3m tall but in better situations may reach 5m. It has many stems 30mm to 100mm thick. Blue Mountains mallee is mostly found in association with silvertop ash *(E. sieberi)*, scribbly gum *(E. racemosa)* and red bloodwood *(E. gummifera)* as well as *Banksia ericifolia* and other heath plants.

A closely related species *E. apiculata* grows near and probably within the area covered by this book although it has not actually been seen in the area by the author. *E. stricta* and *E. apiculata* may also hybridise with the potential of causing some difficulty with this group.

Bark: Smooth, grey and brown mottled.

Leaves: Juvenile — opposite for 4-5 pairs, stalked, narrow lanceolate 30mm to 60mm long, 10mm to 20mm wide. Adult — alternate, stalked, narrow lanceolate, 50mm to 100mm long, 6mm to 10mm wide, thick, equally green on both sides.

Inflorescence: 3-7 flowered umbels in forks of leaves. Buds, club shaped, shortly stalked, 6mm to 10mm long, about 3mm wide. Operculum hemispherical, much shorter than calyx tube. Flowers December-April.

Fruit: Egg shaped to urn shaped, shortly stalked 7mm to 13mm long, 7mm to 10mm across, rim thin, valves deeply enclosed.

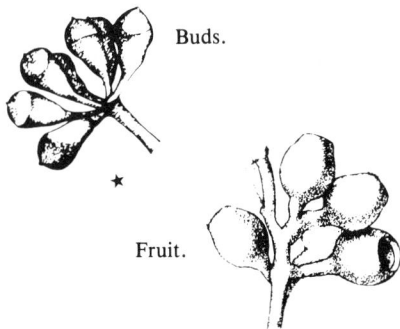

Buds.

Fruit.

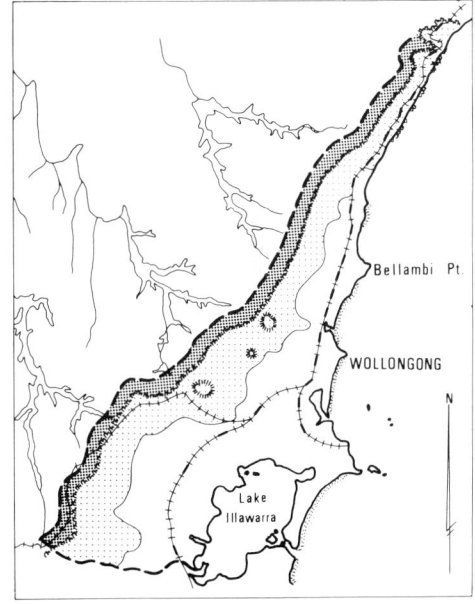

Leaves.

'Tree' in its typical mallee form in shallow soil.

Fruit.

Eucalyptus tereticornis Sm

syn. *E. umbellata* (Gaertn.) Domin.

Forest red gum

Myrtaceae

Forest red gum is the most common and widespread tree of the coastal plain. It extends from the lagoon areas to the foothills of the escarpment and may be found up to about 100m altitude growing in association with *Eucalyptus quadrangulata, E. pilularis* and *E. saligna-botryoides*. On the undulating parts of the coastal plain, *E. tereticornis* forms medium dense to open forests along with *E. longifolia, E. eugenioides* and sometimes *E. paniculata* as well as *Melaleuca decora* and *M. styphelioides*.

With an overall distribution from New Guinea to Victoria along the coastal strip it is not surprising to find that this tree is one of the most adaptable species in cultivation.

Because of the smooth blue-grey to white bark this tree is easily picked out among the other grey rough barked trees on the coastal plain although its close relative *E. amplifolia* looks similar. Forest red gum may grow to a large tree up to 30m tall with an erect habit, but mostly it is found as a medium sized tree up to 12m tall.

Bark: Smooth blue-grey to white, shed in irregularly shaped sheets. Sometimes the old bark is persistent on parts of the trunk.

Leaves: Juvenile — opposite for 2 to 3 pairs, then alternate, stalked rather large ovate to elliptical 60mm to 150mm long, 50mm to 60mm wide but may be found up to 100mm wide. Adult — alternate, stalked, lanceolate, falcate, 80mm to 200mm long, 10mm to 30mm wide, venation regular 40° to 55° to midrib. The colour of both juvenile and adult leaves are green with a slight greyish tinge.

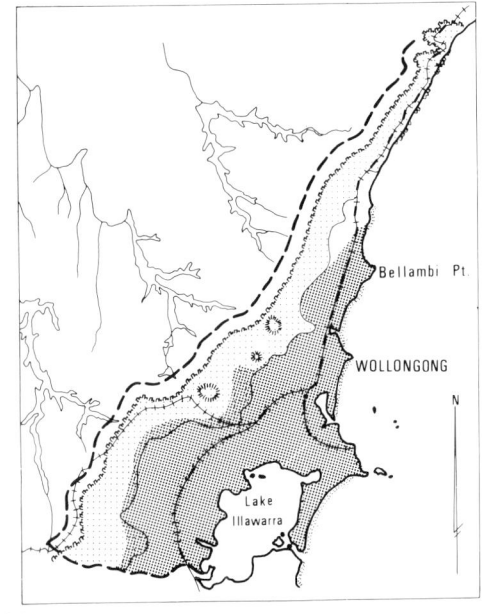

Inflorescence: Umbels born on axillary, cylindrical stalks, 5 to 12 flowers but usually 7, individual flowers possess distinct stalks. Buds have hemispherical bases with an elongated conical operculum. Flowers August-October.

Fruit: Globular, 4mm to 8mm in diameter, with wide disc and 4 to 5 thick raised valves.

Tree.

Bark.

Leaves.

Buds.

★

Fruit.

Eucryphia moorei F. Muell.
Plumwood
Eucryphiaceae

This tree is not common in the Wollongong area. It grows along the crest of the escarpment at West Dapto and below in the rainforest on the upper slopes and occurs in rainforest in gullies on the plateau near Mt. Keira. Plumwood grows to about 15m tall and forms an attractive tree with fern like leaves held more or less horizontally.

Bark: Grey.

Leaves: Pinnate. Leaflets, 5 to 11 but less on flowering stems, narrow oblong to narrow ovate, smooth margin, dark green above, whitish below, thick, 20mm to 60mm long, 5mm to 10mm wide.

Inflorescence: Solitary or small clusters in outer leaf forks.

Flowers: Showy, white, 20mm to 30mm diam., numerous stamens. Flowers February-March.

Fruit: A hard, dry capsule, egg-shaped or oblong, 8mm to 16mm long.

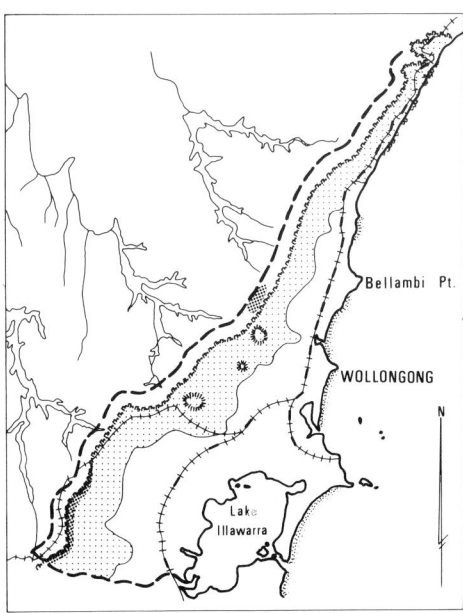

Leaves.

Flower.

Fruit.

Euodia micrococca F. Muell.
White euodia
Rutaceae

About the Wollongong area, *Euodia micrococca* occurs in or at the edges of rainforest and in some tall eucalypt forest. It may be seen up to 10m tall under good conditions with a stem diameter of about 300mm and an umbrella shaped crown. This species can be found on the coastal plain, the escarpment and moist plateau communities.

Bark: Grey.

Leaves: Opposite, mostly clustered at ends of branchlets, trifoliolately compound with a long leaf stalk. Leaflets — oblanceolate, obovate or elliptical, 30mm to 80mm long, 20mm to 40mm wide, obtuse apex.

Inflorescence: Short dense panicles in forks of leaves.

Flowers: Whitish, 4 or 5mm long, sepals 4 petals 4. Flowers summer.

Fruit: Up to 4 carpels about 6mm long which split open. Seeds black and shiny.

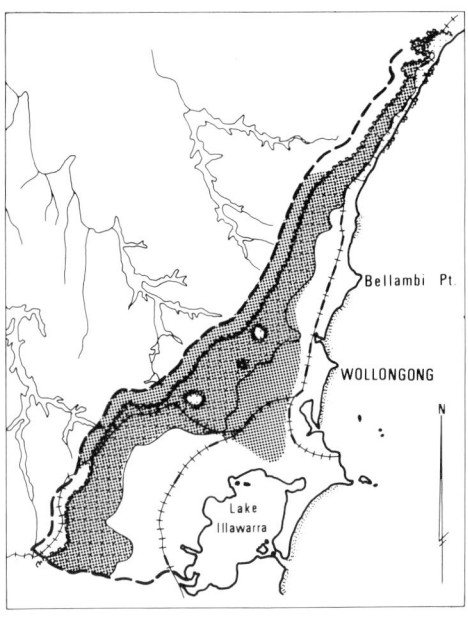

Leaves.

Eupomatia laurina R. Br.
Bolwarra
Eupomatiaceae

Bolwarra is a shrub or small tree, rarely found in the Wollongong area taller than four metres. It usually has weak spreading cane like branches but sometimes forms a definite trunk.

This species is common in rainforest of the escarpment and plateau gullies and is often found as an understorey plant in wet sclerophyll forest.

Bolwarra has very glossy leaves and rather showy white flowers. It fruits and seeds readily and the seed germinates easily. The fruit are edible and pleasant when *ripe*. This tree is a plant ideally suited to cultivation. It does, however, need a protected and shaded place in the garden.

Leaves: Alternate, elliptic to oblong with a short point, 80mm to 150mm long, 30mm to 50mm wide, shiny on upper surface. The leaves are usually arranged in two rows down sides of the stem which are held more or less horizontal.

Inflorescence: Flowers solitary in forks of leaves.

Flowers: 25mm diameter, no petals or sepals. Stamens take place of petals. They are in many rows. The inner stamens are white and broad and petal-like, the outer ones in a few rows with anther cells.

Fruit: The aggregate fruit consists of one or two seeded achenes held in a fleshy receptacle up to 20mm diam. Fruits winter.

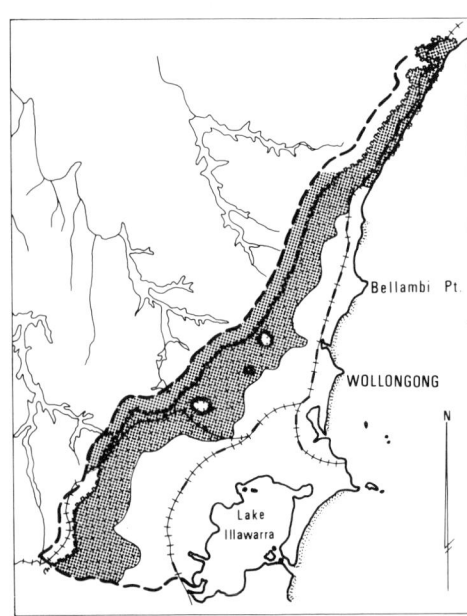

Leaves.

Fruit.

Euroschinus falcata Hook. f.

Blush cudgerie, ribbonwood

Anacardiaceae

This tree is most common in rainforest at the foothills of the escarpment around the Calderwood area. It can be found at Stanwell Park and there is also one specimen growing in the hind dune habitat at Puckey's Estate, North Wollongong.

Ribbonwood is a rather handsome tree with a broad spreading crown and dense pinnate foliage. It grows to about 20m tall and has a rather thick but short trunk. The bark is quite distinctive being dark brown and divided into small segments.

Bark: Dark brown, nearly black, bark on lower parts divided into small segments with deep crevices between.

Leaves: Alternate, pinnate with 4 to 10 leaflets. Each leaflet is unequal sided or oblique (hence specific name falcata), elliptical, 50mm to 70mm long. The whole leaves tend to curl up so that the leaflets are bunched together.

Inflorescence: Terminal or axillary panicles shorter than the leaves.

Flowers: Unisexual, small, petals about 2mm long, stamens 10. Flowers about November.

Fruit: Egg shaped, 6mm to 12mm long.

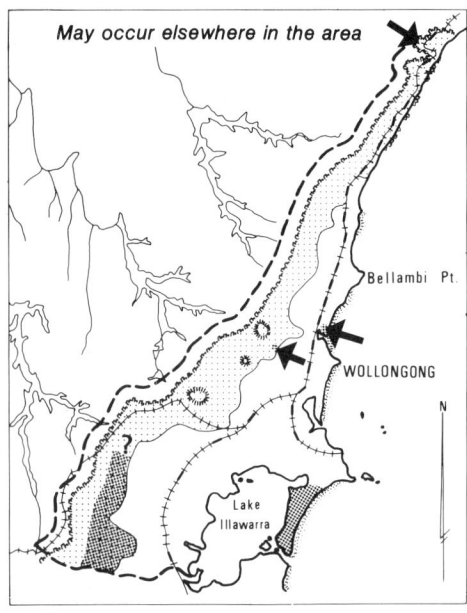

Tree.

Fruit.

A single leaf.

Exocarpos cupressiformis Labill.
Native cherry
Santalaceae

Often mistaken for a casuarina the native cherry has similar thin green branchlets and scale leaves. Its specific name is derived from the cypress which it also resembles.

This species is found in wet sclerophyll forest in Wollongong on the coastal plain and the escarpment. However it is far from a common tree and there are only a few places where there are many individuals of this species. It is believed to be a partial root parasite. Native cherry forms a bushy shrub or tree up to about four metres high.

Bark: Hard, dark brown and furrowed on trunk, greyish on branches.

Leaves: Minute scale leaves, alternate. The branchlets are green and slender.

Inflorescence: Small axillary or terminal spikes up to 7mm long.

Flowers: Minute with 5 perianth segments.

Fruit: Globular dark greenish nut on a swollen, red, succulent stalk.

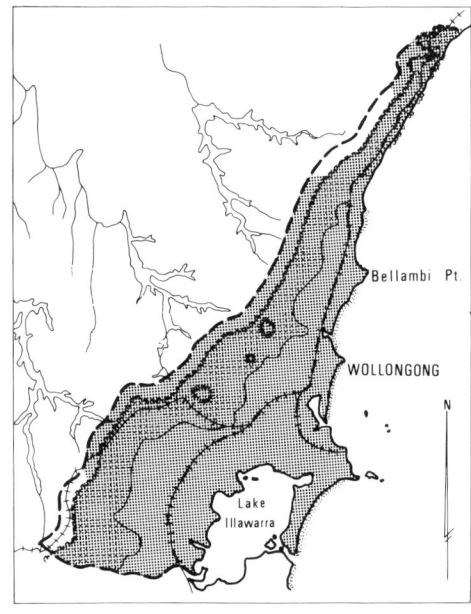

Tree.

Branchlets.

Ficus coronata Spin.
syn. *F. stephanocarpa* Warb.

Sandpaper fig
Moraceae

Sandpaper fig is one of the most easily recognised of the rainforest trees. The rasping roughness of the leaf surface is reputed to have been used by the Aborigines to sharpen their spear points. Also when fruiting from about October on, this tree has the peculiar habit of the fruits arising from the branches and even the main trunk.

This tree is an inhabitant of creek banks usually in rainforest and is typically found hanging out over the water of creeks. It occurs in rainforest on the coastal plain but is most common around the gullies of the lower slopes and the benches of the escarpment.

Where allowed to attain its normal habit it forms a broad little tree about 6m tall (though sometimes taller) with long reaching horizontal or low sweeping branches.

Bark: Grey, fruits often seen protruding from bark of main trunk in fruiting season.

Leaves: Alternate, very rough to the touch, often hairy on underside, elliptical, sometimes with oblique base, 50mm to 100mm long, 20mm to 40mm wide, dark green on top lighter beneath.

Inflorescence: Syconium.

Infructescence: Shortly stalked globular or slightly egg shaped with some bumps, hairy, up to 20mm long. A fig, edible.

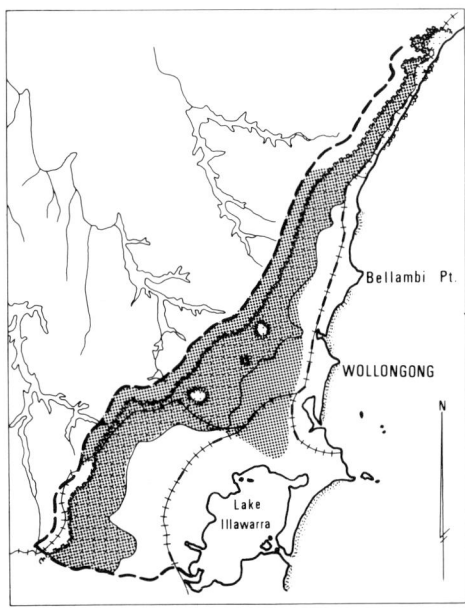

Leaves.

Fruit.

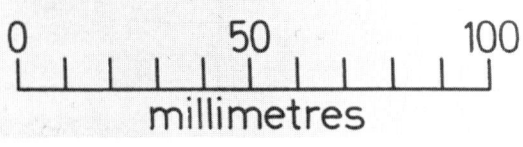

Ficus macrophylla Desf.
Moreton Bay fig
Moraceae

One of giants of the rainforest, this fig is often found as a tree projecting beyond the upper canopy. It grows to about 40m tall and as much across the crown. In old specimens the trunk is often massive being 2m in diameter. It is one of the so-called strangler figs which begin life in the fork of a tree or on a rock and send down a thread-like root to the ground, sometimes 10m or so. Once this single root gains access to the soil on the ground it rapidly grows and more roots descend and fuse together till the host plant becomes enmeshed in aerial roots. As the fig tree grows it strangles its host which actually gave it quick access to the well lit upper canopy.

Moreton Bay fig is found scattered sparsely through the area in rainforest on the escarpment as well as along creeks on the coastal plain. It is also a remnant of rainforest on Berkeley Hills, persisting as scattered specimens in pastureland. It is a Moreton Bay fig which stands proudly at Figtree and gives this suburb its name and identity.

This tree, because of its handsome foliage and large shady habit, has been extensively grown as an ornamental tree. It is easily distinguished by its large dark green leaves with brown tomentum on the underside. It has a typical broad domed fig habit with aerial roots, buttresses and low branches that may touch the ground in specimens grown in the open.

Bark: The bark on both aerial roots and trunk is grey and smooth to more or less rough.

Leaves: Thick, leathery, large, 100mm to 250mm long, 70mm to 100mm wide. Dark glossy green on top, mostly brown on undersurface, midrib prominent. Leaf stalks 50mm to 80mm long.

Inflorescence: A syconium.

Infructescence: Globular or slightly pear shaped, 20mm to 25mm diameter, purplish with light spots when ripe. Fruit stalks thick.

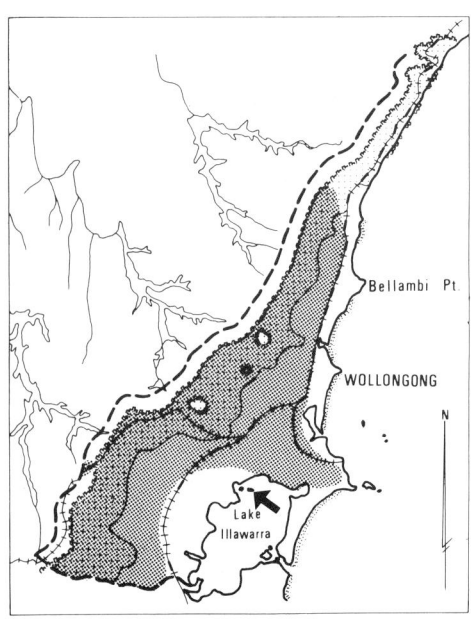

A large tree emerging from rainforest on Flagstaff Hill. Person on right of photograph gives some idea of size.

Trunk of tree showing bark and buttressing.

Leaf showing underside.

Leaves and fruit.

Ficus obliqua Forst. f.
syn. *Ficus eugenioides* F. Muell.

Small-leaved fig

Moraceae

Like Moreton Bay fig, this fig is one of the giants of the rainforest. It grows to about 40m tall and usually stands head and shoulders over the surrounding rainforest. It is easily distinguished from Moreton Bay fig by the small leaves and lack of the brown undersurface on the leaf, although both species are "strangler" figs. Small-leaved fig can look similar to Port Jackson fig *(Ficus rubiginosa)* which has comparable sized leaves and occurs in the Dapto-Berkeley area and northern part of the Wollongong area but this latter species is generally smaller and has a brown undersurface on the leaves.

In the area covered by this book, small-leaved fig occurs in rainforest along the length of the escarpment and occasionally on the coastal plain.

Bark: Grey, more or less smooth, trunk or aerial root column buttressed. Bark when cut exudes milky sap.

Leaves: Alternate, elliptical, 40mm to 80mm long, 20mm to 50mm wide, leaf stalks 6mm to 12mm long. Leaf dark green, hairless on both surfaces and leathery.

Inflorescence: Syconium borne in pairs or sometimes one to three in the forks of leaves; globular, 5mm to 8mm diameter.

Infructescence: Syconium turns yellow or orange when ripe.

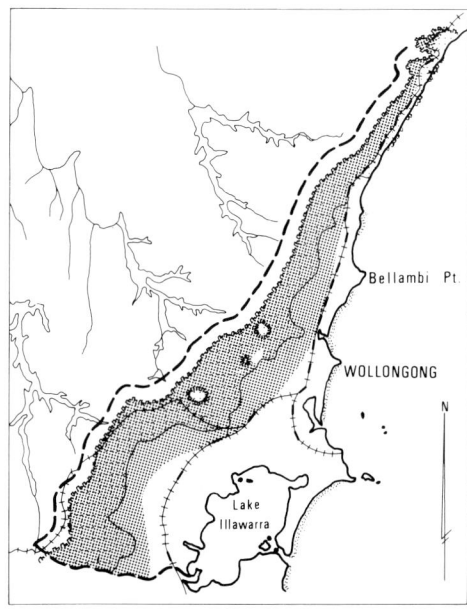

Tree alongside Lawrence Hargrave Drive, Thirroul.

Leaves.

Leaves and fruit.

Ficus rubiginosa Desf. ex Vent.
Port Jackson fig
Moraceae

Port Jackson fig occurs commonly in the Kiama-Jamberoo area where it is usually found on rock shelves near rainforest. In the area covered in this book it only occurs on Berkeley/Flagstaff Hills, Dapto area and in the northern part around Clifton, Coalcliff and Stanwell Park. It can be found on the edge of rainforest or in rainforest which is of low stature, i.e. 1m to 5m tall, and associated with sea cliffs.

This fig is not as large as either Moreton Bay fig or small-leaved fig; in the Wollongong area it grows to about 10m tall.

Bark: Grey, more or less smooth.

Leaves: Alternate, shortly stalked, elliptical, 70mm to 100mm long, 50mm to 60mm wide; smooth on upper surface, rusty pubescent below, leathery.

Inflorescence: Syconia borne in pairs in forks of leaves.

Fruit: Syconium turns yellow.

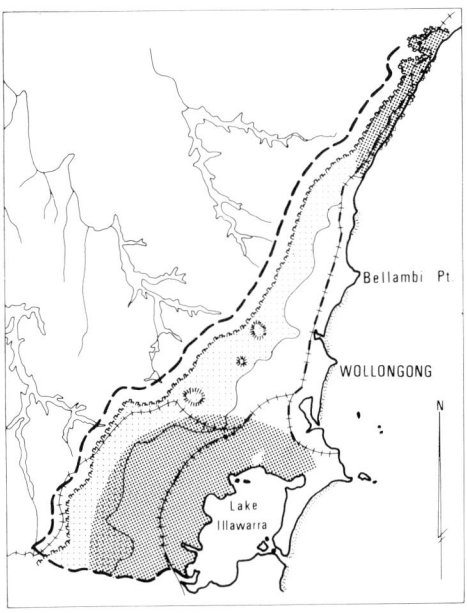

TOP LEFT: Meshwork of aerial roots around a host corkwood.

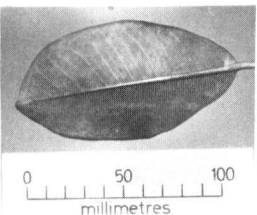

LEFT: Leaf showing underside.

BOTTOM: Leaves and fruit.

Ficus superba var. *henneana*
syn. *F. henneana*

Deciduous fig

Moraceae

It is in the Jamberoo area further to the south where this fig reaches its best development. However, in the area covered by this book, it only occurs in the Calderwood area and on the Berkeley/Flagstaff Hills. Here it is a tree about 20m tall with a spreading crown typical of the figs. It is often found as a so-called strangler fig growing on a host tree or rock with a mesh of roots around its "host".

As the common name suggests this fig loses some or all of its leaves during late winter.

Bark: Grey, smooth or slightly rough.

Leaves: Ovate to elliptical, leaf blade 50mm to 100mm long; leaf stalk 20mm to 50mm long.

Inflorescence: Globular, hollow inflorescence axis, flowers on inside (fig or syconium).

Fruit: 25mm to 30mm diameter, pink when ripe. Figs on thick peduncles. 4mm to 6mm long.

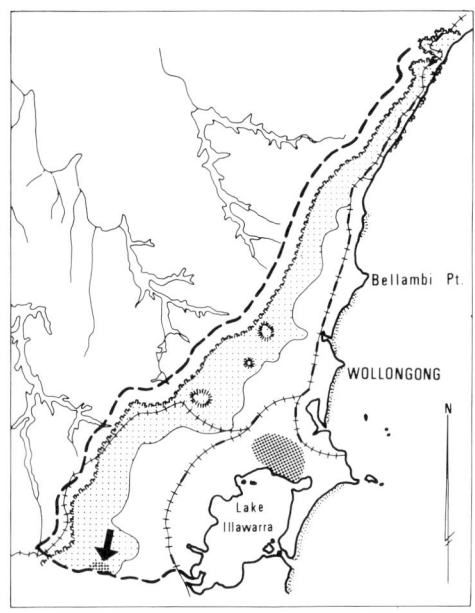

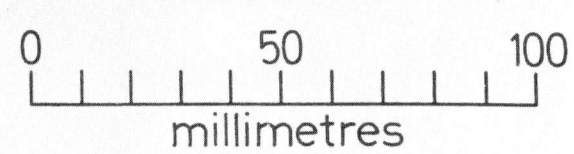

Leaves.

Geijera salicifolia Schott.
Brush wilga
Rutaceae

Brush wilga is a tree uncommon in the area covered by this book, only having been observed at a small number of places. It has little to distinguish it from a distance in the rainforest but on close examination the lateral, regular venation at about 80^0 to the midrib and the slight bump at the leaf blade — petiole junction, are two helpful features.

This tree is seen about 10m tall in this area and typical of most rainforest trees has a dense dark green crown.

Bark: Grey, scaly.

Leaves: Alternate, stalked; size and shape of leaf blade is variable, 70mm to 120mm long, 20mm to 60mm wide, lanceolate to oval. Oil dots present.

Inflorescence: Panicles at the ends of branches.

Flowers: Small, yellowish white.

Fruit: Globular or egg shaped, 4mm to 6mm long.

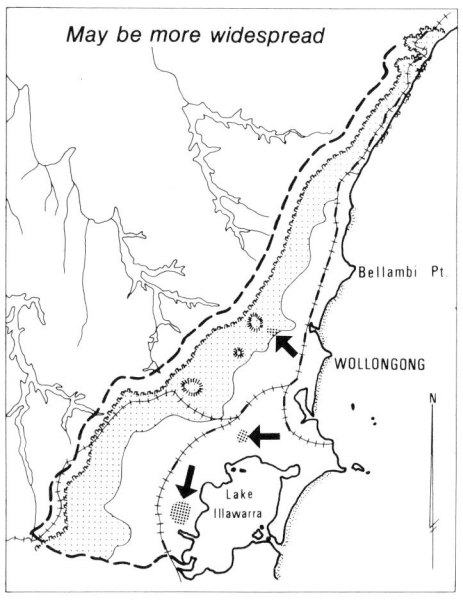

Fruit.

Tree.

Leaves.

Glochidion ferdinandi (J. Muell.) F. M. Bail.
Cheese tree
Euphorbiaceae

Whether growing in the open or in rainforest, cheese tree usually forms a shapely small tree. It can be found up to 15m tall but is usually a much smaller tree at about 6m. This tree is very adaptable and can be found in sheltered eucalypt forest and rainforest commonly throughout the Wollongong region.

The common name cheese tree is derived from the resemblance of the fruit to small cheeses. This tree can also be recognised from its partial deciduous habit in the cooler months with some leaves having a purplish tinge about them.

This species has male and female flowers on separate trees (dioecious).

Bark: Grey with longitudinal fissures, flaky.

Leaves: Alternate and from their being in two rows and on short branchlets often give the appearance of being pinnate. Leaf shape is obovate to elliptic or lanceolate. Size 50mm to 100mm long, 25mm to 50mm wide.

Flowers: In forks of leaves with 6 perianth segments. Male and female flowers on separate trees.

Fruit: Flattened, much depressed in centre, green, 12mm to 20mm diameter, opening to expose bright red seeds. Fruits summer-autumn.

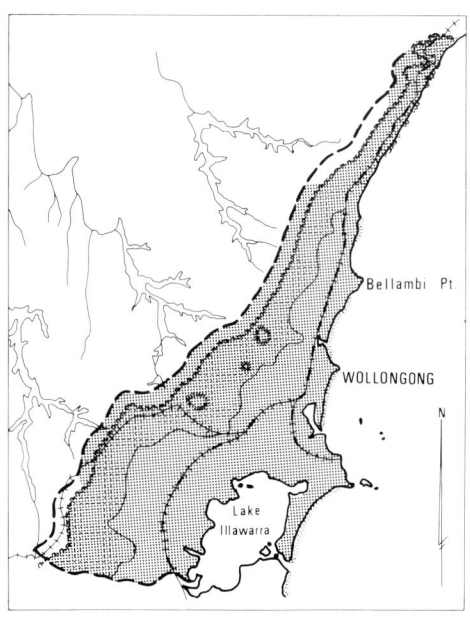

Tree.

Leaves and fruit.

Guioa semiglauca (F. Muell.) Radlk.

syn. *Nephelium semiglaucum* F. Muell.

Sapindaceae

Guioa semiglauca forms a small to medium tree up to about 12m tall in the Wollongong area. It grows in and near rainforest of the escarpment and can also be found along creeks of the coastal plain. It is also tolerant of the seaside environment and may be found on the seacliffs in the northern suburbs where it only grows one or two metres tall.

The most prominent identifying features of this tree are the compound leaves with a lump at the junction of leaflet and rhachis and the pale undersurface of the leaflets. *Alectryon subcinereus* also has these features but this guioa has entire leaflets.

Bark: Grey, more or less smooth.

Leaves: Alternate, pinnate with 2-4 (rarely 6) leaflets. Leaflets, elliptical to lanceolate, ovate to obovate with a blunt rounded end, much paler and glaucous on undersurface. The leaflets measure 40mm to 100mm long, 15mm to 40mm wide. The stalk of the leaflet joins the rhachis in a lump. The rhachis often extends past the last leaflet in a small spike.

Inflorescence: Panicles in forks of leaves shorter than leaves.

Flowers: Small and white.

Fruit: Capsule 8-12mm diameter mostly with 3 flattened lobes.

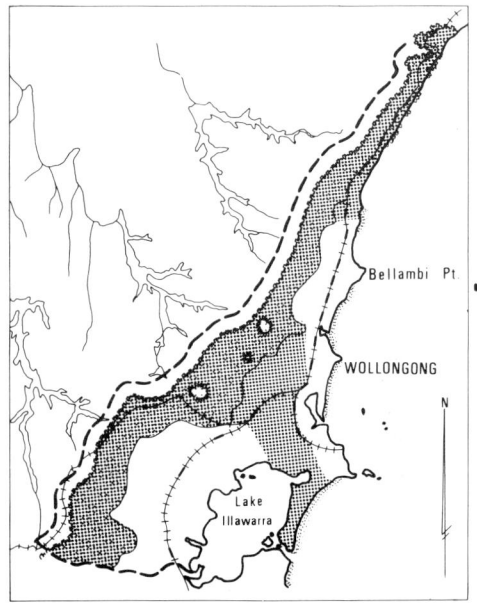

Leaves.

Hedycarya angustifolia A. Cunn.

syn. *H. cunninghamii* Tul.

Native mulberry

Monimiaceae

Native mulberry is to be found as a shrub or small tree up to 6m tall in the Wollongong area. It is an inhabitant of rainforest. The most distinctive features of this tree are the glossy leaves with white or yellow veins and the mulberry-like yellow fruit (or like buttons in the flowering and early stage of development).

Leaves: Opposite, stalked, elliptical to lanceolate, irregularly toothed, 50mm to 100mm long, 30mm to 50mm wide, shiny on upper surface, often with many white veins clearly visible, oil dots, aromatic when crushed.

Inflorescence: Raceme-like cymes, in forks of leaves.

Flowers: Floral tube flat or rounded with numerous small perianth segments. Stamens numerous. Flowers spring.

Fruit: Globular aggregate 6-8mm diameter, 10-20 drupes, closely packed, yellow. Fruits January-April.

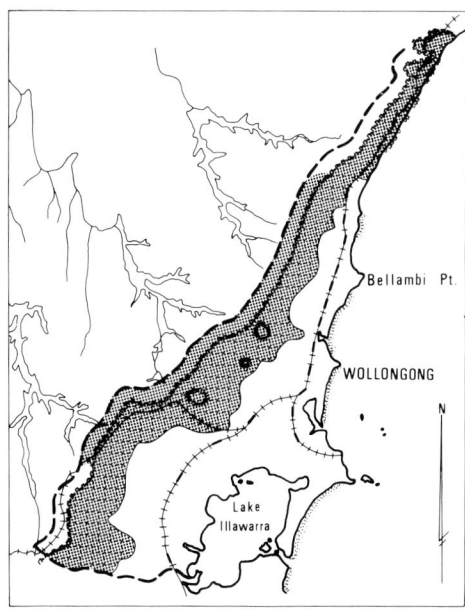

Leaves and fruit.

Hibiscus heterophyllus Vent.
Native hibiscus
Malvaceae

Growing in the open *Hibiscus heterophyllus* tends to form a rounded shrub. However, when it is found growing in forest it may be up to 6m tall with an erect and open tree shape and a trunk diameter of up to 200mm.

This species is quite adaptable and often occurs on cleared land or in regenerating forest. Its natural habitat is the rainforest edge and is to be found in these above situations over the whole area.

Bark: Brown, young stems having short thorns.

Leaves: Alternate, stalked. The leaf shape is quite variable from narrow elliptical to linear up to 150mm long. The leaves may be actually rounded in outline with deep divisions making them 2 to many lobed. There are often small conical prickles on midrib, petiole and stems.

Inflorescence: Axiliary, solitary or in clusters.

Flowers: Large, about 100mm across, calyx green 20mm long. Petals white with a reddish purple strip on one side on undersurface. Staminal column and throat of corolla, deep red.

Fruit: Capsule egg shaped, pointed apex, 20mm long, densely stellate-tomentose (fibreglass-like hairs).

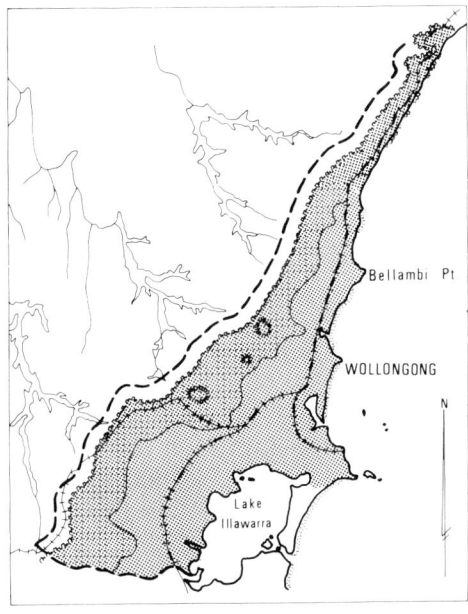

Tree.

Flower and parts of leaves.

Leptospermum laevigatum (Sol. ex Gaertn.) F. Muell.

Coast tea tree

Myrtaceae

Appearing mostly as a shrub along the sea shore, coast tea tree may also be found as a tree or mallee-like shrub up to 6m tall. When reaching larger proportions this tree is quite old and has a fluted trunk often twisted like a corkscrew. The small leaves give the whole tree a fine textured appearance and the foliage is slightly bluish.

Coast tea tree is found within a few hundred metres of the sea and in some places because of development it is the only surviving seaside plant. Dense thickets of this species may be seen at Red Point, Puckey's Estate and along cliffs in the northern suburbs. It grows both on sand dunes and on shaly soils on cliffs.

Bark: Grey-brown, flaky.

Leaves: Alternate, obovate to narrow elliptic, with a rounded end and small mucro, thick, 10mm to 20mm long, 5mm to 7mm wide, grey-green.

Flowers: Solitary in forks of leaves 12mm to 15mm diameter, 5 white conspicuous petals. Flowers spring.

Fruit: A woody capsule 7mm to 8mm diameter with a flat summit.

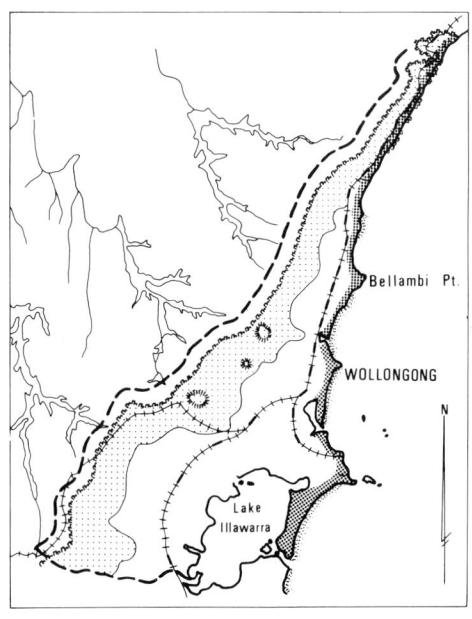

Tree (large shrub 6m tall).

Leaves and fruit.

Litsea reticulata F. Muell.
Bolly gum
Lauraceae

Bolly gum is a rather uncommon tree in the area included in this book. It is a tree of climax rainforest on the escarpment and being a tree 20-odd metres tall the leaves are not often seen near the ground. However, the trunk of this tree is very characteristic with a round cross section and a mottled, brown, fawn, grey and somewhat rough bark, and can be picked out easily from other rainforest tree trunks.

Bark: Brown and grey. The bark is mottled due to rounded patches a few inches across falling off and leaving a different colour on the trunk.

Leaves: Alternate, elliptical, 40mm to 80mm long, 20mm to 40mm wide, with a rounded end or a short point, leathery, conspicuously reticulate on upper surface.

Inflorescence: Short racemes or clusters in forks of leaves.

Flowers: Male and female on separate trees. Flowers about 6mm long in small groups enclosed by four bracts. Flowers April and May.

Fruit: Oval, black, single seeded about 12mm long, seated in a cup shaped receptacle. Fruits autumn.

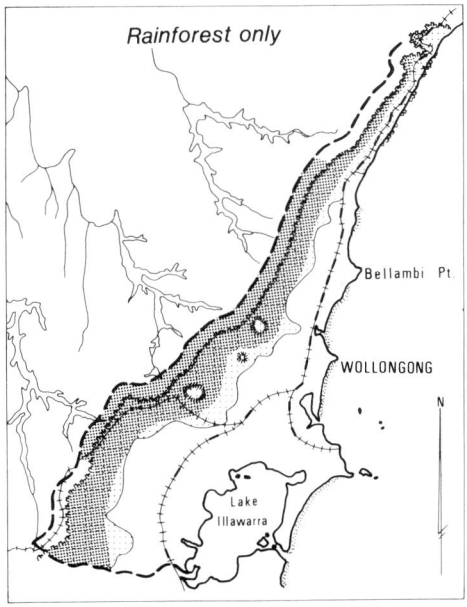

Lower trunk showing bark and buttressing.

Leaves and flower buds.

Livistona australis (R. Br.) Mart.

Cabbage palm
Cabbage tree palm
Palmae

Of all the rainforest trees in Illawarra, the cabbage palm is certainly the most distinctive and conspicuous. This tree is distributed throughout the whole area and can be found taller than 30m with its thin trunk and globular crown. Although it is not confined to the rainforest it is in this community where it is mostly found. Probably the greatest numbers of this species can be found on the upper bench of the escarpment such as just below the elbow on Bulli Pass. During August the numbers of cabbage palms on the escarpment can be appreciated when the trees flower and each tree appears as a white spot. The whole mountainside seems covered in spots. This is repeated in late summer when the trees produce their new foliage. The cabbage palm, because of its adaptability and good looks has been grown commonly in cultivation.

Bark: The outside of the trunk is grey, and rough with more or less circumferential (annular) ridges. The trunk is very fibrous and almost denies cutting with a saw.

Leaves: The leaves are palmately divided and fan shaped, often over 1m across. The leaf stalk can be up to 3m long and may have stout prickles arranged like a saw edge along it.

Inflorescence: The panicle is rather droopy, cream coloured and arises from among the fan arrangement of leaves on top of the stem. Flowers August.

Fruit: Globular, black, 12mm to 20mm in diameter. Fruits in autumn and winter.

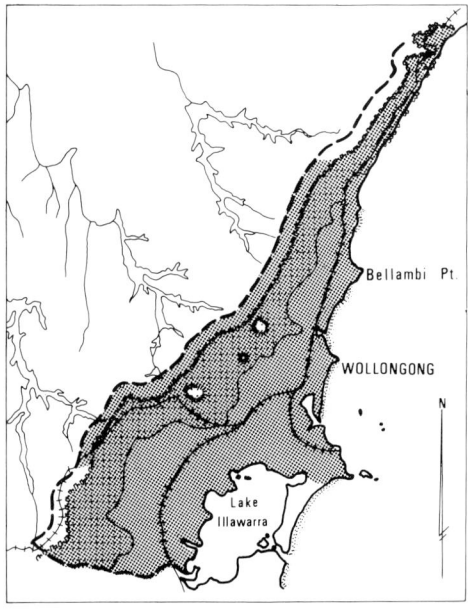

Crown of cabbage palm with fruit.

Cabbage palms in rainforest.

Crowns of two trees with flowers.

THE MELALEUCAS

There are three melaleucas in the Wollongong area which grow to tree size. These are: *Melaleuca decora, M. linariifolia* and *M. styphelioides*. They are all generally small trees although *M. styphelioides* may grow to 25m tall.

Probably the only two of the three melaleucas which could cause difficulty in identification are *M. decora* and *M. styphelioides* since they look alike and grow in the same habitat, often side by side. They are similar in size and shape and overall leaf texture. On close examination, however, the leaves of these two are easily distinguished, with *M. decora* having linear to narrow lanceolate leaves to 20mm long and *M. styphelioides* having ovate leaves with pungent points at the ends, but also 20mm long. In general branching habit *M. decora* has a twisted contorted pattern whereas *M. styphelioides* has an erect or vase shape with relatively straight branches.

Melaleucas usually form well shaped attractive plants and also because of their adaptability, especially to clayey damp conditions of soil, they are extensively grown as ornamental subjects.

The flowers are bottlebrush type and all three species mentioned here have white or creamy coloured flowers. Melaleucas can be separated from callistemons by their flowers having the stamens grouped into 5 bundles or claws whereas callistemon has stamens scattered around the rim of the calyx. If in doubt it is useful to look at this feature since *Callistemon salignus* is a paperbark and can be mistaken for a melaleuca.

Melaleuca decora (Salisb.) Britten

syn. *M. genistifolia* Sm.

Myrtaceae

Melaleuca decora forms a very shapely tree with a rounded head of dense, dark green, small leaves. The upper branches usually have a twisting turning appearance. Its height is usually about 6m but some very old specimens, which are remnants of bygone tall forest, may grow to 15m.

This species is confined to the coastal plain and seems to prefer to grow in forests associated with *E. longifolia, E. tereticornis* and *E. eugenioides*. It is not as adaptable and widespread in the Wollongong area as *M. styphelioides*.

Bark: Thick, soft and papery, more or less white or grey.

Leaves: Alternate, linear to narrow lanceolate, one conspicuous vein, 10mm to 20mm long, 1mm to 3mm wide.

Inflorescence: A spike about 30mm long.

Flowers: Staminate with 5 staminal claws about 4mm long. Flowers summer.

Fruit: A small woody capsule about 2mm or 3mm diameter.

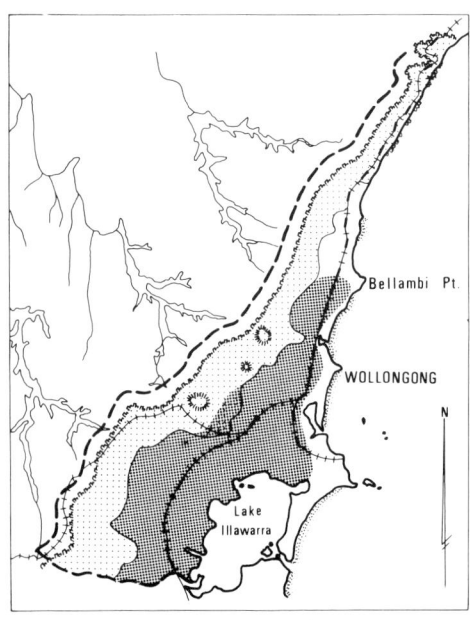

Tree.

Leaves.

Melaleuca linariifolia Sm.

Myrtaceae

This melaleuca is quite uncommon in the Wollongong area, being one of the species to suffer from clearing and urbanisation. It can now only be found in small areas at West Dapto and Towradgi, both on the coastal plain.

Of the three tree melaleucas in Wollongong, *Melaleuca linariifolia* is the most spectacular in flower. The flowers all open together so that the whole tree is topped with dense white. The other melaleucas tend to flower a little more sporadically.

The foliage of this tree has a grey or bluish tinge about it when seen from a distance, at least in comparison to the other melaleucas. The shape of this tree is broader and it is usually only found to about 6m tall but it forms a dense shrub in its young stages.

Bark: Grey or whitish, soft and papery.

Leaves: Opposite, narrow lanecolate, 1 to 3 veined, 15mm to 35mm long, 2mm to 4mm wide. Often faintly blue or grey.

Inflorescence: A spike.

Flowers: White, staminal claw 4mm to 7mm long with pinnately arranged filaments. Flowers spring-summer.

Fruit: A woody capsule about 3mm diameter.

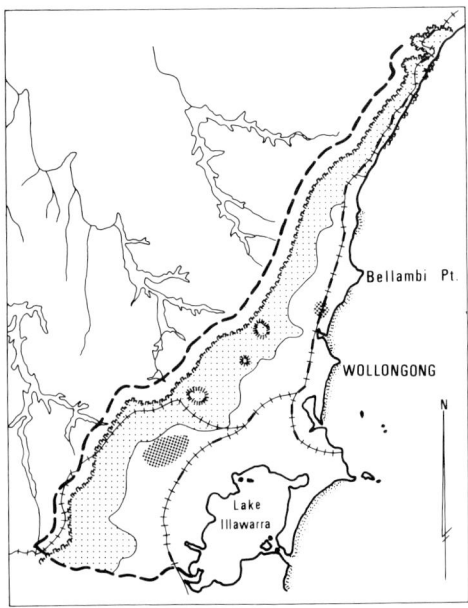

Trees.

Melaleuca styphelioides Sm.
Prickly leaved paperbark
Myrtaceae

This paperbark is probably the most common of the tree paperbarks in the Wollongong area. As the name suggests its prickly leaves make it easy to recognise. It is a common tree of the coastal plain and extends to the foothills of the escarpment. With the ability to tolerate brackish water conditions this Melaleuca is also often found in the lagoon communities behind the beaches. Although it may be found up to 25m tall it is most frequently found growing on coastal flats as a tree 5m to 8m tall with a dense crown.

Melaleuca styphelioides grows in association with *Melaleuca decora, Eucalyptus tereticornis, E. longifolia, E. eugenioides, E. pilularis* and sometimes *E. paniculata* and *E. quadrangulata*.

Bark: Thick, soft and papery, more or less white.

Leaves: Alternate, lanceolate to ovate, often twisted, drawn out to a long, hard sharp point, several longitudinal veins, 10mm to 20mm long, 3mm to 6mm wide.

Inflorescence: Spike up to 50mm long (Bottlebrush).

Flowers: Staminate, 5 staminal claws 3mm to 4mm long, white. Flowers summer.

Fruit: A woody, sessile capsule, 3mm or 4mm diameter.

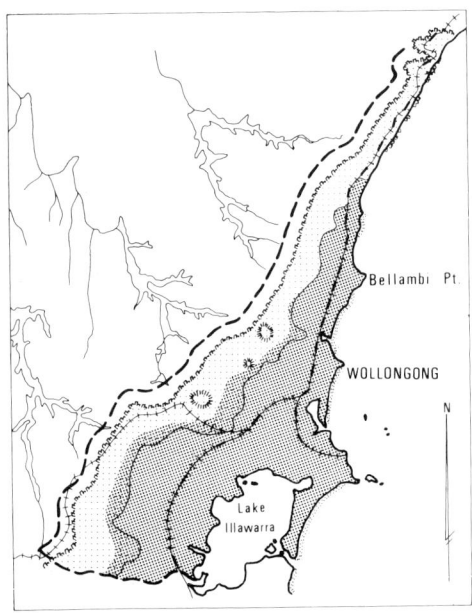

TOP: Trees. BOTTOM LEFT: Paper bark. BOTTOM RIGHT: Leaves and flowers.

Melia azedarach L. var. *australasica* (A. Juss.) C.DC.
syn. *M. dubia* Cav.

White cedar
Meliaceae

The natural distribution of white cedar is difficult to ascertain in the Wollongong area. It occurs naturally in the rainforest of the escarpment but on the coastal plain it is impossible to say whether the occurrence of any specimen is due to cultivation. Even where it does grow naturally, it is not a common tree but is found here and there, usually singly, along most of the escarpment length.

White cedar does not grow large but is usually found as a spreading tree up to about 10m tall. The finer foliage texture due to the bipinnate leaves distinguishes white cedar from red cedar. This tree is grown widely in cultivation and is strangely enough noted for its drought resistance. It is one of the few deciduous trees native to the Wollongong area. In November the white and lilac flowers make quite a show.

Bark: Dark brown, more or less furrowed.

Leaves: Alternate, bipinnate. Leaflets, ovate, drawn out to a point, coarsely serrated or entire 20mm to 50mm long, 15mm to 30mm across.

Inflorescence: Panicles almost as long as leaves.

Flowers: White and lilac in colour, petals arranged like a star, about 25mm across. Stamens united to form a dark coloured tube. Flowers October-November.

Fruit: An egg-shaped drupe, 12mm to 20mm long, yellowish with a fleshy outer covering. The fruit are poisonous.

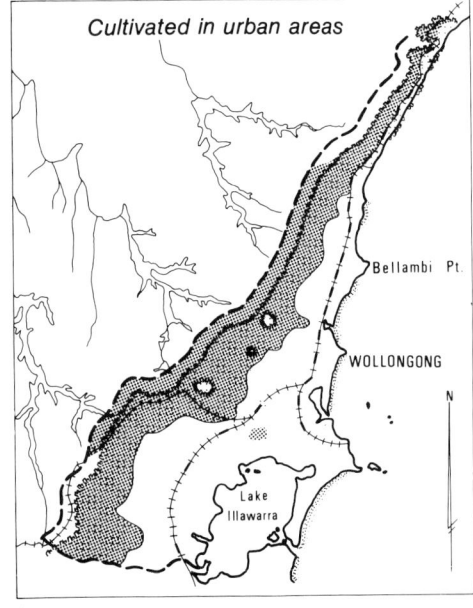

Leaves and flowers.

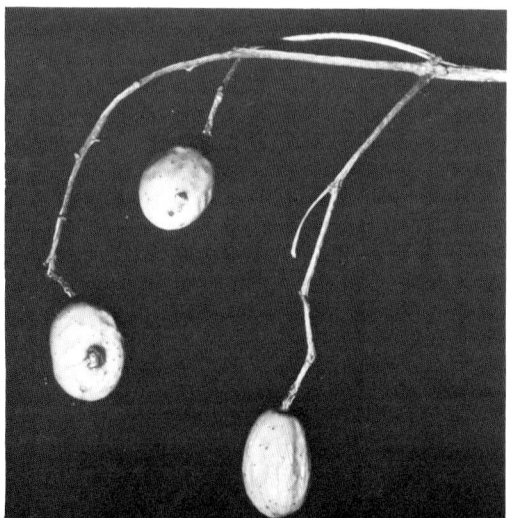

Fruit.

Myoporum acuminatum R. Br.

Boobialla

Myoporaceae

Boobialla is a tree found in the coastline zone and also on the coastal plain of the area considered in this book. It is not a big tree, only reaching about 8m high in rainforest on Flagstaff Hill. It usually forms a many stemmed shrub or tree with corky bark and prefers moister sheltered situations even near the sea. It does not appear as close to the sea as *M. insulare*.

Bark: Grey or usually brown, corky.

Leaves: Alternate, stalked, lanceolate, 50mm to 120mm long, 10mm to 30mm wide, tapering at both ends.

Inflorescence: Clusters of flowers in forks of leaves.

Flowers: About 8mm across, white with purple spots.

Fruit: Globular, black, bluish or purplish about 5mm diameter.

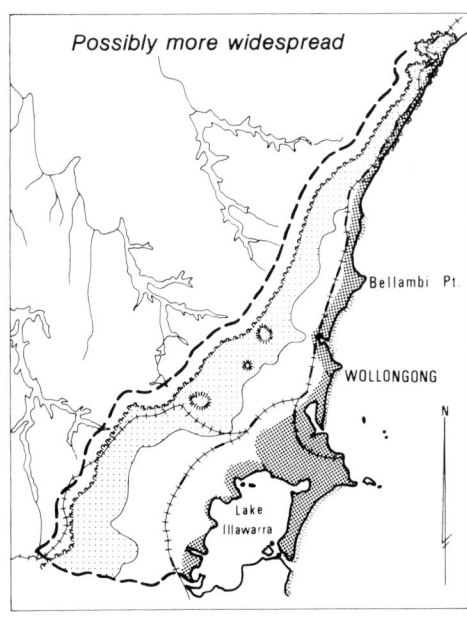

Leaves and fruit.

Bark.

Neolitsea dealbata (R. Br.) Merrill

syn. *Litsea dealbata* Nees

Lauraceae

Neolitsea dealbata is not a common tree in the Wollongong area occurring only in the Mt. Keira-Brokers Nose area. It can be readily observed at the Rhododendron Park at Mt. Pleasant, being most common in the vicinity of the benches on the escarpment. It grows to about 8m tall in rainforest and is easily distinguished by its oval leaves with pale or white undersurface.

Leaves: Alternate, ovate or elliptical, white or pale (glaucous) undersurface, basal pair of veins prominent, 100mm to 200mm long, 50mm to 100mm wide.

Inflorescence: Axillary clusters surrounded by deciduous bracts.

Flowers: Dioecious. Male — 4 perianth segments, 6 stamens. Female — stamens reduced to staminodes.

Fruit: A globular berry about 7mm diameter.

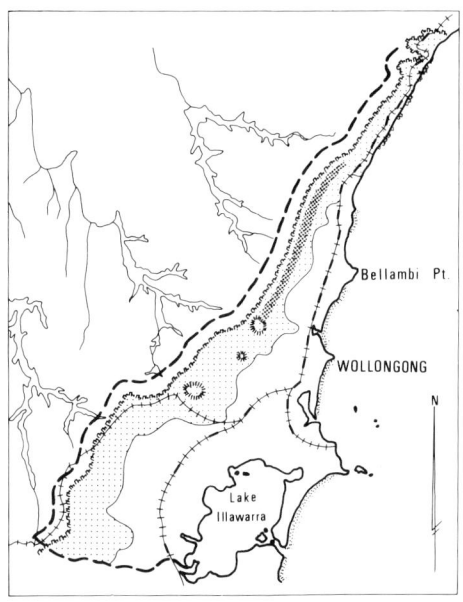

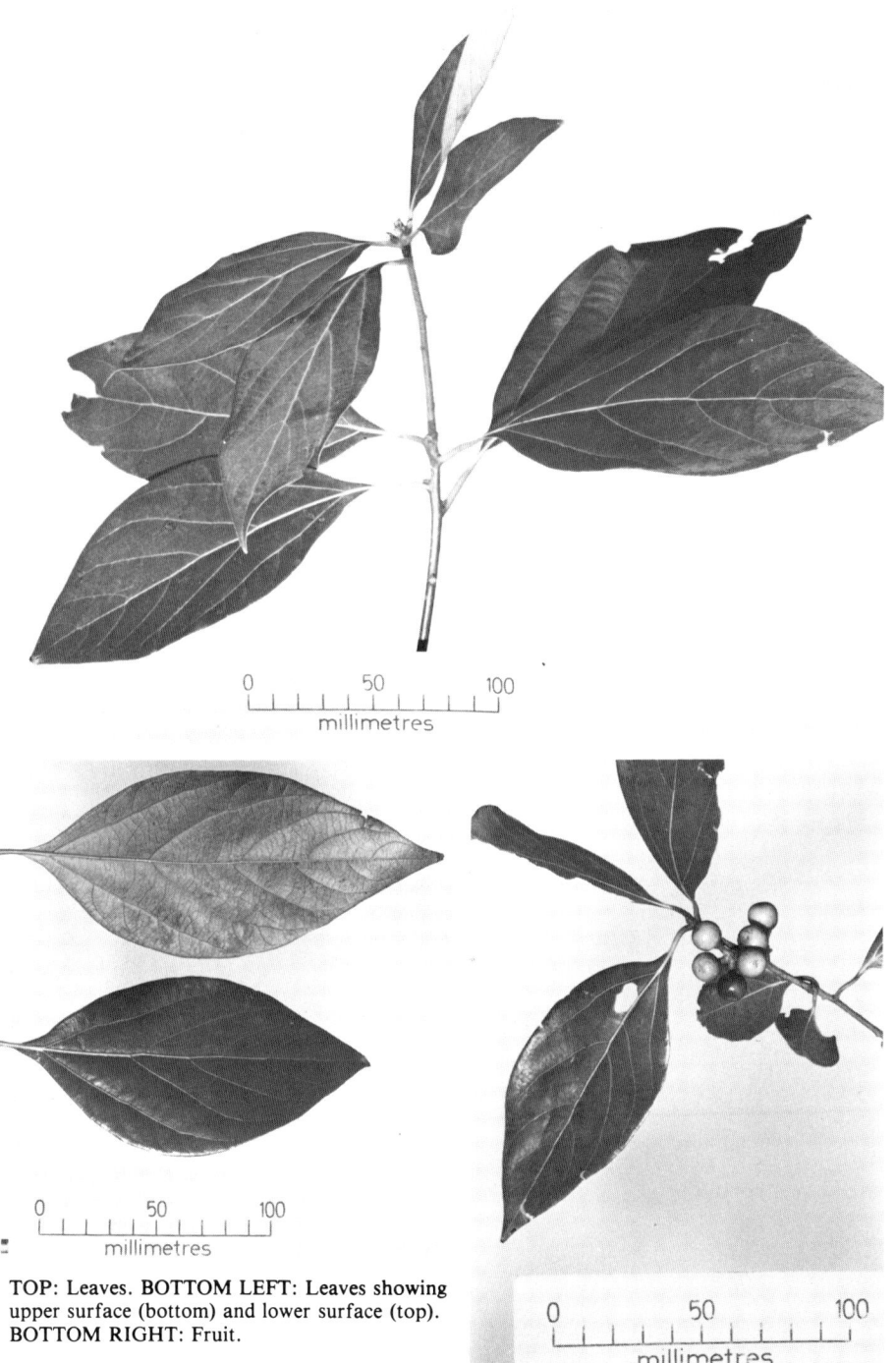

TOP: Leaves. BOTTOM LEFT: Leaves showing upper surface (bottom) and lower surface (top). BOTTOM RIGHT: Fruit.

Notelaea longifolia Vent.
Notelaea venosa R. Br.

Native olive
Oleaceae

Because these two species exhibit wide and overlapping variation in their characters, it is very difficult to separate them. They both occur throughout the area in various habitats from the hind-dune situation to climax rainforest on the escarpment. The most distinctive characteristics of these *Notelaea spp.*, despite the variation in leaf size, is the stiff texture and dull green surface of the leaves.

Both species are usually found as bushy shrubs or small trees up to about 3m in height but occasionally reach 6m. One conspicuous feature of these species is their commonness; they are almost always found in any piece of bushland, indeed they are often the last remnant of forest to survive after clearing, burning etc.

Bark: Brown or grey, or corky on large specimens. Twigs have conspicuous lenticels.

Leaves: Opposite, shortly stalked, lanceolate to broadly ovate, 50mm to 200mm long, 20mm to 70mm wide; thick, leathery; reticulate venation clearly visible. Surface varies from velvety hairy to hairless.

Inflorescence: Short clusters in forks of leaves.

Flowers: Small, about 2mm long, white.

Fruit: Black, 5mm to 20mm long, fleshy layer variable in thickness, single seed.

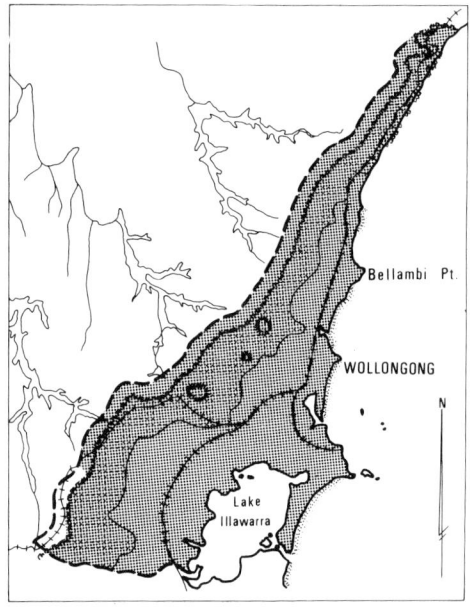

Leaves and flowers.

Leaves.

These three photographs show variation in leaf size.

Leaves and fruit.

Omalanthus populifolius Grah.
Native bleeding heart
Euphorbiaceae

Native bleeding heart grows on the edge of rainforest or as an understorey plant in eucalypt forest and is often found on disused land and in regenerating bush. It is likely to be found over most of the area but is most common on the escarpment.

This species only just makes it to tree status, usually about 3m to 4m tall. However it nearly always has a single main trunk with a bushy crown. The older leaves turn bright red and cause native bleeding heart to stand out against the green of the bush. There is usually a greater number of red leaves in the winter months. The shape of the leaves being distinctly deltoid is another easily recognised feature of this plant.

Bark: Brown or buff coloured, slightly rough.

Leaves: Alternate, deltoid to ovate, tapering to a point, dull surface, leaf stalks rather long, leaf blade 50mm to 120mm long, about as broad as long. Older leaves turning bright red.

Inflorescence: Terminal raceme (tassel-like), about 120mm long.

Flowers: Small. Male — 2mm to 3mm diameter, numerous. Female — few. Perianth irregularly truncate or 2 lobed.

Fruit: Glaucous, flattened 8mm to 10mm wide.

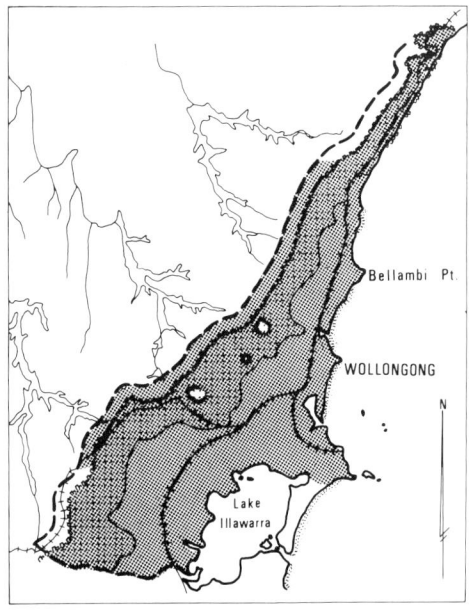

Flowers and upper surface of leaves.

Fruit and lower surface of leaves.

Pennantia cunninghamii Miers
Brown beech
Icacinaceae

The most distinctive features of brown beech are the fluted, twisted and often leaning trunk, and the small hollow glands in the leaves. It grows to a medium sized tree about 10m tall and is mainly found in the complex rainforest in gullies of the lower slopes and on the benches. It is particularly found along the banks of watercourses in rainforest. This species is not found anywhere on the coastal plain.

Bark: Brown or grey, rough, main trunk fluted and twisted, often leaning.

Leaves: Alternately arranged on a zig-zag stem. Oval in outline, entire margin, bright green, with glands (domatia) on the undersurface at junction of lateral veins. Leaf size 80mm to 150mm long, 50mm to 100mm wide.

Inflorescence: Panicles at ends of branches or in forks of leaves, shorter than the leaves.

Flowers: Small, 4mm long, 5 petals, male and female organs sometimes in different flowers. Flowers November-December.

Fruit: An egg shaped berry about 12mm long, black. Fruits winter and spring.

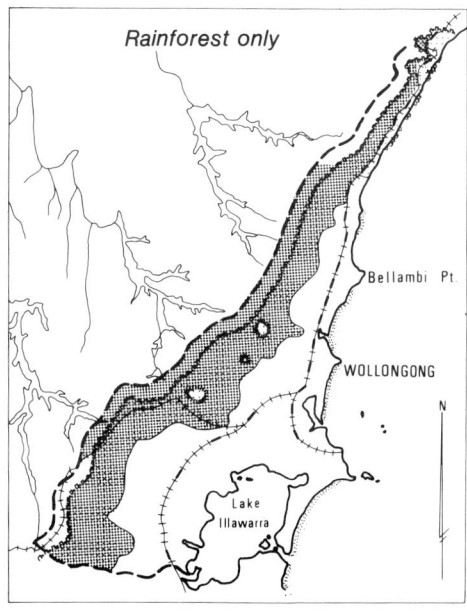

Tree in rainforest at Wombarra.

Fruit.

Lower trunk showing irregular fluting and bark.

Leaves.

Pisonia umbellifera (Forst. et F.) Seem.
Bird-lime tree
Nyctaginaceae

This tree takes its common name from the very sticky fruit which adheres to birds' feathers and feet and effects seed dispersal for this species. In the Jamberoo area there is evidence that flying foxes transport the seeds and spread this species.

In the Wollongong area the Bird-lime tree is only to be found in rainforest. It grows to about 6m tall but often has a many stemmed or bushy habit. It is quite an uncommon tree in the area included in this book and all observations of it have been at the rear of the upper bench on the escarpment.

Bark: Whitish.

Leaves: Alternate or in groups of 2-5, lanceolate or egg shaped in outline, mostly 100mm to 200mm long but sometimes longer, 60mm to 100mm wide. The leaf stalks are often an attractive purple colour.

Inflorescence: Terminal leafless cymose panicles.

Flowers: Funnel shaped calyx about 10mm long.

Fruit: About 25mm long, 4 or 5 ribbed exuding a very viscid (sticky) substance.

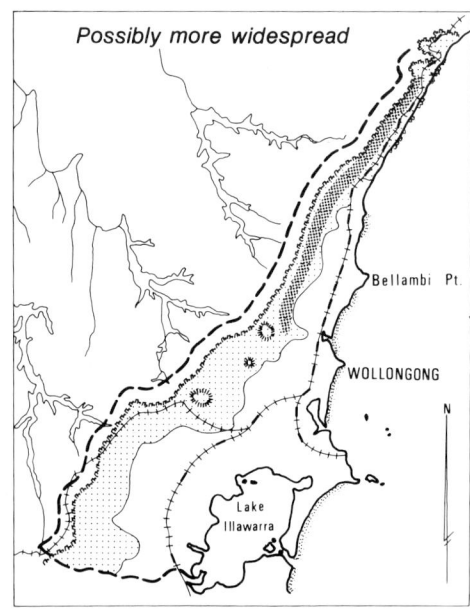

Leaves.

Fruit (very sticky).

Pittosporum undulatum Vent.

Native daphne
Pittosporum
Pittosporaceae

Pittosporum undulatum is very widespread in the Wollongong area. It occurs in almost every plant community, from dry sclerophyll to rainforest, where it reaches its best development. In rainforest it may be found up to 10m tall and a trunk diameter of 300mm. In eucalypt forest pittosporum grows to about 6m tall and is a spreading little tree.

This tree is most conspicuous in August-September when the new foliage opens and is brilliant green against the darker green of its old leaves and surrounding foliage. Pittosporum, because it is a very adaptable tree and a rainforest pioneer, is often found in regenerating vegetation on hillsides where en masse, the bright green new foliage is quite outstanding. Also in August-September the perfume of the flowers is heavy in the air about these trees.

Bark: Grey to dark grey and almost black with conspicuous lenticels on the younger branches.

Leaves: Alternate, lanceolate to narrow elliptical, drawn out to a point, 80mm to 130mm long, 25mm to 40mm wide, mostly with an undulate margin, prominent midrib and usually has round spots 5mm in diameter which are damage from a white fly.

Inflorescence: Compound clusters shorter than leaves at ends of branches.

Flowers: 10mm to 12mm long and wide, white, petals curled back, perfumed. Flowers September.

Fruit: A berry-like capsule 12mm diameter, orange, when open exposing orange sticky seeds. Fruits January-February.

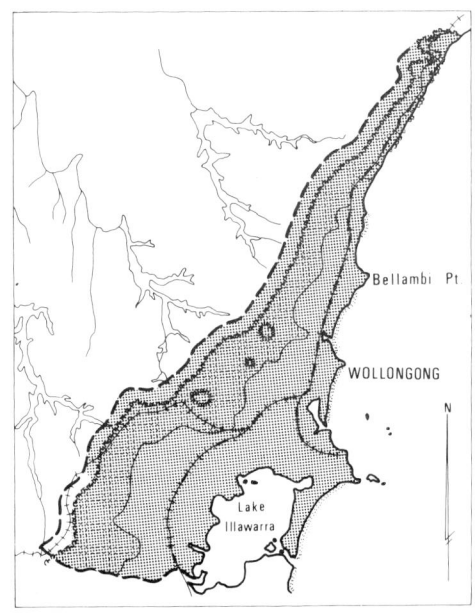

TOP: Tree. MIDDLE: Leaves. LEFT: Fruit.

Planchonella australis (R. Br.) Pierre

syn. *Sideroxylon australe* (R. Br.) F. Muell.

Black apple

Sapotaceae

The "black apples" which this tree bears can be seen hanging from the tree or littering the ground beneath during December-January. These fruit are quite palatable when *ripe* and serve as a good identifying feature. The tree itself grows up to about 15m tall in the Wollongong area and has typical large rainforest laurel-like leaves. It occurs on the escarpment and foothills and at least on the western side of the coastal plain in the area covered by this book.

Bark: Grey, somewhat scaly.

Leaves: Alternate, stalked, elliptical to oblanceolate, 60mm to 100mm long, 20mm to 50mm wide, rather thick with conspicuous reticulate venation.

Inflorescence: Flowers clustered in forks of leaves.

Flowers: About 5mm long, sepals 5, corolla tube with 5 lobes. Five fertile and 5 infertile stamens ovary surrounded by long brown hairs. Flowers December.

Fruit: A globular black berry up to 50mm diameter. Seeds, 3-5 about 25mm long, 10mm across, brown and shiny. Fruits December-January, a year after flowering.

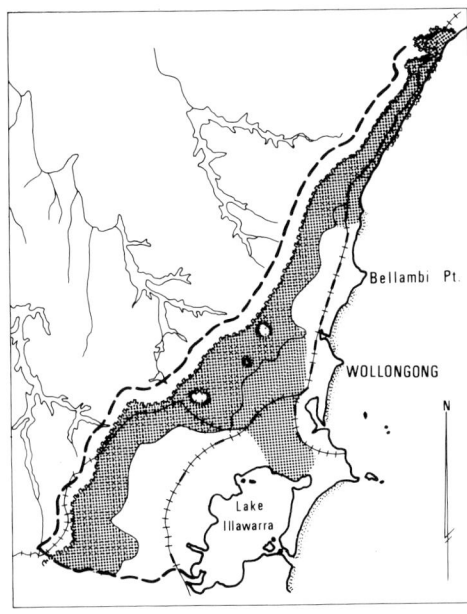

Leaves and fruit.

Podocarpus elatus R. Br. ex Endl.

Plum pine
Brown pine
Podocarpaceae

Plum pine is the only conifer (Gymnosperm) which occurs in the area covered by this book. The next nearest conifer is the Port Jackson pine of the Cypress family to be found just outside the western boundary on the plateau. Plum pine is an inhabitant of the rainforest of the area but is usually not common. However, there is a good population of this species in the rainforest gully immediately south of the ridge of Brokers Nose. There are also many trees in the Berkeley-Flagstaff Hills area. Just south of the area at Bass Point this tree grows in rainforest on poor sandy soil in an almost seaside environment.

Podocarpus elatus is generally a medium sized tree but may grow up to about 30m tall with a stem diameter of 500mm. The grey-brown fissured bark is the most distinctive feature when confronted with this tree in the rainforest. The narrow leaves also stand out among the laurel-like leaves of the other rainforest trees.

Bark: Brown, finely fissured, fibrous main stem often irregularly fluted.

Leaves: Alternate, thick, narrow, oblong-linear to linear-lanceolate, 50mm to 100mm long, 6mm to 12mm wide. Midrib prominent.

Cones: Male and female on different trees. Male Cones — 10mm to 30mm long in axillary clusters. Female Cones — single on stalks in forks of the leaves. Flowers October.

Fruit: The seed, 8mm to 12mm diameter sits atop a fleshy "plum" derived from the swollen stalk of the female cone.

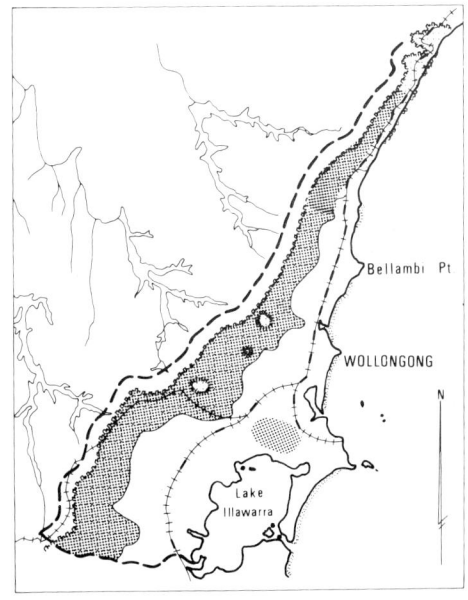

TOP: Trees. BOTTOM LEFT: Bark. BOTTOM RIGHT: Leaves.

Polyosma cunninghamii J. J. Benn

Featherwood

Escalloniaceae

The shiny elegant leaves and regular shape of this small tree make it very attractive in the rainforest. Featherwood grows to about 10m tall in the rainforest of the escarpment and plateau gullies, often as an understorey to taller forest. It has quite a pyramidal shape where allowed to grow unimpaired.

Bark: Grey or brown.

Leaves: Opposite, stalked, elliptical to oblanceolate, tapering gradually at base, coarsely serrated, very shiny on upper surface, 50mm to 100mm long, 20mm to 40mm wide.

Inflorescence: Racemes shorter than the leaves.

Flowers: White or greenish, perfumed, 4 calyx lobes, 4 petals about 10mm long forming a tube for half their length. Flared at ends. Flowers spring and summer.

Fruit: Egg shaped, black or purplish, 12mm to 20mm long, with 8-10 longitudinal ribs.

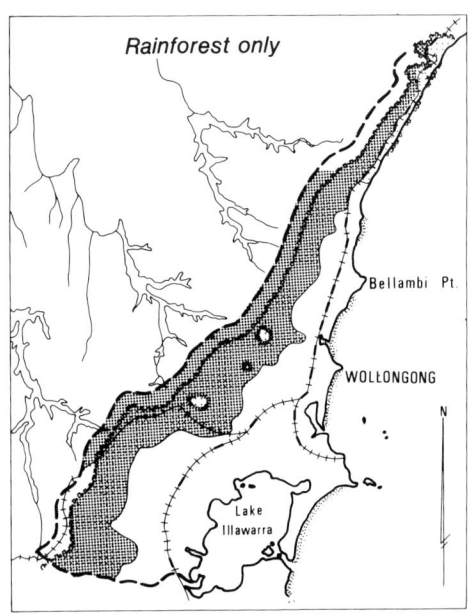

Leaves.

Polyscias elegans (C. Moore et F. Muell.) Harms

syn. *Tieghemopanax elegans* R. Viguier
Panax elegans C. Moore et F. Muell.

Celery-wood

Araliaceae

As the specific name suggests this is an elegant little tree with an umbrella-like habit. It is grown in cultivation chiefly about Sydney because of its habit and crown of glossy dark green and bipinnate leaves. So called celery-wood because of the smell of the young shoots when broken, this tree grows to about 6 metres tall and is found scattered in and about the edges of rainforest on the escarpment and the coastal plain. It is very uncommon in the Wollongong area.

Bark: Grey, slightly rough.

Leaves: Alternate pinnate or bipinnate, large. Leaflets opposite, ovate with an abrupt point, 50mm to 100mm long, dark green and shiny.

Inflorescence: Terminal, large panicle with raceme like subdivisions, carried above the foliage. Flowering period — irregular.

Fruit: Circular with two curved styles at its apex, flattened, black, 7mm diameter containing two seeds.

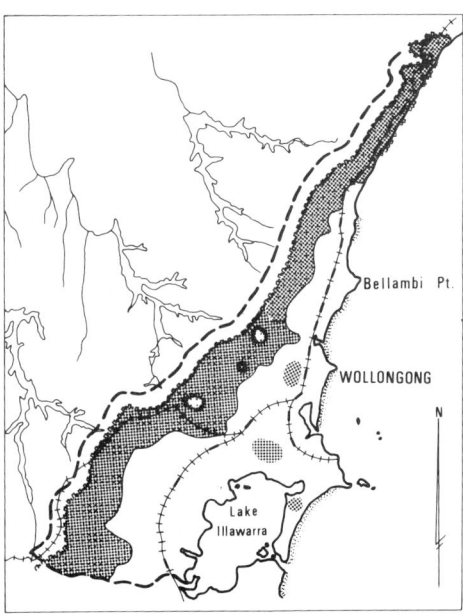

TOP: Tree. BOTTOM: A single leaf.

Polyscias murrayi (F. Muell.) Harms.

syn. *Tieghemopanax murrayi* (F. Muell.) Viguier
Panax murrayi F. Muell.

Umbrella tree
Pencil cedar
Araliaceae

The habit of this tree when young makes it unmistakable in the forest. It has a central straight stem for 6m or so with large pinnate leaves radiating off it. As an older tree it may be seen up to 15m tall with an arching umbrella-like canopy.

Polyscias murrayi grows on the edges of and in the rainforest of the escarpment and the plateau. It sometimes grows in the moister, more sheltered wet sclerophyll forest also.

Bark: Grey-brown.

Leaves: Alternate, large pinnate; often over 1m long, with 9 to 31 or more leaflets. Leaflets: Shortly stalked, oblong-elliptic, oblique, drawn out to a point, margins may be toothed, 50mm to 200mm long, 20mm to 60mm wide.

Inflorescence: Large pyramidal panicles subdivided in umbels.

Flowers: Numerous.

Fruit: Two, sometimes three lobed, 6mm or 7mm diameter surmounted by a minute fork.

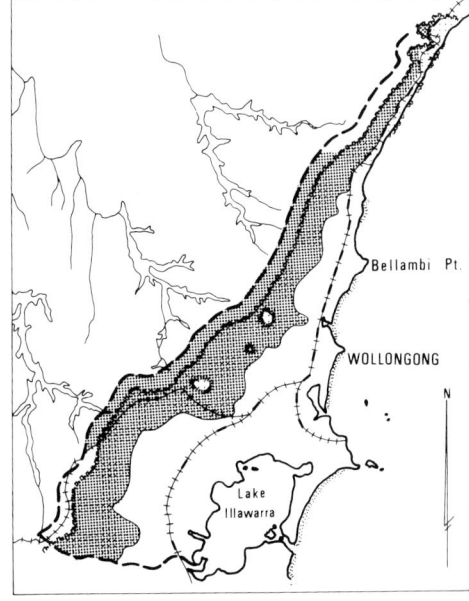

TOP LEFT: Young tree. TOP RIGHT: A mature tree. The person standing at base of tree gives an idea of its height. BOTTOM: The long pinnate leaves.

Quintinia sieberi A.DC.

Possum wood

Escalloniaceae

Possum wood is not a common tree in the Wollongong area, occurring only on the upper part of the escarpment in rainforest or sheltered eucalypt forest. It is mainly found on the talus material immediately below the escarpment cliffs or sometimes on the cliffs and crest.

This species grows to a small bushy tree reaching about 8m high in the area included in this book. Possum wood is most easily distinguished by its oval, thick glossy leaves and corky bark.

Bark: Brown wrinkled and often corky.

Leaves: Alternate, somewhat leathery, elliptical 60mm to 120mm long, with a short point, veins quite visible on both surfaces, the margin has a fine clear line at the edge.

Inflorescence: Panicles with raceme-like subdivisions, about as long as leaves, at the ends of branches.

Flowers: White, about 10mm diameter. Five calyx lobes, five petals and five stamens. Flowers October-November.

Fruit: A small 3-5 celled capsule opening at the top. Fruits December-January.

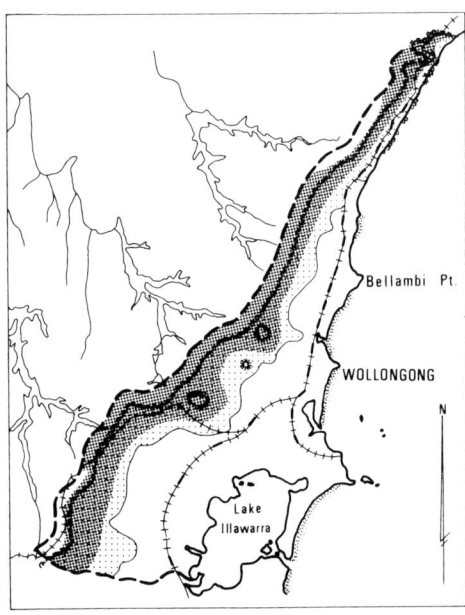

Leaves of *Quintinia sieberi*.

Rapanea howittiana Mez

Myrsinaceae

This *Rapanea* differs from the following one in the narrower leaves with a more rounded end and no serrations (except on juvenile foliage). This species also grows more often in rainforest and bears a profusion of blue or purplish berries when in fruit. It grows to a small tree about 8m tall. It is not as common as *Rapanea variabilis*.

Stems: The two *Rapanea* in the Wollongong area have short stubs left after old leaves fall which make the stems rough to touch.

Leaves: Alternate, shortly stalked, narrow elliptical to oblanceolate, 50mm to 100mm long, shiny upper surface and a softer leaf than *Rapanea variabilis*.

Inflorescence: Clusters in forks of leaves, mostly an old wood.

Flowers: Small.

Fruit: Blue or purple, globular drupe, about 5mm diameter.

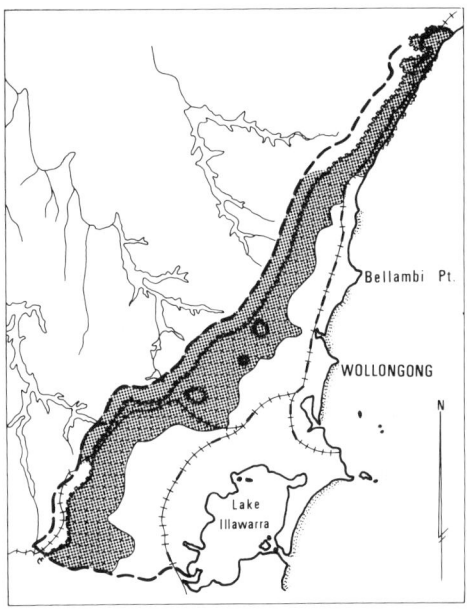

Leaves of *Rapanea howittiana*.

Rapanea variabilis (R. Br.) Mez
Mutton wood
Myrsinaceae

Mutton wood is a widespread shrub or small tree found in sclerophyll forest and sometimes rainforest. In fact it extends from the hind dune area to the plateau. It grows to about 8m tall and usually has a rather open habit.

The leaves of this species as the name implies are variable in size, shape and degree of serration of the margin. The stems are distinctive and after leaves have fallen, the short projections left make the stems somewhat rasp-like.

Leaves: Alternate, shortly stalked, elliptical to obovate or oblanceolate, 30mm to 80mm long, 15mm to 60mm wide, leathery often shiny on upper surface. Irregularly toothed, serrate or entire, sometimes wavy (undulate).

Inflorescence: Clusters in forks of leaves.

Flowers: Small, greenish white, petals united into four-lobed tube about 5mm long.

Fruit: Globular, whitish to purplish about 7mm diameter.

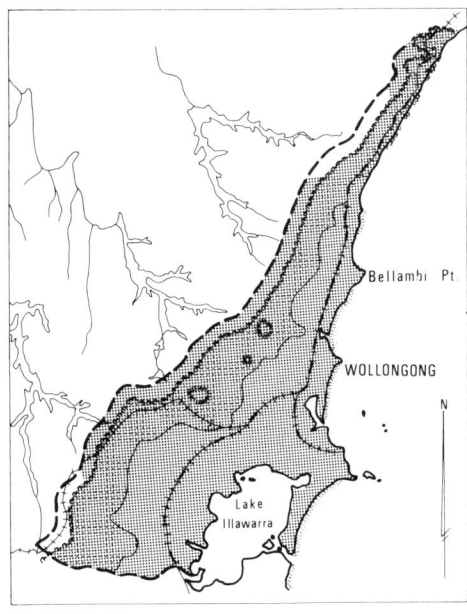

Leaves of *Rapanea variabilis*.

Rhodamnia rubescens (Benth.) Miq.

syn. *R. trinervia* (Sm.) Bl.

Scrub stringybark

Myrtaceae

Scrub stringybark derives its common name from the stringy appearance of the bark which is an odd occurrence in the rainforest. This tree often grows at the edge of, or may be found in rainforest. It is only a small tree up to about 8m tall with a rather open crown.

The three veined leaves are quite distinctive as well as the stringy bark of the tree.

Bark: Brown, stringy-flaky.

Leaves: Stalked, opposite, broadly lanceolate to elliptical drawn out to a point at the apex. There are three conspicuous parallel veins running the length of the leaf, net veins conspicuous on undersurface, hairy on undersurface.

Inflorescence: Axillary cymes, shorter than the leaves.

Flowers: 8mm diameter, white, numerous stamens. Flowers spring and summer.

Fruit: Berry about 6mm diameter, crowned by 4 old calyx lobes.

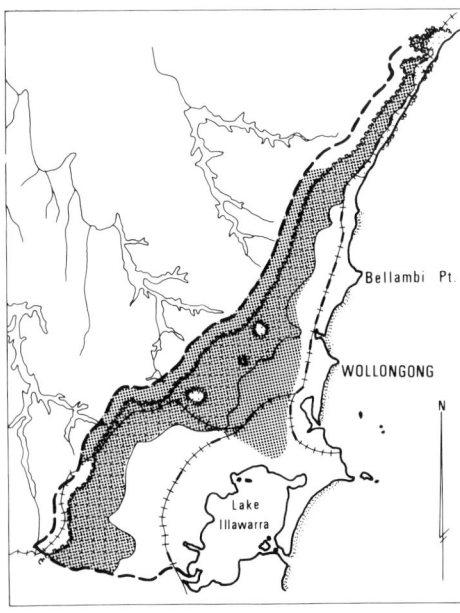

Leaves.

Sarcomelicope simplicifolia (Endl.) Hartley subsp. *simplificifolia*

syn. *Bauerella simplicifolia* (Endl.) Hartley subsp. *simplicifolia*
    syn. *Acronychia simplicifolia* (Endl.) McGillivray et Green subsp. *simplicifolia* A. *baueri* Schott.

Rutaceae

This species is rare in the Wollongong area, only having been observed at the Rhododendron Park at Mt. Pleasant and on Flagstaff Hill. South of the area covered in this book it grows more commonly and is found at Bass Point and Whispering Galleries. It occurs in rainforest, has a rather open branching habit and is found up to about 10m tall.

This tree, like *Acronychia oblongifolia*, has a leaf blade which articulates on the leaf stalk but it has a longer petiole and a broader elliptical leaf blade.

Leaves: Opposite, stalks up to 30mm long, leaf blade elliptical to obovate, 50mm to 120mm long, 30mm to 60mm wide, leaf blade articulates on petiole.

Inflorescence: Single or in spike-like panicles in forks of leaves.

Flowers: About 5mm across.

Fruit: Globular, or egg-shaped to 20mm long; orange coloured; 4 lobed. Fruits January to February.

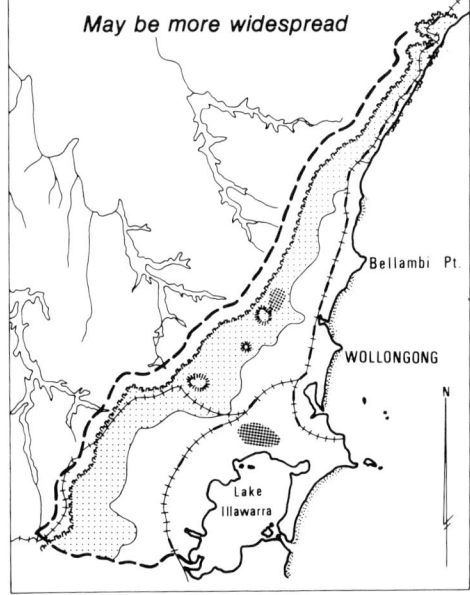

Leaves.

Fruit.

Schizomeria ovata D. Don
Crab apple
Cunoniaceae

This tree is found chiefly in the rainforest of the area as a tall tree. In good conditions it may be found over 25m high. It is also found as a small tree in moist sandstone gullies.

The steel grey fissured bark is reminiscent of *Citronella moorei* but the roundness of the trunk along with these other features set white cherry apart. The trunk is often 1m in diameter in good forest.

The coarse serrations on the leaf are somewhat like sassafras but the base of the leaf tapers gradually into a long petiole.

Schizomeria ovata is not a common tree but it is reasonably easy to find and occurs generally in simple rainforest on the upper part of the escarpment.

Bark: Grey, longitudinal fissures.

Leaves: Opposite, serrated margin, broadly lanceolate, 80mm to 200mm long, 30mm to 80mm wide, acute to acuminate apex. Darker green on top than below.

Inflorescence: In forks of leaves.

Flowers: Small. Flowers spring.

Fruit: White, egg shaped, drupe, outer part fleshy about 12mm diameter.

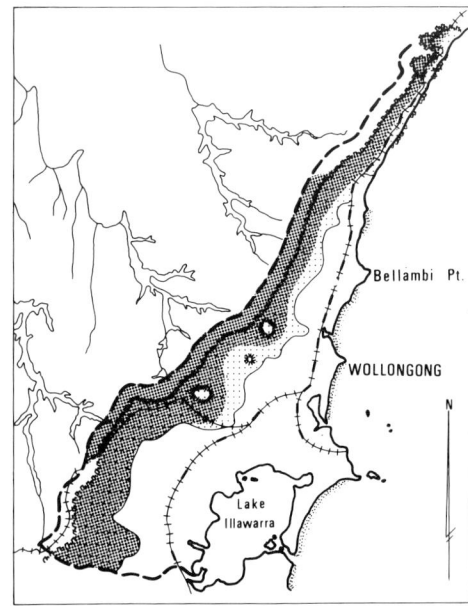

Leaves and flowers.

Scolopia braunii (Klotzsch) Sleumer
syn. *Scolopia brownii* F. Muell.

Flacourtiaceae

As a young tree the leaves of this species often have an angular or irregularly toothed margin which serves as an identifying feature. It forms a small shapely tree and may be found in and near rainforest in the area, particularly on the lower part of the escarpment. R. H. Anderson recommends this species for cultivation, it having a dense shapely crown and being easily propagated from seed.

Bark: Brown, slightly scaly.

Leaves: Alternate, stalked, 30mm to 80mm long, 15mm to 40mm wide, often with one or two angles along the margin. The basal pair of veins run parallel to the margin for some distance. The leaves are hairless and shiny on top.

Inflorescence: Short racemes in forks of leaves.

Flowers: White, about 4mm across.

Fruit: Globular, about 12mm in diameter containing several angular seeds embedded in the pulp.

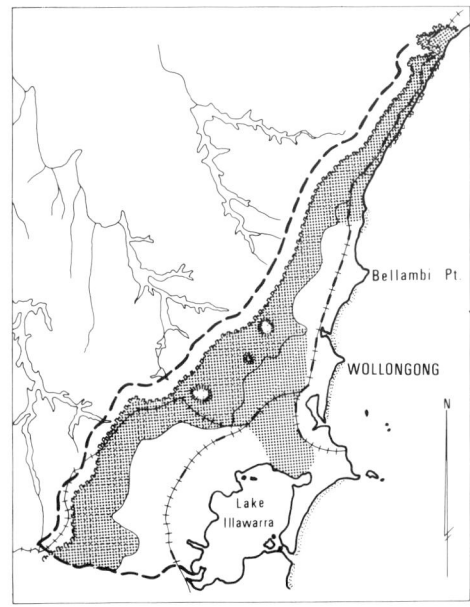

Leaves of *Scolopia braunii*.

Sloanea australis (Benth.) F. Muell.

syn. *Echinocarpus australis* Benth.

Maiden's blush

Elaeocarpaceae

The trunk of maiden's blush is similar to that of *Pennantia cunninghamii*, being often crooked and leaning with irregular fluting. It does however grow to about 15m tall and is usually easy to pick out by its large obovate leaves. This tree is particularly found along watercourse banks in rainforest on the escarpment.

The crooked trunk and leaves are the most distinctive parts of this tree.

Bark: Grey or light brown, somewhat scaly.

Leaves: Alternate, obovate to elliptic, 120mm to 300mm long, 70mm to 120mm wide, leaf blade narrow and cordate at base with a second articulation point at junction of leaf blade and leaf stalk.

Inflorescence: Flowers solitary or in short racemes in forks of leaves.

Flowers: Pendulous, cream coloured, about 25mm across, numerous bristle-like stamens in centre of flower. Flowers October-November.

Fruit: A light brown coloured woody capsule covered in dense soft bristles. Fruit opening by 4 woody valves. Seeds black enveloped in a bright orange-red aril. Fruits winter.

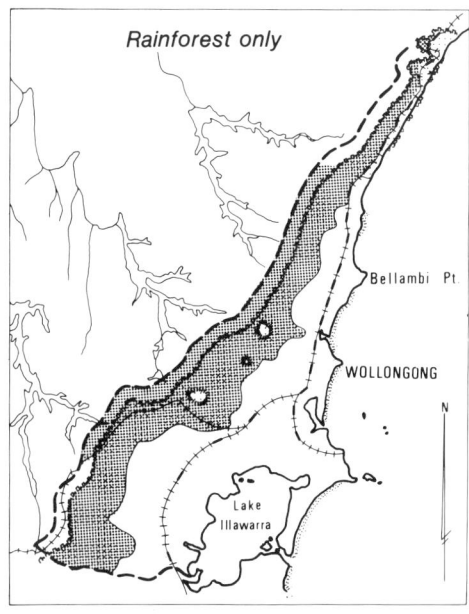

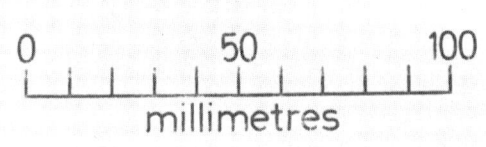

Leaves.

Stenocarpus salignus R. Br.
Scrub beefwood
Proteaceae

Although this tree does not have the showy flowers of its close relative fire wheel tree *(Stenocarpus sinuatus)*, it does have rather distinctive leaves with the venation more or less parallel. In the Wollongong area it occurs in or on the edges of rainforest associated with the escarpment and lower slopes and at least the western side of the coastal plain. Scrub beefwood grows up to 10m tall with a stem diameter of 200mm but is usually smaller.

Bark: Grey or brown often finely wrinkled.

Leaves: Alternate, stalked, elliptical to lanceolate, narrowing at either end. "There appears to be a considerable amount of variation in this species. In some cases there are one or two longitudinal nerves (veins) on each side of the midrib, in others these nerves are suppressed and the leaves are penninerved. Sometimes the reticulate veins are obscured. Bentham recognises two varieties as under: Var. *moorei*. Leaves broader than the typical form with one or two longitudinal nerves (veins) on each side of the midrib, ovary minutely hairy — Illawarra. . . ." (Francis, 1970). Leaves measure 80mm to 120mm long, 30mm to 50mm wide.

Inflorescence: 15 to 30 flowered umbels on stalks singly or several together terminal or in forks of leaves.

Flowers: White or greenish "spider flower" 10mm long when unopened, 20mm to 30mm long when opened. Flowers October-January.

Fruit: A long narrow boat-shaped follicle, 50mm to 100mm long, 25mm wide.

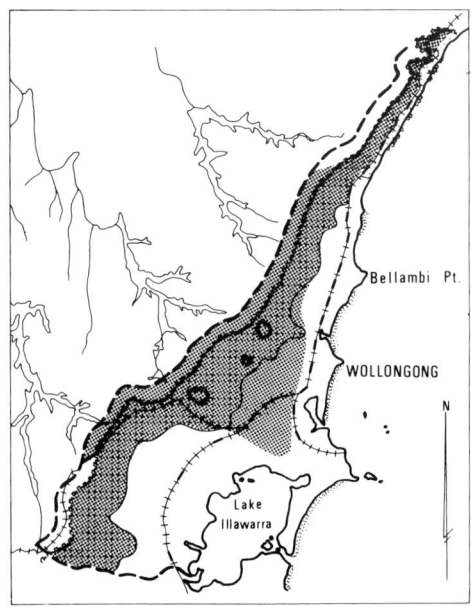

Leaves

Streblus brunonianus (Endl.) F. Muell.

syn. *Pseudomorus brunoniana* (Endl.) Bur.

Whalebone tree
Moraceae

Whalebone tree, in the Wollongong area, grows to a large shrub or a small tree about 6m tall. It grows in or on the edge of rainforest and also in wet sclerophyll forest on the escarpment and on the coastal plain. This species is most abundant as with well formed trees in rainforest of the Berkeley and Flagstaff Hills. The leaves of this tree are extremely variable so a close look must be had when attempting to identify it. Young twigs when broken exude a milky sap.

Bark: Grey.

Leaves: Alternate, quite variable, elliptical ovate or lanceolate, usually 10mm to 70mm long, often drawn out to a point, margins toothed, glossy on upper surface but rough to touch. Leaves of sucker shoots may be abnormally long.

Flowers: Male — In dense spikes 10mm to 50mm in forks of leaves. Female — Short spikes or clusters with 3 or 4 flowers. Perianth segments about 1mm long. Flowers March and April.

Fruit: Egg-shaped drupe about 6mm long, surmounted by a forked style.

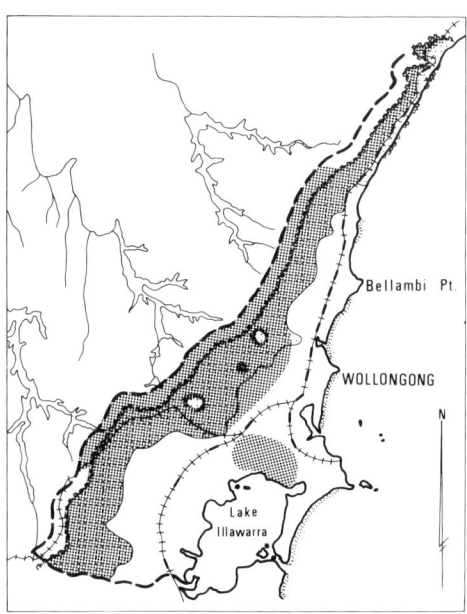

Trees.

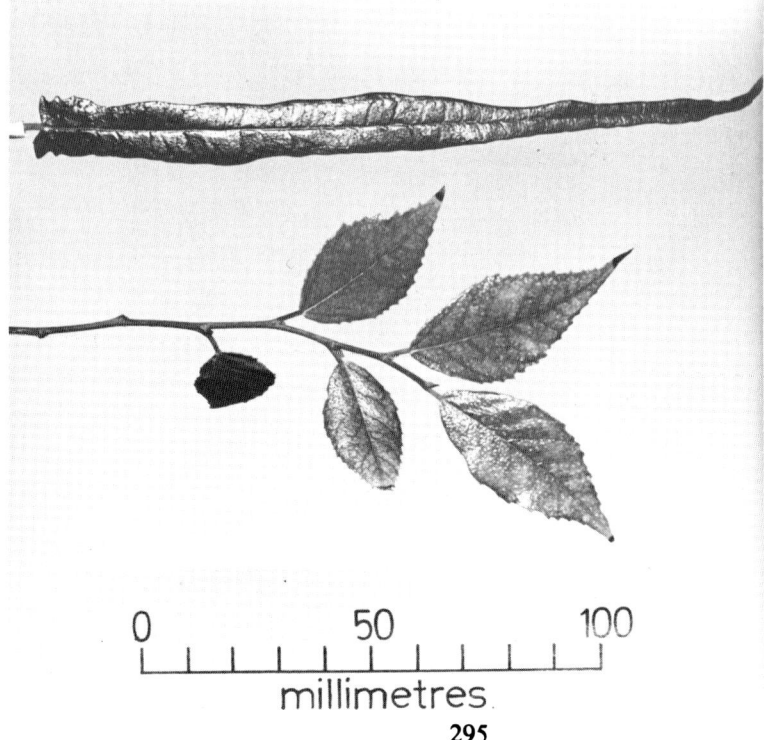

Leaves. The long top leaf is a juvenile one.

Symplocos thwaitesii F. Muell.

Symplocaceae

Symplocos thwaitesii is a very uncommon tree in the Wollongong area. It is to be found in rainforest on the escarpment, in the gullies of the plateau and in the Berkeley/Flagstaff Hills area. One of the few good sized mature specimens can be found in the Rhododendron Park in Parrish Avenue, Mount Pleasant. This species forms a rather heavy looking tree with thick branches and dense, coarse, thick leaves. It may be found up to about 15m tall.

Bark: Grey or brown.

Leaves: Alternate, narrow elliptical to oblanceolate, 100mm to 150mm long, 20mm to 35mm wide, stiff almost rigid, thick, margins often toothed. The leaves are so thick that they rattle when a branch is shaken.

Inflorescence: Racemes or panicles in forks of leaves.

Flowers: Calyx lobes 5, petals 5, stamens numerous, flowers to 10mm across.

Fruit: Egg-shaped drupe to 12mm long with persistent calyx lobes at apex.

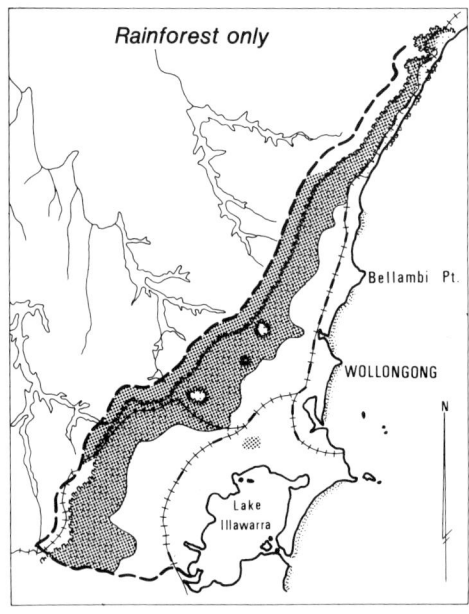

Leaves.

Syncarpia glomulifera (Sm.) Niedenzu
syn. *S. laurifolia*

Turpentine

Myrtaceae

Turpentine is a tree which can attain a great deal of character in its old age. In the open it forms a spreading tree often with gnarled branches, however, it also grows as a tall forest tree and is often found in the zone immediately outside rainforest. It occurs across the coastal plain, on the escarpment and the plateau but only north of Mt. Keira and the Berkeley Hills. It is, surprisingly, absent or rare in the West Dapto area, only to reappear in abundance at Macquarie Pass.

In tall wet sclerophyll forest turpentine may attain a height well over 30m in the Wollongong area. It is most commonly found in association with blackbutt *(Eucalyptus pilularis)* and Sydney blue gum *(Eucalyptus saligna]*.

There are some magnificent forests of turpentine on the escarpment foothills at Balgownie. Other splendid old trees may be seen at the Wollongong Botanic Gardens.

Bark: Grey, fibrous, can be pulled off in long strips (stringy).

Leaves: Opposite, lanceolate to elliptical, 50mm to 120mm long, 20mm to 60mm wide, with a short point; white or grey hairy undersurface; margins often curved under.

Inflorescence: Flowers united by their calyces into dense round heads on long peduncles.

Flowers: White; 5 calyx lobes, 4 petals. Numerous prominent stamens in 2 whorls. Flowers spring and summer.

Fruit: A woody, hard, compound capsule about 15mm across.

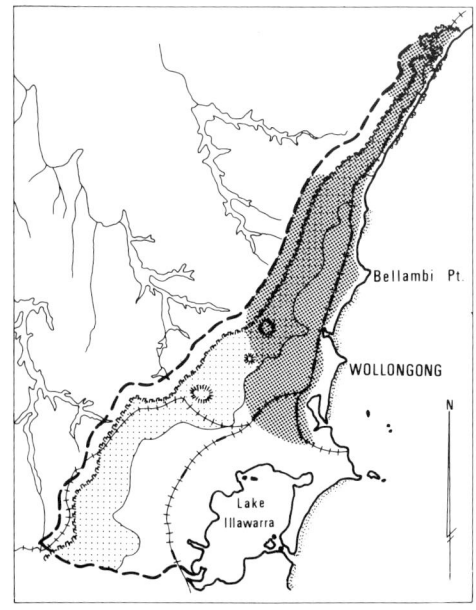

Tree.

Bark.

Fruit.

Leaves.

Synoum glandulosum (Sm.) A. Juss.

Bastard rosewood
Meliaceae

In the Wollongong region bastard rosewood can be found in or on the edges of most rainforest patches as well as being common in wet sclerophyll forest. It also grows in hind dune areas such as Puckey's Estate where conditions favour a moister community.

This species often grows as a large shrub but reaches tree proportions in several places such as just east of Mt. Ousley Road at the crest of the escarpment. Here it grows to about 8m tall with a stem diameter of 200m.

The main identifying feature is the compound leaves, with oblanceolate leaflets which have a mucronate apex. The terminal leaflet is often larger than the others.

Bark: Grey-brown, shed in small angular patches.

Leaves: Alternate, imparipinnate, 5 to 9 leaflets. Leaflets oblanceolate with mucronate apex, 30mm to 80mm long, 15mm to 40mm wide. At the intersection of several lateral veins and the midrib can be found small sunken hairy glands.

Inflorescence: Panicles, up to 25mm long in forks of leaves.

Flowers: White, reddish on outside about 7mm across. 4 or 5 petals. Flowers most of the year.

Fruit: A one, two or mostly three lobed capsule about 25mm in diameter. Green ripening to orange. Seeds about 6mm diameter embedded in a fleshy aril.

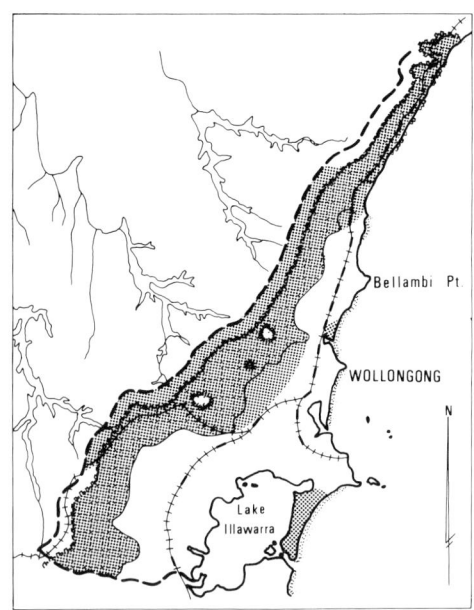

TOP LEFT: Fruit among leaves. TOP RIGHT: Tree.   BOTTOM: Leaves.

Syzygium australe (Wend. ex Link) B. Hyland
syn. *Syzygium paniculatum Gaertn.*
syn. *Eugenia australis* Wendl. et Link.

Brush cherry
Myrtaceae

Brush cherry is confined to rainforest in the Wollongong area and is most commonly found along watercourses of the lower half of the escarpment. It occurs also on the western part of the coastal plain and on Berkeley and Flagstaff Hills. It often overhangs watercourses.

This species grows up to 20m tall but is usually found as a small tree 6-10m high. When in fruit the bright red elongated berries are attractive and pleasantly edible. The small shiny leaves are also a distinctive feature of this tree.

Bark: Brown, greyish, somewhat scaly.

Leaves: Opposite, narrow, ovate or obovate, drawn out to a short point, 25mm to 80mm long, 15mm to 30mm wide.

Inflorescence: Singly or in clusters of three in forks of leaves or panicles at end of branchlets.

Flowers: Up to 25mm across, 4 small petals, numerous white stamens about 12mm long.

Fruit: Egg shaped or elongated to 25mm long, bright red with purplish tinge. Fruit January-March.

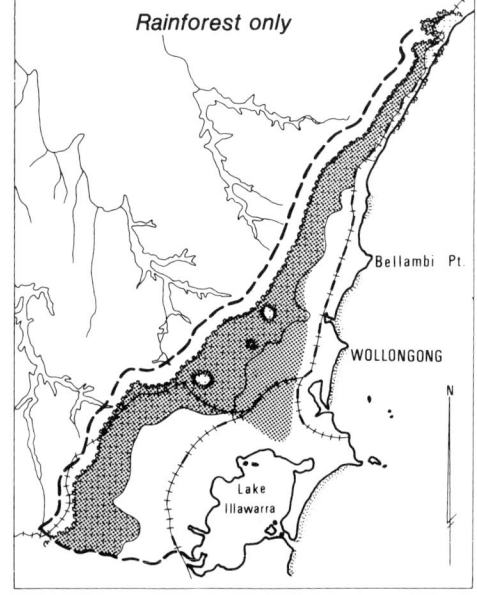

TOP: Tree. MIDDLE LEFT: Flower. BOTTOM LEFT: Fruit. BOTTOM RIGHT: Leaves.

Syzygium oleosum (F. Muell.) B. Hyland
syn. *S. coolminianum*

Myrtaceae

The inclusion of this species is based on one specimen found in the area covered by this book at Mt. Kembla by Mr. K. Mills. There is possibly more of this species to be found but it is rare in this area. As with most of the rainforest Myrtaceae it is an attractive small tree with distinctively coloured fruits although the leaves are similar to others of *Syzygium*. The specimen referred to is a bushy small tree about four metres tall and is growing in rainforest.

Bark: Brown, more or less smooth (on branches up to 100mm diameter).

Leaves: Opposite, shortly stalked, lanceolate, tapering gradually at both ends, with a pointed apex. 50mm to 100mm long, 15mm to 30mm wide.

Inflorescence: Panicles at ends of branchlets or in forks of leaves.

Flowers: White, about 10mm diameter.

Fruit: Globular or urn-shaped purplish-blue, 10mm to 20mm diameter.

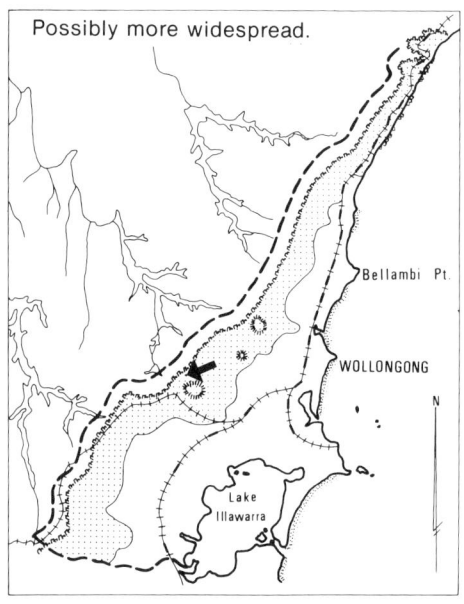

Leaves.

Fruit.

Toona australis (F. Muell.) Harms

syn. *Cedrela toona* Roxb. ex Rottler var. *australis* F. Muell. C.DC.

Red cedar
Meliaceae

Red cedar, famous for its fine furniture timber, occurs abundantly in the Wollongong area but only as small or medium sized trees. Gone are the past giants of the rainforest which were mercilessly exploited during the last century. There is also little hope of this species ever again attaining the size it did in pre-European times due to the completely changed environment. There are odd specimens which can still be found up to 40m in height and a stem diameter of 1m but mostly it is a tree of 15m to 20m high with a stem diameter of 300mm to 400mm. When found in the open red cedar has a rounded crown and its distinctive pinnate leaves separate it from most trees. However *Polyscias murrayi* looks similar to the red cedar and care must be taken with these two species.

Toona australis is conspicuous in winter when the leaves turn yellow and finally fall off and in springtime the new shoots are pink with good specimens being quite colourful in this condition.

Red cedar is found in rainforest and suitable wet sclerophyll forest from the foot of the escarpment to the plateau, although it is somewhat less common in the rainforest of the plateau. It reaches its best development in the complex rainforest in the vicinity of the benches and gullies of the escarpment foothills.

Bark: Smooth fawn coloured to very flaky. The flakes are hard and on large specimens quite prominent.

Leaves: Alternate, pinnate, 11 to 17 leaflets, each leaflet; oblique, ovate-lanceolate, stalked, drawn out to a long point, 60mm to 120mm long, 20mm to 60mm wide.

Inflorescence: Large panicles at the ends of branches.

Flowers: Fragrant, about 5mm long, white or pinkish. Flowers September-October.

Fruit: A dry capsule 20mm to 25mm long splitting into 5 pieces exposing seeds which are winged. Fruits late summer and autumn.

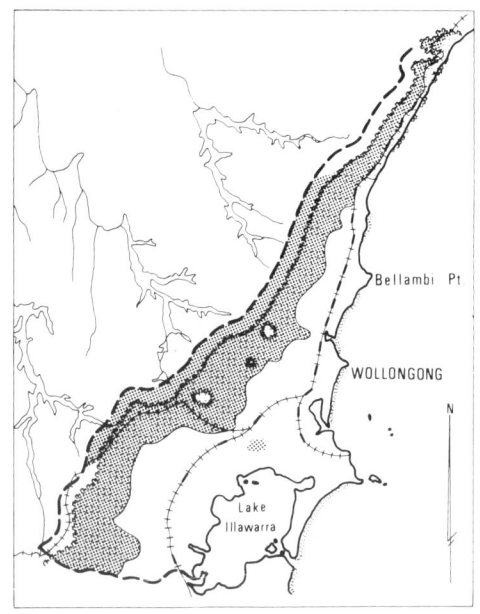

TOP LEFT: Flowers. TOP RIGHT: Tree. MIDDLE LEFT: Bark (pencil wedged in flakes serves as scale). BOTTOM: Leaves.

Tristaniopsis collina P. G. Wilson et J. T. Waterhouse

Formerly known under *Tristania laurina*

Myrtaceae

Although closely related to *T. laurina* this species occupies a hillside habitat rather than a streamside one. In the Wollongong area it is rarely more than a shrub up to about three metres and although the species has a fibrous bark it does not attain a stem diameter large enough to exhibit this character in this area. *T. collina* can be found on the escarpment, usually on ridges as an understorey plant to eucalypts, and also on the plateau, particularly near the crest of the escarpment, again as an understorey plant in eucalypt forest. It can be readily distinguished from *T. laurina* by the elliptical almost rhomboidal shaped leaves, which are also smaller.

Bark: Fibrous on larger trees but smooth on shrubbier specimens.

Leaves: Alternate, shortly stalked, narrow elliptical, acuminate, paler on underside, hairless, 40mm to 120mm long, 10mm to 40mm wide. Oil glands very numerous.

Inflorescence: Axillary cymes, 3-7 flowered.

Flowers: Yellow, about 8mm long, 5 petals, stamens fused into 5 bundles opposite the petals.

Fruit: Capsule, plitting into three valves. Flattened seeds.

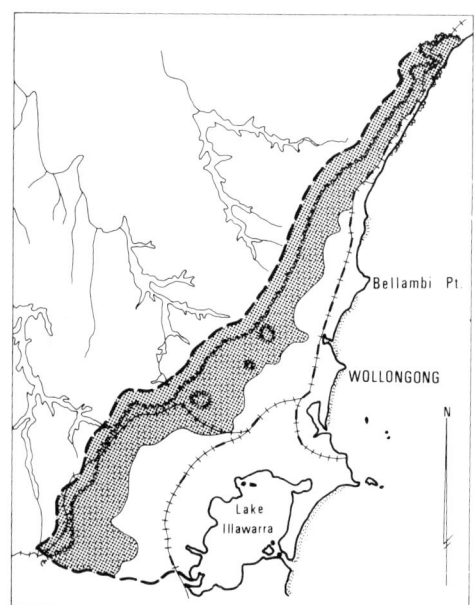

Leaves

Fruit.

Tristaniopsis laurina (Sm.) P. G. Wilson & J. T. Waterhouse

Formerly known under *Tristania laurina*

Water gum

Myrtaceae

Tristaniopsis laurina typically grows along watercourses. In the area covered by this book it occurs only in the northern part around Coalcliff and Stanwell Park. Along Stanwell Creek which drains eastward down the escarpment this tree grows abundantly as a rainforest tree attaining a height of up to 15m. *T. laurina* occurs to the north commonly in Royal National Park and in gullies draining westward from the Illawarra escarpment. However it has not been observed in the one kilometre wide strip just west of the escarpment crest that is covered by this book. Also south of Stanwell Creek it does not occur east of the escarpment crest.

This tree with its handsome foliage and yellow flowers is commonly grown as an ornamental.

Bark: Small stems, smooth white and brown blotched. On older and larger stems; orange, brown or grey mottled, more or less smooth.

Leaves: Alternate, lanceolate to narrow elliptic, broader near the end or sometimes narrow rhomboid.

Inflorescence: Cymes about 12mm long in forks of leaves.

Flowers: Small, yellow, fragrant about 7mm long, staminal claws 2mm long or less, petals 3mm long. Flowers December-January.

Fruit: An oval capsule about 10mm long with 3 valves.

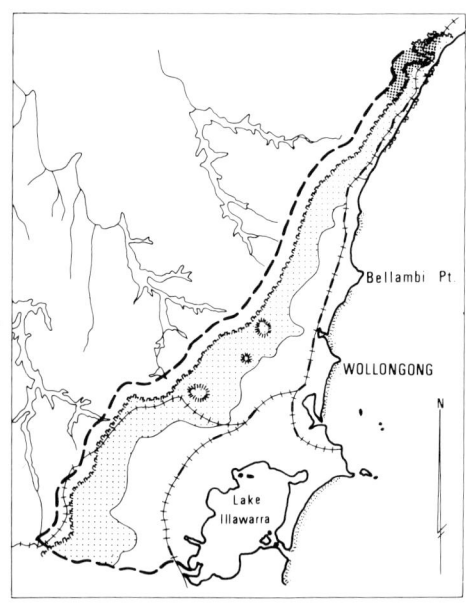

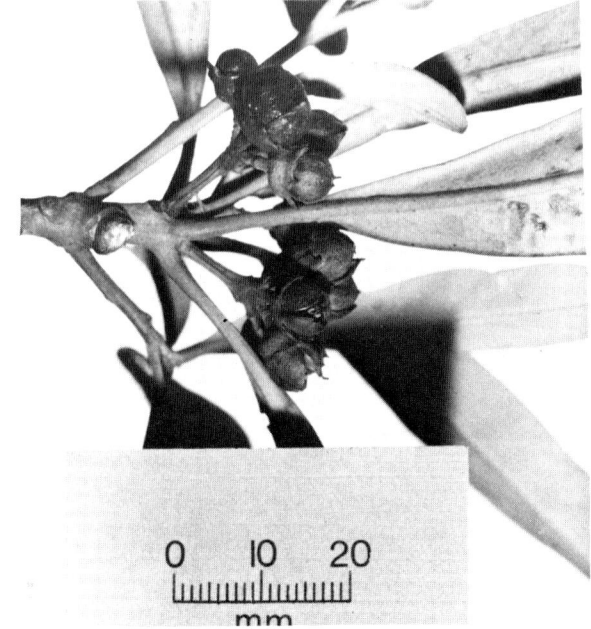

Leaves.

Fruit.

Trochocarpa laurina R. Br.
Epacridaceae

This species is the largest of the epacrids in the Wollongong area. It grows up to about 6m and is usually to be found in wet sclerophyll or rainforest on Hawkesbury Sandstone and the Narrabeen Series. It is a common feature of the forest directly at the base of the escarpment at the top of the Narrabeen Series. Although it does descend onto the Coal Measures it is largely absent under 300m.

Trochocarpa laurina usually forms a crooked, spreading, little tree and its small, shiny, parallel veined leaves set it apart in the rainforest. It is also found as a rounded shrub in more open forest.

Bark: Dark grey, rough.

Leaves: Alternate oval to lanceolate with a drawn out point at the apex, glossy upper surface with 5 to 7 parallel veins 40mm to 80mm long, 20mm to 30mm wide.

Inflorescence: Terminal spikes, 20mm to 40mm long, solitary or in clusters.

Flowers: Small, 3mm long, tubular, white. Flowers December-January.

Fruit: Gobular drupe, dark blue-black about 5mm diameter.

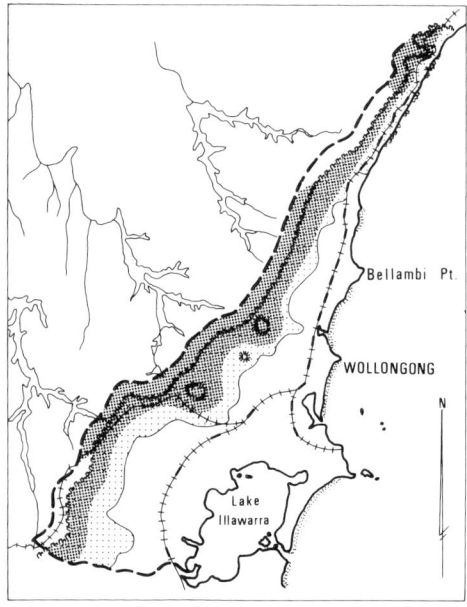

Leaves. Leaf laid across stem shows undersurface.

Wilkiea huegeliana (Tul.) A.DC.

syn. *Mollinedia huegeliana* Tul.

Monimiaceae

In this area *Wilkiea huegeliana* is usually found as a shrub but occasionally grows to 4m tall. It occurs as an understorey plant in rainforest and wet sclerophyll forest over most of the area. This plant stands out, when encountered, by virtue of its leaves.

Leaves: Opposite, thick, rigid and wavy, elliptic to oblong lanceolate, 40mm to 150mm long, 20mm to 60mm wide, coarsely and irregularly toothed, venation conspicuous on both surfaces but raised on undersurface.

Inflorescence: Short racemes or panicles in forks of leaves.

Flowers: Male and female often on different trees, globose 2mm diameter with a small terminal opening. Flowers summer.

Fruit: Egg-shaped, black 12mm diameter seated on an enlarged receptacle.

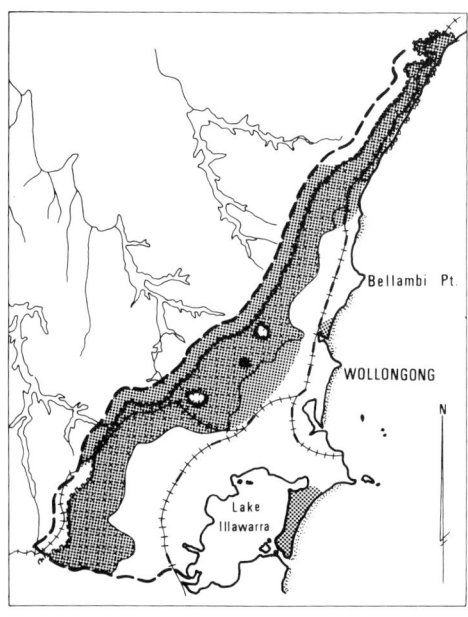

Leaves of *Wilkiea huegeliana*.

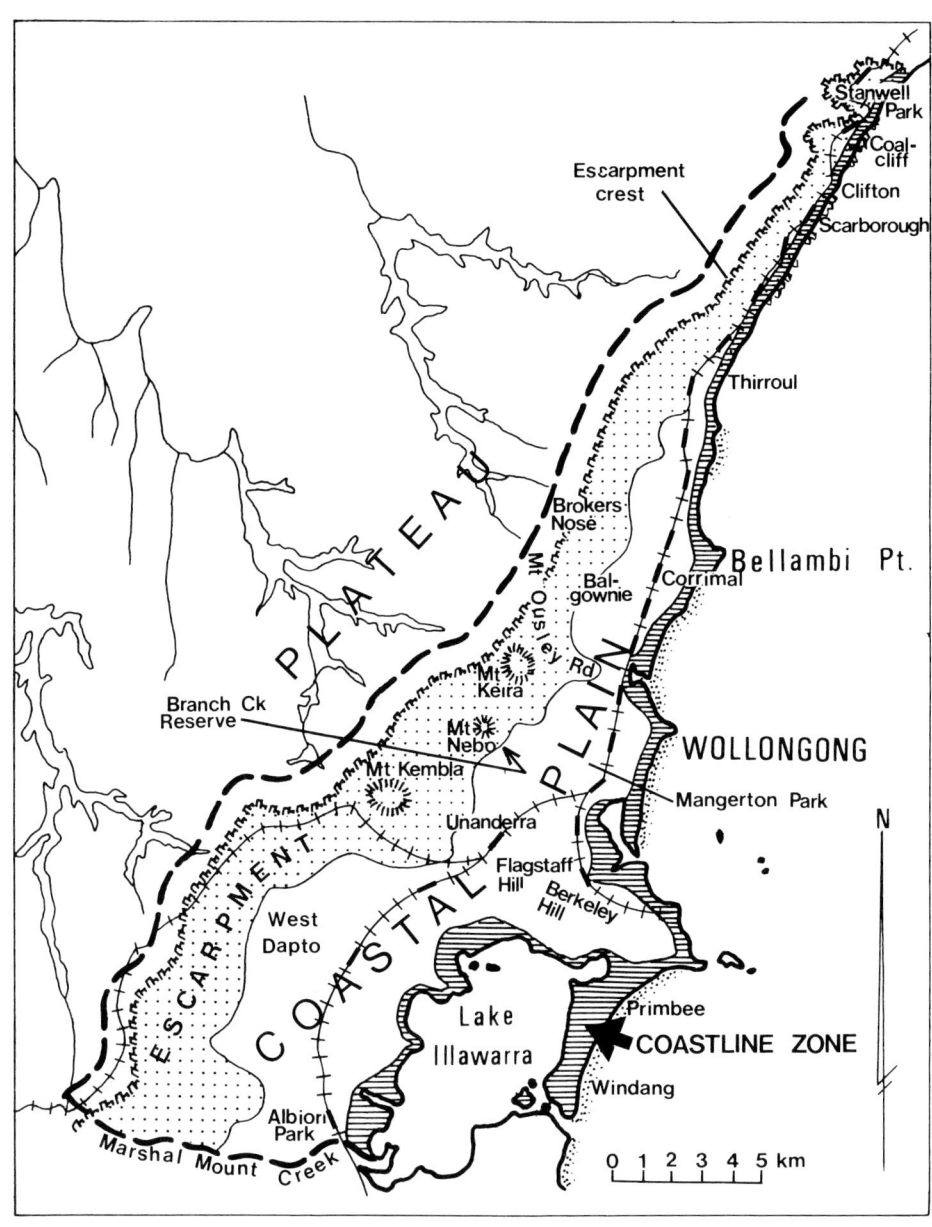

Fig. 6.1. Reference map for following lists.

Trees Listed in Community Groups

NOTE: Where there are qualifying notes after any species they only refer to the species in that community or section of the overall area, e.g., in **Coastline Zone** *Eucalyptus pilularis* occurs at Primbee and Windang, however, it is also a common tree elsewhere in the Wollongong area.

Coastline Zone
(Including Hind Dune, Lagoon and Sea Cliff)

Acacia maidenii
Alectryon subcinereus
Allocasuarina littoralis
Alphitonia excelsa
Angophora floribunda
Avicennia marina var. *australasica* (tidal lagoons only)
Banksia integrifolia
B.   serrata
Casuarina glauca
Choricarpia leptopetala (Stanwell Park only)
Clerodendrum tomentosum
Commersonia frazeri
Duboisia myoporoides
Elaeocarpus reticulatus
Elaeodendron australe
Endiandra sieberi (Windang)
Eucalyptus botryoides
E.   globoidea
E.   paniculata (characteristic of Coastal Plain but often close to lagoon areas)
E.   pilularis (Primbee-Windang only)
E.   robusta
E.   tereticornis
Euroschinus falcata
Exocarpus cupressiformis
Glochidion ferdinandi
Guioa semiglauca
Hibiscus heterophyllus
Leptospermum laevigatum
Melaleuca linariifolia (Towradgi only)
M.   styphelioides
Myoporum acuminatum
Notelaea longifolia
N.   venosa
Pittosporum undulatum
Rapanea variabilis
Synoum glandulosum

Seacliff Communities North of Thirroul

Acmena smithii
Allocasuarina verticillata
Backhousia myrtifolia
Banksia integrifolia
Casuarina glauca
Clerodendrum tomentosum
Elaeodendron australe
Eucalyptus botryoides
Eupomatia laurina
Ficus rubiginosa
Glochidion ferdinandi
Guioa semiglauca
Leptospermum laevigatum
Livistona australis
Omalanthus populifolius
Pittosporum undulatum
Rapanea variabilis
Sambucus australasica
Scolopia braunii
Synoum glandulosum
Wilkiea huegeliana

Coastal Plain Sclerophyll Forest

Acacia binervata
A.   maidenii
A.   mearnsii
Allocasuarina littoralis (rare on coastal plain)
A.   torulosa (uncommon on coastal plain)
Angophora floribunda (south of Unanderra)
Brachychiton populneum (Mt. Brown only)
Callistemon salignus
Choricarpia leptopetala (Stanwell Park only and bordering rainforest)
Commersonia fraseri
Eucalyptus amplifolia (poorly drained sutuations only)
E.   bosistoana (south of Unanderra)
E.   botryoides (usually associated with creeks or near sea)
E.   eugenioides
E.   globoidea
E.   longifolia
E.   maculata
E.   paniculata
E.   pilularis
E.   robusta (Wet or poorly drained situations only)
E.   saligna (usually associated with creeks)
E.   saligna/botryoides
E.   tereticornis
Exocarpos cupressiformis (uncommon on Coastal Plain)

Melaleuca decora
M.   linariifolia
M.   styphelioides
Notelaea longifolia
N.   venosa
Syncarpia glomulifera

Rainforest along Coastal Plain Creeks

Abarema sapindoides
Acmena smithii
Alphitonia excelsa
Backhousia myrtifolia
Claoxylon australe
Clerodendrum tomentosum
Commersonia frazeri
Croton verreauxii
Diospyros australis
Doryphora sassafras (only at Mangerton Park)
Elaeodendron australe
Ficus macrophylla
F.   obliqua
Glochidion ferdinandi
Guioa semiglauca
Hibiscus heterophyllus
Livistona australis
Notelaea longifolia
N.   venosa
Omalanthus populifolius
Pittosporum undulatum
Rapanea howittiana
R.   variabilis
Rhodamnia trinervia
Scolopia braunii
Streblus brunonianus
Synoum glandulosum

NOTE: *Casuarina cunninghamiana* grows along the banks of Marshall Mount Creek

Rainforest on Volcanic Soils on Coastal Plain (Berkeley and Flagstaff Hills)

Abarema sapindoides
Acacia binervata
A.   maidenii
A.   mearnsii
A.   melanoxylon

Acmena smithii
Alectryon tomentosum
Baloghia lucida
Brachychiton acerifolium
Clerodendrum tomentosum
Coelebogyne ilicifolia
Croton verreauxii
Dendrocnide excelsa
Diospyros australis
Duboisia myoporoides
Ehretia acuminata
Elaeodendron australe
Euodia micrococca
Ficus macrophylla
F.   rubiginosa
F.   superba var. *henneana*
Geijera salicifolia (also Mt. Brown)
Guioa semiglauca
Hibiscus heterophyllus
Myoporum acuminatum
Notelaea longifolia
N.   venosa
Planchonella australis
Podocarpus elatus
Rapanea variabilis
Sarcomelicope simplicifolia
Scolopia braunii
Stenocarpus salignus
Streblus brunonianus
Symplocos thwaitesii
Syzygium australe
Toona australis

Escarpment Foothills (Sclerophyll Forest)

Acacia binervata
A.   maidenii
A.   mearnsii
A.   melanoxylon
Allocasuarina torulosa
Angophora costata (Stanwell Park)
Brachychiton populneum
Callistemon salignus (West Dapto)
Clerodendrum tomentosum
Commersonia frazeri
Eucalyptus botryoides (north of Thirroul)
E.   maculata (Corrimal only)
E.   paniculata (north of Mt. Keira)
E.   pilularis (north of Mt. Keira)

E. quadrangulata (south of Balgownie)
E. saligna
E. saligna/botryoides
E. tereticornis (south of Mt. Keira)
Melaleuca styphelioides
Notelaea longifolia
N. venosa
Pittosporum undulatum
P. revolutum
Rapanea howittiana
Rapanea variabilis
Rhodamnia trinervia
Scolopia braunii
Syncarpia glomulifera (north of Mt. Kembla)
Synoum glandulosum
Tristaniopsis collina

Upper Slopes of Escarpment (Sclerophyll Forest)

Acacia binervata
A. maidenii
A. melanoxylon
Allocasuarina torulosa
Angophora costata (north of Coalcliff)
Endiandra sieberi
Eucalyptus botryoides (north of Thirroul)
E. elata (Mt. Kembla area)
E. muellerana (south of Mt. Kembla)
E. paniculata (north of Mt. Keira)
E. pilularis (north of Mt. Nebo)
E. quadrangulata
E. saligna
E. smithii (south of Mt. Ousley Road)
Exocarpos cupressiformis
Omalanthus populifolius
Pittosporum undulatum
Rapanea howittiana
R. variabilis
Rhodamnia trinervia
Syncarpia glomulifera
Synoum glandulosum
Tristaniopsis collina
Trochocarpa laurina

Escarpment Cliffs
(Trees Often Growing as Shrubs)

Acmena smithii
Allocasuarina littoralis
Angophora costata (Stanwell Park only)
Backhousia myrtifolia

Banksia integrifolia (north of Scarborough)
B. serrata
Callicoma serratifolia
Ceratopetalum apetalum
Elaeocarpus reticulatus
Endiandra sieberi
Eucalyptus dendromorpha (at top of cliffs)
E. gummifera
E. ligustrina (Brokers Nose and Albion Park West)
E. sieberi
Eucryphia moorei (West Dapto)
Quintinia sieberi
Syncarpia glomulifera (north of Mt. Keira)
Tristaniopsis collina
Trochocarpa laurina

NOTE: The escarpment cliffs accept other trees from neighbouring communities but only in localised situations. Therefore it should not be surprising to find species other than those listed above.

Rainforest of the Escarpment and Plateau Gullies

Abarema sapindoides
Acacia maidenii
A. melanoxylon
Acmena smithii
Acronychia oblongifolia
Alectryon subcinereus
Archontophoenix cunninghamiana
Backhousia myrtifolia
Baloghia lucida
Brachychiton acerifolium
Callicoma serratifolia
Ceratopetalum apetalum
Citronella moorei
Claoxylon australe
Clerodendrum tomentosum
Croton verreauxii
Cryptocarya glaucescens
C. microneura
Cyathea australis
C. cooperi
C. leichhardtiana
Dendrocnide excelsa
Dicksonia antarctica
Diospyros australis
D. pentamera
Diploglottis australis
Doryphora sassafras
Ehretia acuminata

Elaeocarpus kirtonii
E.   reticulatus
Elaeodendron australe
Emmenosperma alphitonioides
Endiandra sieberi
Euodia micrococca
Eupomatia laurina
Ficus coronata
F.   macrophylla
F.   obliqua
F.   rubiginosa
F.   superba var. *henneana*
Glochidion ferdinandi
Guioa semiglauca
Hedycarya angustifolia
Litsea reticulata
Livistona australis
Neolitsea dealbata
Notelaea longifolia
N.   venosa
Pennantia cunninghamii
Pisonia umbellifera
Pittosporum undulatum
Planchonella australis
Podocarpus elatus
Polyosma cunninghamii
Polyscias elegans
P.   murrayi
Quintinia sieberi
Rapanea howittiana
R.   variabilis
Sarcomelicope simplicifolia
Schizomeria ovata
Scolopia braunii
Sloanea australis
Stenocarpus salignus
Symplocos thwaitesii
Synoum glandulosum
Syzygium oleosum
S.   australe
Toona australis
Tristaniopsis collina
T.   laurina (Stanwell Park only)
Trochocarpa laurina
Wilkiea huegeliana

Plateau (Sclerophyll Forest on Hawkesbury Sandstone)

Allocasuarina littoralis
Angophora costata (north of Clifton West)
Banksia integrifolia (north of Clifton West)

B. serrata
Ceratopetalum gummiferum
Commersonia frazeri (occasionally)
Elaeocarpus reticulatus
Eucalyptus dendromorpha
E. gummifera
E. ligustrina
E. piperita
E. racemosa — *E. haemastoma*
E. sieberi
E. stricta

Sclerophyll Forest of Plateau (On Soils Below Hawkesbury Sandstone)

Acacia binervata
A. maidenii
A. mearnsii
A. melanoxylon
Elaeocarpus reticulatus
Eucalyptus cypellocarpa
E. elata
E. muellerana
E. pilularis
E. piperita
E. quadrangulata
E. saligna
E. smithii
Exocarpos cupressiformis
Notelaea longifolia
N. venosa
Pittosporum undulatum
Rapanea howittiana (edge of rainforest)
R. variabilis
Rhodamnia trinervia
Syncarpia glomulifera
Synoum glandulosum
Tristaniopsis collina
Trochocarpa laurina

Rainforest Trees found in Sclerophyll Forest and More Exposed Situations

Acmena smithii
Alphitonia excelsa
Backhousia myrtifolia
Clerodendrum tomentosum
Commersonia frazeri
Croton verreauxii

Elaeodendron australe
Glochidion ferdinandi
Guioa semiglauca
Hibiscus heterophyllus
Notelaea longifolia
N.   venosa
Pittosporum undulatum
Rapanea variabilis
Rhodamnia trinervia
Streblus brunonianus
Synoum glandulosum
Trochocarpa laurina

Miscellany

Shrubs which Occasionally Reach Tree Proportions in the Wollongong Area

Acacia terminalis
A.   longifolia
Abrophyllum ornans
Astrotricha latifolia
Breynia oblongifolia
Canthium coprosmoides
Citriobatus multiflorus
Coelebogyne ilicifolia
Hymenanthera dentata
Leptospermum flavescens
Hakea dactyloides
H.   salicifolia
Lomatia myricoides
Monotoca elliptica
Olearia argophylla
Pittosporum revolutum
Pomaderris aspera
Prostanthera lasianthos
Psychotria loniceroides
Sambucus australasica
Tasmannia insipida
Trema aspera
Tristania neriifolia

Coelebogyne ilicifolia.

Additional Trees found just Outside the Area Covered in this Book

Acacia elata
Callitris rhomboidea
Celtis paniculata
Daphnandra micrantha
Eucalyptus fastigata
E.   apiculata
E.   globoidea
E.   luehmanniana
E.   obliqua
Gmelina leichhardtii
Melaleuca armillaris

Glossary

Achene: A dry, one seeded fruit formed from a single carpel, with no special method for liberating the seed.
Acuminate: Drawn out into a fairly long point (Fig. 8.3a), as for leaf apex.
Acute: (Leaf apex) pointed but not an elongated point. (Fig. 8.3b.)
Aril: Swollen fleshy seed stalk (funicle) which largely covers the seed.
Articulate: Having joints where separation takes place or where parts move with respect to each other.
Axil: (Of leaf) angle between upper side of leaf stalk (petiole) and the stem to which it is attached. Fork between stem and leaf.
Berry: A succulent fruit with pericarp separated into skin of the fruit and pulp containing one or more seeds e.g. passionfruit, grape, black apple, lilly pilly.
Bipinnate: Leaf twice divided (Fig. 8.2a).
Bract: Leaf-like structure at the base of an inflorescence or flower. (Fig. 8.8d.)
Branchlets: Small branches.
Buttress: Flaring of base of tree stem into narrow "planks" where trunk meets roots.
Calyx: Collective term for sepals. (Fig. 8.9.)
Calyx tube: Sepals formed into a tube-like structure. (Fig. 8.10.)
Capsule: A dry fruit opening to release seed and consisting of two or more joined carpels.
Carpel: Female unit of flower consisting of ovary, style and stigma. (Fig. 8.9.)
Compound leaf: Leaf subdivided into leaflets. (Fig. 8.2.)
Cordate: Heart shaped, often applied to base of leaf only. (See Fig. 8.4a.)
Corolla: Collective term for petals. (Fig. 8.9.)
Corymb: A raceme-like inflorescence in which the flower stalks arise from different levels but are of different lengths, so that the flowers are held at the same level. (Fig. 8.8f.)
Cyme: Inflorescence where main and all lower axes terminate in flowers and each bears no more than one pair of leaves or bracts. (Figs. 8.8g, h and i.)
Deltoid: (Leaf shape) broad at the base, tapering to a point, triangular. Shape of Greek letter   . (Fig. 8.1h.)
Dentate: Toothed or with toothed margin. (Fig. 8.5b.)
Dioecious: Having male and female flowers borne on separate trees.
Disc: A usually circular plate found between whorls of floral segments. (Fig. 8.10.)
Domatia: Pits or depressions on undersurface of leaf usually at the junction of veins and often inhabited by minute insects or mites, e.g. *Pennantia cunninghamii*.
Drip tip: Pointed end of leaf where water accumulates from mist or rain (acuminate or mucronate apex, Fig. 8.3a, b, c).
Drupe: A succulent fruit with a single seed and consisting of skin (epicarp) fleshy layer (mesocarp) and hard layer around seed (endocarp).
Dry sclerophyll forest: Forest dominated by sclerophyllous trees, usually eucalypts, and having a dense undergrowth of plants resistant to dry conditions.
Ecotone: Vegetation zone where two communities adjoin.
Elliptical: Shaped like an ellipse. (Fig. 8.1g.)
Ephphyte: A plant using another plant, rock, log etc. for physical support but not parasitic on it.
Exserted: Protruding, as in valves of eucalypt fruit protruding beyond rim of capsule.
Falcate: Sickle shaped (Fig. 8.1k).
Filament: Stalk of stamen which supports anther. (Fig. 8.9.)
Fluting: Thick longitudinal ridges along stem of trees.
Follicle: A dry fruit which splits open along one side, derived from one carpel.
Glabrous: Smooth, without hairs or scales.
Gland: A small structure on the surface or embedded in the tissue of plants; often secreting nectar, oil or other matter.
Glaucous: Pale, white, bluish or greyish covering an otherwise green surface. Often covered with a fine bloom.
Globose, globular: Spherical.
Heterophylly: Leaves which vary considerably in size and shape on one plant, e.g. *Brachychiton acerifolium*.
Imparipinnate: Pinnate but having an odd terminal leaflet. (Fig. 8.2b.)
Inflorescence: A head of flowers. (Fig. 8.8.)
Insolation: Exposure to sun's rays.
Internode: Area on a stem between two nodes.

Isohyet: Line on a map joining points of equal rainfall.
Kino: Astringent vegetable exudation from eucalypts, commonly known as gum.
Lanceolate: Lance shaped (Fig. 8.1c).
Leaflet: Subdivision of a compound leaf (Fig. 8.2b).
Legume: A dry fruit formed from one carpel and splitting open along both sides.
Lenticel: Pore for gas exchange on stems.
Linear: (Leaf shape) long, narrow and with parallel sides. (Fig. 8.1a.)
Mallee: Form of eucalypt having many thin stems arising from a basal woody structure (ligno-tuber).
Mesophyte: Plant which grows under average conditions of water availability.
Mucro: A short beak.
Mucronate: Having a short point or beak. (Fig. 8.3c.)
Node: Point on a stem where a leaf and bud arise.
Oblanceolate: Reverse lance-shaped, wider towards the apex than the base. (Fig. 8.1d.)
Oblique: (Leaf base) where the sides of the leaf blade joins the stalk at different levels. (Fig. 8.4b.)
Oblong: More or less rectangular shaped. (Fig. 8.1b.)
Obovate: Reverse-ovate, being wider towards the apex than the base. (Fig. 8.1f.)
Obtuse: Blunt or rounded at the apex. (Fig. 8.3e.)
Operculum: Cap which covers the floral parts of a eucalypt flower when in bud stage. (Fig. 8.11.)
Orbicular: Rounded in outline. (Fig. 8.1e.)
Orographic: Due to the effects of mountains.
Ovate: Outline of an egg shape. (Fig. 8.1e.). With leaf shape this term usually includes a pointed apex.
Palmate: Compound leaf shape with leaflets diverging from one point (hand-like). (Fig. 8.2d.)
Palmately lobed: With lobes radiating from one point. (Fig. 8.5d.)
Panicle: A much branched inflorescence. (Fig. 8.8a.)
Parallel veined: Having major veins or nerves running more or less parallel.
Pedicel: Stalk of an individual flower.
Peduncle: Stalk of an inflorescence.
Peltate: having the leaf stalk attached to the leaf in from the margin. (Fig. 8.1j.)
Penninerved; penniveined: Closely pinnately veined. (Fig. 8.6c.)
Perianth: The calyx and corolla collectively, especially when joined or similar.
Petiole: Leaf stalk.
Petiolate: Having a leaf stalk. (Fig. 8.7a.)
Petiolule: Stalk of a leaflet.
Phyllode: Petiole of a leaf modified so as to carry out the function of a leaf, e.g. *Acacia binervata*.
Physiography: Description of physical features.
Pinnate leaf: Having leaflets arranged in rows on opposite sides of the midrib or rhachis. (Fig. 8.2b, c.)
Pubescent: Densely covered with soft hairs.
Pustule: Raised warty outgrowth.

Raceme: An inflorescence of stalked flowers along an axis or central stem, the oldest flowers toward the base. (Fig. 8.8c.)
Rachis: See rhachis.
Reticulate venation: Having veins arranged in a close net-like pattern. (Fig. 8.6b.)
Rhachis: Central stem of a pinnate leaf. (Fig. 8.2a.) Also main axis of an inflorescence.
Rhomboid: Diamond shape. (Fig. 8.1i.)
Scale: Any thin, dry and membranous structure, e.g. tree ferns scales on base of stipe.
Sclerophyll: A plant with hard stiff leaves.
Scurfy: Scaly.
Sepal: Green, leaf-like structure forming outer part of flower and usually covering it in bud. (Fig. 8.9.)
Serrate: Saw-like, or with saw-like margin. (Fig. 8.5a.)
Sessile: Having no stalk. (Fig. 8.7b.)
Sorus: Fruiting structure of ferns. A group of sporangia.
Spike: An inflorescence having flowers without stalks arranged along a central stem. (Fig. 8.8b.)
Stamen: Male unit of a flower, consisting of filament and anther. (Fig. 8.9.)
Staminate: With stamens, applied to male flowers.
Staminode: A sterile modified stamen.
Stellate: Star-like.
Stigma: Sticky receptive part of carpel at the end of the style. (Fig. 8.9.)
Stipe: A stalk.
Stipule: Small appendage at base of leaf often protecting axillary bud.

Style: Part of carpel which supports the stigma. (Fig. 8.9.)
Syconium: Flowering and fruiting structure of the fig family, having an invaginated floral axis bearing many minute flowers.
Talus: Slope of mountain below crest, often covered in material eroded from above.
Terete: Narrow-cylindrical.
Terminal: (Of inflorescences) borne at end of branches.
Tesselated: Divided into small squarish pieces (snakeskin-like).
Tomentose: Covered with closely matted short hairs.
Transpire: To lose water, usually from leaves.
Trichotomous: Repeatedly dividing into three equal branches.
Trifoliolate: Compound leaf having three leaflets. (Fig. 8.2e.)
Trilobed: Having three lobes.
Truncate: Cut off abruptly. (Fig. 8.3d.)
Umbel: An inflorescence having many flowers on stalks originating from one point.
Undulate: Wavy.
Urceolate: Urn shaped.
Valve: Structure which breaks apart or opens to release seed from fruit. (Fig. 8.10.)
Vascular: Having a conducting system to transport water, consisting mainly of xylem and phloem.
Wet sclerophyll forest: Tall forest dominated by sclerophyll trees, usually eucalypts, and having an open understorey often of ferns, grasses, wattles or mesophytic plants.
Whorl: Three or more leaves originating from the same node.

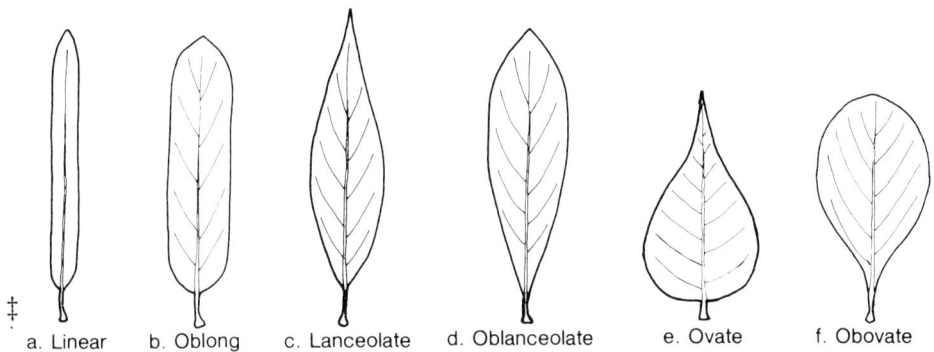

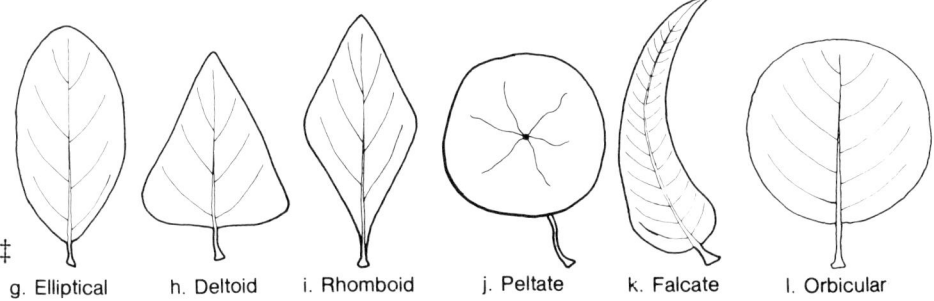

FIG. 8.1   SIMPLE LEAF SHAPES

a. Bipinnate b. Imparipinnate c. Paripinnate d. Palmate e. Trifoliolate

Pinnate

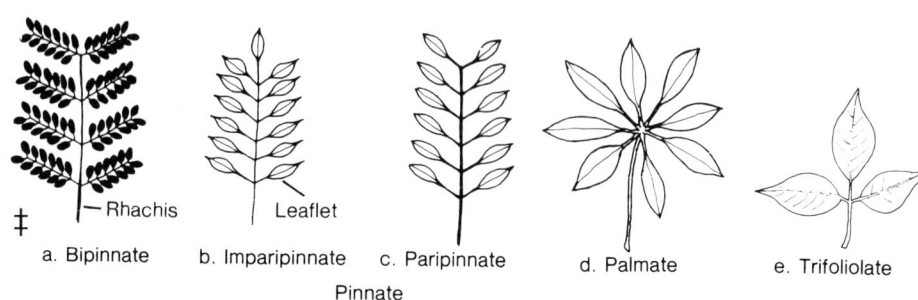

FIG. 8.2 COMPOUND LEAF SHAPES

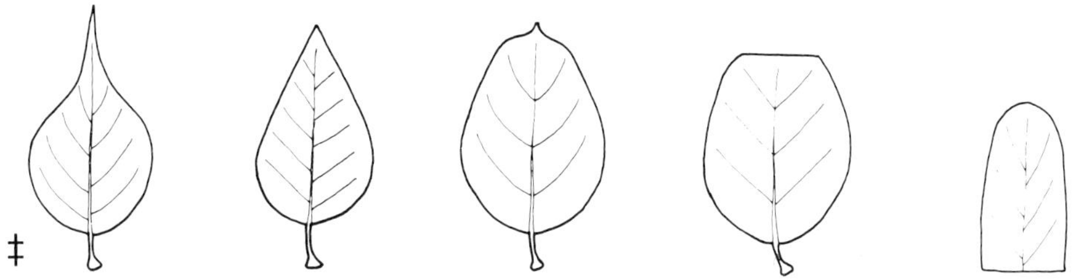

a. Acuminate b. Acute c. Mucronate d. Truncate e. Obtuse

FIG. 8.3 LEAF APICES

a. Cordate b. Oblique

FIG. 8.4 LEAF BASES

a. Serrate b. Dentate c. Trilobed d. Palmately lobed

FIG. 8.5 LEAF MARGINS

a. Linear b. Reticulate c. Penniveined Penninerved

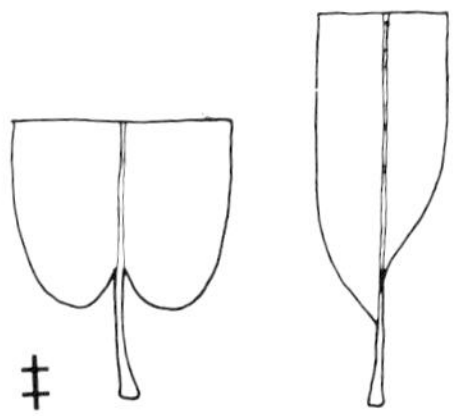

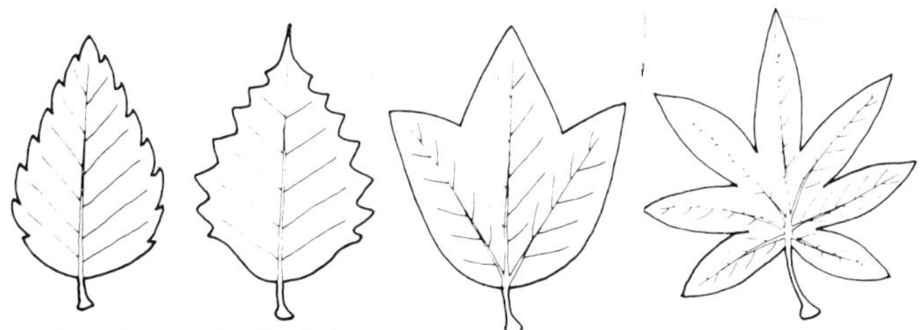

FIG. 8.6 LEAF VENATION

a. Petiolate b. Sessile c. Decurrent

FIG. 8.7 LEAF ATTACHMENT TO STEM

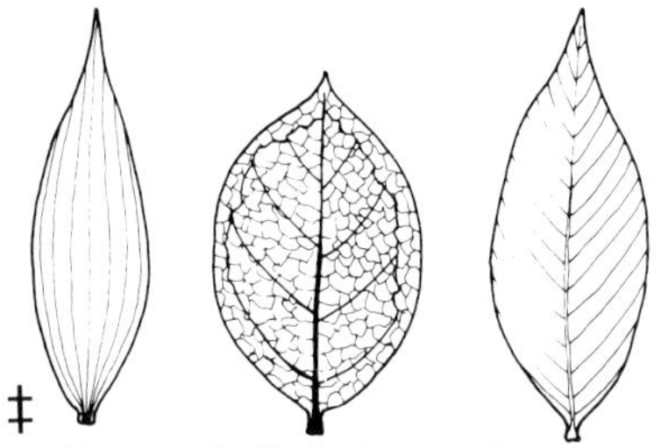

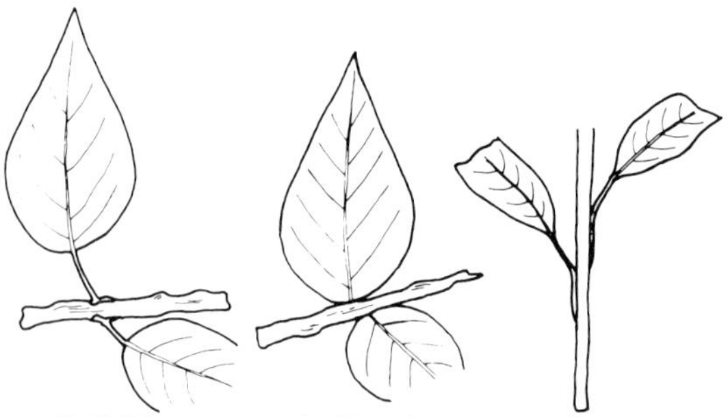

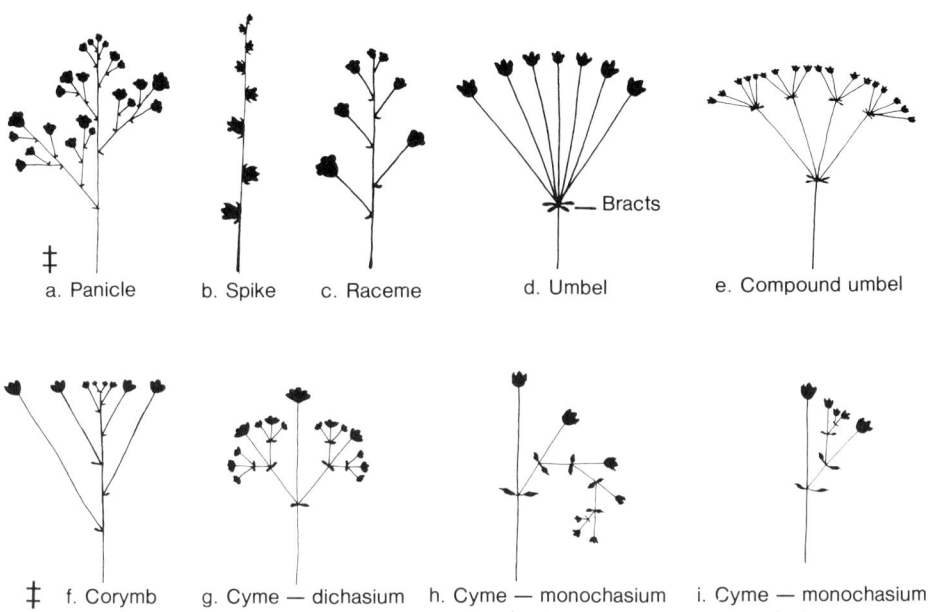

FIG. 8.8   INFLORESCENCES

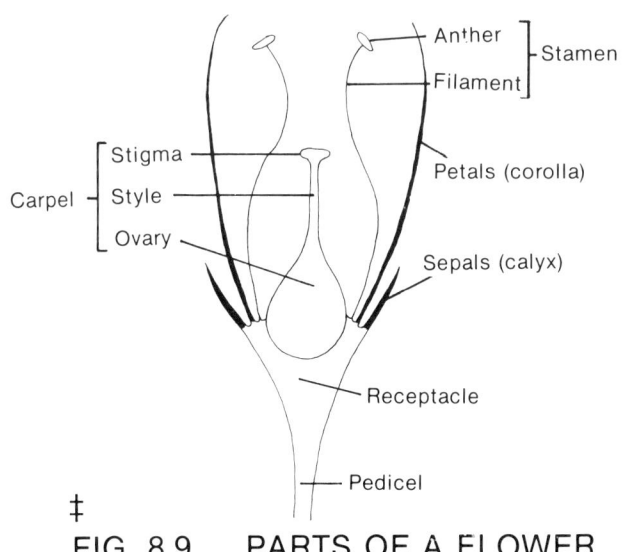

FIG. 8.9   PARTS OF A FLOWER

References and Further Reading

ANDERSON: R.H.: *The Trees of N.S.W.* Government Printing Office, Sydney 1968.
AUDAS, J. W.: *Native Trees of Australia.* Whitcombe and Tombs Pty. Ltd., Melbourne.

BEADLE, N. C. W., EVANS, O. D., CAROLIN, R. C. & TINDALE, M. D.: *Flora of the Sydney Region.* A. H. & A. W. Reed, Sydney 1972.
BLAKELY, W. F.: *A Key to the Eucalypts.* Forestry & Timber Bureau, Canberra 1965.
BOWMAN, H. N.: *Wollongong, Kiama and Robertson 1:50,000 Geological.* Sheets Geological Survey of N.S.W. Government Printer N.S.W., Sydney 1974.
BURBIDGE, N. T.: *The Wattles of the A.C.T.* Verity Hewitt, Canberra 1961.
BYWATER, J.: *Distribution and Ecology of Rainforest Vegetation and Fauna in the Illawarra* (Thesis). University of Wollongong 1978.

CHIPPENDALE, G. M.: *Eucalyptus Buds and Fruit.* Forestry and Timber Bureau, Canberra 1968.
COOK, A. C., et al.: *Geology of the Illawarra District.* University of Wollongong 1978.
COUSINS, A.: *The Garden of N.S.W.* Producers' Co-op. Distributing Society Ltd., Sydney 1948.

DAVIS, C.: Plant Ecology of the Bulli District, Part 1 — *Proceedings of the Linnean Society*, Vol. 61, pp. 285-297 1936.
DAVIS, C.: Plant Ecology of the Bulli District, Part 2 — *Proceedings of the Linnean Society*, Vol. 66, pp. 1-19 1941.
DAVIS, C.: Plant Ecology of the Bulli District, Part 3 — *Proceedings of the Linnean Society*, Vol. 66, pp. 20-32 1941.

FRANCIS, W. D.: *Australian Rainforest Trees.* Forestry and Timber Bureau, Sydney 1951.

GARNET, J. R.: The Family Casuarinaceae, *Australian Plants*, Vol. 3, No. 25. Soc. for Growing Aust. Plants, Sydney 1965.
GENTILLI, J.: *Australian Climate Patterns.* Nelson, Melbourne 1972.
GIBSON, J. D.: Birds of the County of Camden (Including the Illawarra District), *Australian Birds*, Vol. 11, No. 3, pp. 41-80. N.S.W. Field Ornithologists Club, Sydney 1977.

HALL, N., et al.: *Forest Tree Series*, Nos. 9, 19, 29, 33, 38, 93. Aust. Government Publishing Service, Canberra.
HALL, N., JOHNSON, R. D., CHIPPENDALE, G. M.: *Forest Trees of Australia.* Australian Government Publishing Service, Canberra 1975.
HAMILTON, A. G.: Flora of the South Coast, *British Assn. for the Advancement of Science: Handbook for N.S.W.* Edward Lee & Co., Sydney 1914.
HARRIS, A. (Emigrant Mechanic): *Settlers and Convicts.* Melbourne University Press 1969.
HARRISON, R. E.: *Handbook of Trees and Shrubs for the Southern Hemisphere.* A. H. & A. W. Reed, Wellington, N.Z. 1967.
HARTLEY, T. G.: The Taxonomic Status of the Genus *Bauerella* (Rutaceae), *Journal of the Arnold Arboretum*, Vol. 56, No. 1, pp. 164-170, 1975.

JERVIS, J.: Cedars and Cedar Getters, *Royal Historical Journal and Proceedings*, Vol. 25, Part 2, pp. 131-156.
JOHNSON, L. A. S. and BLAXELL, D. F.: New Taxa and Combinations in *Eucalyptus* I, Contributions From the N.S.W. National Herbarium, Vo. 4, No. 5, p. 286. N.S.W. Dept. Agric., Sydney 1972.
JOHNSON, L. A. S. and BLAXELL, D. F.: New Taxa and Combinations in *Eucalyptus* II, Contributions From the N.S.W. National Herbarium, Vol. 4, No. 6, p. 379. N.S.W. Dept. Agric., Sydney 1973.
JONES, D. L. and CLEMESHA, S. C.: *Australian Ferns and Fern Allies.* A. H. & A. W. Reed, Sydney 1977.

LEAR, R. and TURNER, T.: *Mangroves of Australia.* University of Queensland Press 1977.
LEE, I.: *Early Explorers in Australia.* Methuen, London 1927.
LINACRE, E. and HOBBS, J.: *The Australian Climatic Environment.* J. Wisley & Sons, Sydney 1977.
LINDSAY, B.: *A Story of Early Land Settlement in Illawarra.* Mitchell Library, Sydney.

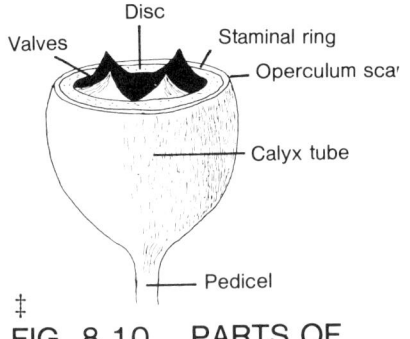

FIG. 8.10 PARTS OF EUCALYPTUS FRUIT

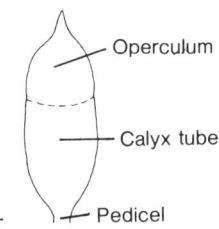

FIG. 8.11 EUCALYPTUS BUD

MAIDEN, J. H.: Critical Revision of the Genus Eucalyptus. Government Printer, Sydney.
McDONALD, W. G.: *Earliest Illawarra.* Illawarra Historical Society 1966.
McDONALD, W. G.: *The First Footers.* Illawarra Historical Society.
MILLET, M.: *Native Trees of Australia.* Lansdowne Press, Melbourne 1971.

PRYOR, L.D.: *Biology of Eucalypts.* Edward Arnold, London 1976.
PRYOR, L. D. and JOHNSON, L. A. S.: *A Classification of the Eucalypts.* A.N.U., Canberra 1971.

ROBINSON, R.: *Urban Illawarra.* Sorrett Publishing, Melbourne 1977.

SHAW, H. J.: *200 Facts About Historic Illawarra.* Illawarra Historical Society 1970.

WEBB, L. J.: Environmental Relationships of the Structural Types of Australian Rain Forest Vegetation. *Ecology,* Vol. 49, No. 2, pp. 296-311.
WEBB, L. J.: A General Classification of Australian Rainforests. *Australian Plants,* Vol. 9, No. 76, pp. 349-363. Soc. for Growing Aust. Plants, Sydney 1978.
WEBB, L. J.: A Physiognomic Classification of Australian Rainforests. *Journal of Ecology,* Vol. 47, pp. 551-570. 1959.

YOUNG, R. W. and JOHNSON, A. R. M.: The Physical Setting. *Urban Illawarra* ed. R. Robinson. Sorrett Publishing, Melbourne 1977.

Index

Abarema sapindoides, 54
Aborigines, effect of, 8
Acacia,
  binervata, 56
  maidenii, 58
  mearnsii, 60
  melanoxylon, 62
  mollissima, 60
Acknowledgements, 1
Acmena smithii, 64
Acronychia,
  baueri, 284
  laevis, 66
  oblongifolia, 66
  simplicifolia subsp. *simplicifolia*, 284
Alectryon subcinereus, 68
Allocasuarina,
  littoralis, 70
  torulosa, 72
  verticillata, 74
Alphitonia excelsa, 76
Altitude, effects of, 38
Angophora,
  costata, 78
  floribunda, 80
  intermedia, 80
  lanceolata, 78
Archontophoenix cunninghamiana, 82
Avicennia,
  marina var. *australasica*, 84
  marina var. *resinifera*, 84
  officinalis, 84

Backhousia myrtifolia, 86
Baloghia lucida, 88
Bangalay, 162
Bangalow palm, 82
Banksia,
  integrifolia, 90
  serrata, 92
Bass and Flinders, 8
Bastard rosewood, 300
Bauerella simplicifolia subsp. *simplicifolia*, 284
Benches, 17
Berkeley Hills, 19, 31, 32
Bird lime tree, 262
Birds, 46
  and blossoms, 46
Black,
  apple, 266
  ash, 200
  myrtle, 138
  plum, 136
  she-oak, 70
  wattle, 60, 98
Blackbutt, 186
  peppermint, 202
Blackwood, 62

Blueberry ash, 150
Blue Mountains mallee, 204
Blush cudgerie, 214
Bolly gum, 240
Bolwarra, 212
Bonewood, 154
Boobialla, 252
Boundaries of area, 5
Brachychiton,
  acerifolium, 94
  populneum, 96
Brown,
  beech, 260
  kurrajong, 118
  pine, 268
Brush,
  bloodwood, 88
  cherry, 302
  wilga, 228
Bushfire, 12, 25

Cabbage,
  gum, 158
  palm, 242
Callicoma serratifolia, 98
Callistemon salignus, 100
Captain Cook, 8
Cargillia,
  australis, 136
  pentamera, 138
Casuarina,
  cunninghamiana, 102
  glauca, 104
  littoralis, 70
  stricta, 74
  suberosa, 70
  torulosa, 72
Casuarinas, 102
Cedar getters, 9
Cedrela toona var. *australis*, 306
Celery wood, 272
Ceratopetalum,
  apetalum, 17, 106
  gummiferum, 108
Cheese tree, 230
Choricarpia leptopetala, 110
Churnwood, 112
Citronella moorei, 112
Claoxylon australe, 114
Clearing leases, 11
Clerodendrum tomentosum, 116
Climate, 19
Coachwood, 17, 106
Coal Measures, 17
Coal Mining, 11
Coast,
  banksia, 90

grey box, 160
  tea tree, 238
  white box, 190
Coastline, 19, 26
Coastal plain, 18, 31
Commersonia fraseri, 118
Corkwood, 144, 156
Crab apple, 286
Croton verreauxii, 120
Cryptocarya,
  glaucescens, 122
  microneura, 124
Cyathea,
  australis, 126
  cooperi, 128
  leichhardtiana, 130
Dairy farms, 11
Davis, Consett, 10
Deciduous fig, 226
Dendrocnide excelsa, 132
Description of trees, 53
Dicksonia antarctica, 134
Diospyros,
  australis, 136
  pentamera, 138
Diploglottis,
  australis, 140
  cunninghamii, 140
Distribution of trees, 25
Doryphora sassafras, 142
Drooping she-oak, 74
Drying winds, 23
Duboisia myoporoides, 144
Echinocarpus australis, 290
Ehretia acuminata, 146
Elaeocarpus,
  bauerlenii, 148
  cyaneus, 150
  kirtonii, 148
  longifolius, 148
  reticulatus, 150
Elaeodendron australe, 152
Emmenosperma alphitonioides, 154
Endiandra sieberi, 156
Escarpment,
  benches, 17
  cliffs, 40
  drainage of, 18
  foothills, 18
  stratigraphy, 17
  vegetation, 34
Eucalypts, 7
Eucalyptus,
  amplifolia, 158
  andreana, 168
  bosistoana, 160
  botryoides, 162
  corymbosa, 174
  cypellocarpa, 164
  dendromorpha, 166
  elata, 168

  eugenioides, 170
  globoidea, 172
  gummifera, 174
  haemastoma, 192
  ligustrina, 176
  lindleyana, 168
  longifolia, 178
  maculata, 180
  micrantha, 192
  muellerana, 182
  multiflora, 194
  numerosa, 168
  obtusiflora var. *dendromorpha*, 166
  paniculata, 184
  pilularis, 186
  piperita, 188
  quadrangulata, 190
  racemosa, 192
  robusta, 194
  saligna, 196
  saligna/botryoides, 198
  sieberi, 200
  smithii, 202
  stricta, 204
  tereticornis, 206
  umbellata, 206
  wilkinsoniana, 170
Eucryphia moorei, 208
Eugenia,
  australis, 302
  smithii, 64
Euodia micrococca, 210
Eupomatia laurina, 212
Euroschinus falcata, 214
Evans, G. W., journey of, 8
Exocarpos cupressiformis, 216

Featherwood, 270
Ficus,
  coronata, 218
  eugenioides, 222
  macrophylla, 220
  henneana, 226
  obliqua, 222
  rubiginosa, 224
  stephanocarpa, 218
  superba var. *henneana*, 226
Fig,
  deciduous, 226
  Moreton Bay, 220
  Port Jackson, 224
  sandpaper, 218
  small leaved, 222
First settlers, 9
Flagstaff Hill, 19, 31, 32
Flame tree, 94
Forest oak, 72
Forest red gum, 206

Geijera salicifolia, 228
Geology, 15
Giant stinging tree, 132

Glochidion ferdinandi, 230
Green wattle, 60
Grey,
  ironbark, 184
  mangrove, 84
  myrtle, 86
Guioa semiglauca, 232
Gully gum, 202
Hawkesbury Sandstone, 15
Hedycarya,
  angustifolia, 234
  cunninghamii, 234
Hibiscus heterophyllus, 236
Hind dune community, 26
History, 7
Ice ages, 7
Illawarra,
  flame tree, 94
  geology, 16
  just prior to arrival of Europeans, 8
  landforms, 15
  origin of landforms, 7
Industrial development, 12
Insect suppression, 48
Insolation, 23
Introduced plants and animals, 12
Ironwood, 86
Koda, 146
Kurrajong, 96
Lagoon community, 28
Land,
  clearing, 11
  grants, 10
  settlement, 10
Laportea gigas, 132
Leatherjacket, 106
Leptospermum laevigatum, 238
Lilly pilly, 64
Litsea,
  dealbata, 254
  reticulata, 240
Livistona australis, 242
Maiden's,
  blush, 290
  wattle, 58
Melaleuca,
  decora, 244
  genistifolia, 244
  linariifolia, 246
  styphelioides, 248
Melaleucas, 244
Melia,
  azedarach, 250
  dubia, 250
Mollinedia huegeliana, 314
Monkey gum, 164
Moorlands, 8, 15
Moreton Bay fig, 220
Mountain grey gum, 164
Murrogun, 124

Mutton wood, 280
Myoporum acuminatum, 252
Myrtle ebony, 138
Narrabeen Group, 17
Native,
  bleeding heart, 258
  cascarilla, 120
  cherry, 216
  clerodendrum, 116
  daphne, 264
  hibiscus, 236
  laurel, 122
  mulberry, 234
  olive, 256
  quince, 68
  tamarind, 140
Neolitsea dealbata, 254
Nephelium,
  semiglaucum, 232
  tomentosum, 68
Notelaea,
  longifolia, 256
  venosa, 256
N.S.W. Christmas bush, 108
Old man banksia, 92
Omalanthus populifolius, 258
Origin of Illawarra landforms, 7
Overall patterns of distribution, 26
Palm,
  bangalow, 82
  cabbage, 242
Panax,
  elegans, 272
  murrayi, 274
Pencil cedar, 274
Pennantia cunninghamii, 260
Permian, 7
Piccabeen palm, 82
Pigeonberry ash, 148
Pink tips, 100
Pisonia umbellifera, 262
Pittosporum undulatum, 264
Planchonella australis, 266
Plateau, 15, 40
Plum pine, 268
Plum wood, 208
Podocarpus elatus, 268
Polyosma cunninghamii, 270
Polyscias,
  elegans, 272
  murrayi, 274
Port Jackson fig, 224
Possum wood, 276
Prickly leaved paperbark, 248
Prickly tree fern, 130
Privet leaved stringybark, 176
Pseudomorus brunoniana, 294
Quintinia sieberi, 276
Rainfall, 19, 20, 22

Rainforest, 42
  characteristics of, 43
  classification and distribution of, 44
  on escarpment, 34
  origin, 7
  self perpetuation, 25
Rapanea,
  howittiana, 278
  variabilis, 280
Red,
  ash, 76
  bloodwood, 174
  cedar, 306
  honeysuckle, 92
Red-fruited olive plum, 152
Rhodamnia,
  rubescens, 282
  trinervia, 282
Ribbonwood, 214
River,
  oak, 102
  peppermint, 168
Rough,
  barked apple, 80
  tree fern, 126
Sand,
  deposition, 7
  dunes, 26
Sandpaper fig, 218
Sarcomelicope simplicifolia subsp. *simplicifolia*, 284
Sassafras, 142
Schizomeria ovata, 286
Scolopia,
  braunii, 288
  brownii, 288
Scribbly gum, 192
Scrub,
  beefwood, 292
  stringybark, 282
Sea cliff, 28
Sea level, rise in, 7
Seed dispersal, 47
She-oak,
  black, 70
  drooping, 74
  forest, 72
  river, 102
  swamp, 104
Shoalhaven Group, 17
Sideroxylon australe, 266
Silvertop ash, 200
Sloanea australis, 290
Smooth barked apple, 78
Snappy gum, 192
Snow wood, 54
Soft tree fern, 134
Spotted gum, 180
Stanwell Park, 40
Stenocarpus salignus, 292
Streblus brunonianus, 294

Stink wood, 54
Swamp,
  mahogany, 194
  oak, 104
  she-oak, 104
Sydney,
  blue gum, 196
  peppermint, 188
  red gum, 78
Symplocos thwaitesii, 296
Syncarpia,
  glomulifera, 298
  laurifolia, 298
Synoum glandulosum, 300
Syzygium,
  australe, 302
  coolminianum, 304
  oleosum, 304
  paniculatum, 302
Talus slope, 17
Taluvium, 18
Temperature, 20, 23
Tertiary period, 7
Thin leaved stringybark, 170
Throsby-Smith Charles, 9
Tieghemopanax,
  elegans, 272
  murrayi, 274
Tom Thumb lagoon, 12
Toona australis, 306
Tree, definition of, 6
Tree distribution, 25
  effects of altitude on, 38
Tree ferns, 126
Trees,
  and birds, 46
  in the garden, 49
Triassic, 7
Tristania laurina, 308, 310
Tristaniopsis,
  collina, 308
  laurina, 310
Trochocarpa laurina, 312
Turpentine, 298
Two-veined hickory, 56
Umbrella tree, 274
Water gum, 310
Whalebone tree, 294
White cedar, 250
White euodia, 210
White stringybark, 172
White topped box, 190
Whitewood, 148
Wilde, Joseph, 10
Wilkiea huegeliana, 314
Winds, 19
Woollybutt, 178
Yellow,
  sassafras, 142
  stringybark, 182